Judge Knot

ANTHEM FRONTIERS OF GLOBAL POLITICAL ECONOMY

The **Anthem Frontiers of Global Political Economy** series seeks to trigger and attract new thinking in global political economy, with particular reference to the prospects of emerging markets and developing countries. Written by renowned scholars from different parts of the world, books in this series provide historical, analytical and empirical perspectives on national economic strategies and processes, the implications of global and regional economic integration, the changing nature of the development project, and the diverse global-to-local forces that drive change. Scholars featured in the series extend earlier economic insights to provide fresh interpretations that allow new understandings of contemporary economic processes.

Judge Knot

Politics and Development
in International Investment Law

Todd N. Tucker

ANTHEM PRESS

Anthem Press
An imprint of Wimbledon Publishing Company
www.anthempress.com

This edition first published in UK and USA 2018
by ANTHEM PRESS
75–76 Blackfriars Road, London SE1 8HA, UK
or PO Box 9779, London SW19 7ZG, UK
and
244 Madison Ave #116, New York, NY 10016, USA

British Library Cataloguing-in-Publication Data
A catalogue record for this book is available from the British Library.

ISBN-13: 978-1-78308-790-7 (Hbk)
ISBN-10: 1-78308-790-0 (Hbk)
ISBN-13: 978-1-78308-791-4 (Pbk)
ISBN-10: 1-78308-791-9 (Pbk)

This title is also available as an e-book.

To Gail and Dale, who taught me when to judge
and when to laugh it off.

CONTENTS

ILLUSTRATIONS

ACKNOWLEDGMENTS

This book is about the obscure world of investment law. It is also about a journey: my own.

When I started writing this, I was coming off 12 years as a global justice advocate. Protests against the World Bank? Check. Marching against the Iraq War? Check. Loads of intemperate remarks about capitalism and corporations? You bet.

Despite our hard-fought campaigns, my advocacy coalition ended up on the losing side of congressional votes on US trade agreements that we worried would undermine US well-being and sovereignty. A regional trade deal with six Central American countries (2005), followed by bilateral ones with Bahrain (2005), Oman (2006), Peru (2007), Colombia (2011), South Korea (2011) and Panama (2011)—each passed at the insistence of big business and presidents of both political parties, and over the howls of labor unions, environmentalists and consumer groups.

It was time for a reset. Back in 2002, I had completed a master's degree in development studies at Cambridge University. At the time, word was just breaking about a string of new cases under an obscure legal system known cryptically as investor–state dispute settlement, or ISDS, whereby multinational corporations were suing sovereign governments such as Argentina over various regulatory policies. As a kid, I had lived in Argentina, so this piqued my interest. I briefly considered doing a PhD then, but there were hardly any cases to study. Fast forward to 2012, and the number of lawsuits had piled up in the hundreds. Corporations were catching on to this new remedy.

I wanted to get to the bottom of whether this novel investment law mattered, and if so, how. That endeavor became my PhD dissertation (2012–16), which led me to reexamine long-held assumptions from my advocacy days. This book is an elaboration of that work, updated to include new chapters putting the research in a broader comparative context and taking account of the post-2016 changes in politics.

I could not have done any of this without the ongoing support of my loving friends and family. I thank foremost my wife, best friend and volunteer editor, Heather Boushey. She uprooted herself from a very productive think-tank career to work remotely alongside me in England for my course work and has helped me through the stress and exhilarations of this project with patience and love. My parents, Gail and Dale, brother Daniel and sister-in-law Emily Bunker were relentless encouragers, as was Heather's family.

I also thank the scores of arbitrators who took time to help me better understand their work. They fly to Washington, DC, and around the world to arbitrate, working from early in the morning until late at night. Despite such demanding hours, they took time from their grueling schedules to share perspectives with a graduate student not even in their field. Even if they do not agree with the conclusions I draw, I hope they find the outsider perspective informative as they contemplate the future of the system they helped build.

My supervisor Ha-Joon Chang was instrumental in shaping my research interests back when I was a master's student in 2001, and then encouraged me to return to Cambridge over a decade later to write down my strange ideas that fell between the gaps of what traditional disciplinary departments could offer. I thank him, Walter Mattli and Michael Waibel, who served on my *viva* committee and provided invaluable feedback. Lesley Dingle at the Squire Law Library and Diana Kazemi of the Centre of Development Studies provided valuable help navigating Cambridge resources. The Gates Cambridge Trust generously supported me throughout my PhD research, while Sarah Pray and the Open Society Foundations provided the boost of financial and moral support needed to take the manuscript and associated reports over the finish line from my perch at the Roosevelt Institute. In recent years, Roosevelt fellows have published *Rewriting the Rules of the American Economy* and *Hidden Rules of Race*; I'm pleased to extend the institutionalist framework of those two books to the global economy.

My editor Ed Paisley read the entire manuscript several times and made it much better. Kevin Gallagher helped champion me at Anthem Press, where Abi Pandey, Tej Sood, Nisha Vetrivel and their teams doggedly ushered the manuscript through. Daniel Tucker and Kelsea Henson helped conceive the cover art. Pete Morelewicz swept in literally just hours before submission to help rescue me from my sorry attempts at amateur graphic design; his expert work on Figures 2.3, 4.1, 5.2, 5.3, and 6.3 will be (I believe) among the central contributions of the overall project. I also thank the two anonymous peer reviewers who gave detailed comments.

I benefited tremendously from feedback from participants at the Institute for New Economic Thinking's Advanced Graduate Workshop in Bangalore in 2014; the seminars convened by Ha-Joon Chang and the Centre of Development Studies; Gates Cambridge Scholar symposia; the Cambridge Replication Workshop; the World Trade Institute's 2013 conference on the "Role of the State in Investor-State Arbitration"; the *International Organization* / iCourts 2015–16 conferences on "The Judicialization of International Relations"; the 2016 PluriCourts Arbitrator Behavior Workshop; and the 2013–16 annual meetings of the American Political Science Association and International Studies Association.

I was lucky enough to get advice, brainstorms, comments, tweets and needed encouragement from many great scholars, thinkers and practitioners across numerous disciplines at various stages of the five-and-a-half-year writing process, including Nellie Abernathy, Paul Adler, Todd Allee, Karen Alter, Wolfgang Alschner, Daniel Behn, Sam Bell, Eric Harris Bernstein, Jonathan Bonnitcha, Gabriel Bottini, Greg Brown, Julia Calvert, Jeff Colgan, Nathan Converse, Cosette Creamer, Brendan Duke, David Edeli, Haley Edwards, Michelle Egan, Isabel Estevez, Shailaja Fennell, Andrea Flynn, Susan Franck, Kevin Gallagher, Bryant Garth, David Gaukrodger, Timi Gerson, Geoffrey Gertz, Anna Ghosh, Nils Petter Gleditsch, Andy Green, Andrew Gruen, Emilie Hafner-Burton, Jennifer Harris, Jostein Hauge, Martin Hearson, Sue Holmberg, Heather Hurlburt, Andrew Hwang, John Ishiyama, Nicole Janz, Lise Johnson, Nikhil Kalyanpur, Anna Katselas, Robert Keohane, Andrew Kerner, Mike Konzcal, Ming Leong Kuan,

Shaheeza Lalani, Olof Larsson, Simon Lester, Carlos Lopez-Gomez, Barry C. Lynn, J. W. Mason, Juan Mayoral, Benjamin McKean, Tim Meyer, Domna Michailidou, Katy Milani, Andrew Mitchell, Sara Mitchell, Avanti Mukherjee, Cecilia Nahon, Suresh Naidu, Fernanda Nicola, Peter Nolan, Andy Oswiak, Lenore Palladino, Clint Peinhardt, Krzysztof Pelc, Luke Eric Peterson, Cam Phillips, Mona Pinchis, Rodrigo Polanco, Mark Pollack, Mihaela Popescu, Matt Porterfield, Lauge Poulsen, Sergio Puig, Mike Pyle, Tonya Lee Putnam, Jose Quiroga, K. Sabeel Rahman, Brishen Rogers, David Rosnick, Virginia Rutter, Lisa Sachs, John Schmitt, Mark Schmitt, Thomas Schultz, Brad Setser, Ganesh Sitaraman, Anne-Marie Slaughter, Benjamin Smith, Jeff Staton, Marshall Steinbaum, Taylor St John, Joseph Stiglitz, Bob Stumberg, Anton Strezhnev, Steve Teles, Kyla Tienhaara, Joel Trachtman, Elisabeth Tuerk, Gunes Unuvar, Gus Van Harten, Pierre Verdier, Erik Voeten, Tania Voon, Lori Wallach, Dorian Warren, Zoe Williams, Will Winecoff, Felicia Wong and others I am inadvertently leaving out. Thanks also to the staff of Filter Coffeehouse, Pleasant Pops, Tryst, Cove DC and Hot Numbers, where I wrote much of the early drafts.

Finally, I thank Oxford University Press and the editors at the *Journal of International Dispute Settlement* for generously granting permission to reprint material first published there, refashioned as chapter 4. Also, chapters 2 and 6 include material first published in reports for the Roosevelt Institute.

INTRODUCTION

Judge not, lest ye may be judged

For the judgment ye judge ye shall surely be judged, you gets no love

—KRS One

Since classical times, international law has focused on restraining states' freedom of action on the global and regional stages, from setting rules on protection of diplomats to ensuring non-interference with commerce on the high seas.

In recent decades, however, international legal constraints have shifted far behind national borders. Multilateral lending institutions' structural adjustment programs require sovereign nations to slash budgets, privatize public enterprises and cut pensions. Tax treaties limit how and when countries can collect revenue from multinational business enterprises operating in their borders. Trade agreements have shifted from simply locking in low tariffs to forbidding policies that today's rich countries once deployed to climb up the economic developmental ladder themselves. And all of these constraints are backed up by developed countries' bilateral foreign-aid programs.

One newly controversial instrument in this arsenal is the investor–state dispute-settlement (ISDS) system contained in thousands of trade and investment treaties. Its defining feature: allowing foreign investors to sue host states outside of national courts before transnational tribunals. These disputes are triggered by multinational companies that are unhappy with host-state regulations. The tribunals themselves are comprised of arbitrators hired by the litigating company and country on a case-by-case basis. Corporations have employed this dispute-settlement instrument to launch aggressive claims against states over environmental conservation, financial stabilization and public-service provisions.

Since a tribunal issued the first investment treaty award in 1990, more than 700 investor–state dispute-settlement lawsuits have been launched—most of them in just the past few years. And criticisms of the system are growing in number. The online news-site *BuzzFeed* ran a four-part investigative series by Pulitzer Prize–winning author Chris Hanby, titled "Global Super Court: The Secret Threat That Makes Companies More Powerful than Countries" (Hanby 2016a). *Time* magazine's Washington correspondent Haley Edwards published a popular book for Columbia Global Reports, called *Shadow Courts: The Tribunals That Rule Global Trade* (Edwards 2016). *New York Times* now regularly runs articles on developments in ISDS practices, featuring titles such as "Trans-Pacific Partnership Seen as Door for Foreign Suits Against U.S." (Weisman 2015).

Critics worry that ISDS tribunals represent a type of corporate-driven implosion of democracy. Former Secretary of State Hillary Clinton, during her 2016 presidential campaign, called for a fundamental reexamination of these dispute-settlement practices, saying, "We need to have a new paradigm for trade agreements that doesn't give special rights to corporations that workers and NGOs [non-governmental organizations] don't get" (Conahan 2016). President Donald Trump's trade representative, Robert Lighthizer, told the US Senate that he is "always troubled by the fact that nonelected non-Americans can make the final decision that the United States law is invalid" in ISDS tribunals (Swanson 2017). Indeed, their inclusion in international trade treaties has generated outrage on the left and the right, in legislatures and in the streets—stalling conclusion of major new trade deals such as the Trans-Pacific Partnership (TPP) and the Trans-Atlantic Trade and Investment Partnership (TTIP) (Hanby 2016b).

But proponents of investor–state suits had a running start defending a system that has existed on treaty paper since the 1960s. First, they point out that governments win more than they lose—and that the United States has never lost a case. Second, they argue that investment treaties bring the rule of law to developing nations, which is good for them and for US multinationals. Third, they argue arbitration is faster and more flexible than domestic courts, which might be corrupt or favor the national government. Finally, proponents note this dispute-settlement system has been around for decades without major problems for governance or defections by governments. As investment law proponent President Barack Obama noted, they are "not new. There are over 3,000 different ISDS agreements among countries across the globe. And this neutral arbitration system has existed since the 1950s. The United States has investment agreements with 54 different countries over the last 30 years" (Sargent 2015). In other words, the system is deeply entrenched: recent trade deals did not create it and rejecting a given trade deal (as is being contemplated as of early 2018 in the context of North American Free Trade Agreement renegotiations) will not eliminate it.

Judge Knot argues that both sides of the debate miss what international investment law is really doing and why it matters.

The ISDS template was introduced, and thrives today, because it builds on three longer-standing projects of Western liberalism. Reforms of the system will have a difficult time gaining analytical traction if they do not somehow address these three pillars (either by finding alternative means of fulfilling their functions or by demonstrating their functions are not essential).

First, this template extends late twentieth-century ideas from law and social science that prescribe a minimal state role as the best recipe for economic growth. The formula involves independent courts and central banks, low inflation, balanced budgets, lowered trade tariffs accompanied by the privatization of state-owned enterprises and the lowering of barriers to foreign direct investment (Williamson 1990). Sometimes called *neoliberalism*, sometimes the "Washington Consensus," this suite of policies was colorfully termed a "golden straitjacket" by columnist Thomas Friedman:

> As your country puts on the Golden Straitjacket, two things tend to happen: your economy grows and your politics shrinks. That is, on the economic front the Golden Straitjacket usually

fosters more growth and higher average incomes—through more trade, foreign investment, privatization and more efficient use of resources under the pressure of global competition. But on the political front, the Golden Straitjacket narrows the political and economic policy choices of those in power to relatively tight parameters. That is why it is increasingly difficult these days to find any real differences between ruling and opposition parties in those countries that have put on the Golden Straitjacket. Once your country puts it on, its political choices get reduced to Pepsi or Coke—to slight nuances of taste, slight nuances of policy, slight alterations in design to account for local traditions, some loosening here or there, but never any major deviation from the core golden rules" of deregulation. (T. L. Friedman 1999, 105–6)

Second, investment arbitration reflects a nineteenth- and twentieth-century notion that international lawyers can and should help states "de-politicize" economic disputes. In this view, law is an alternative to the evils of war, colonialism and gunboat diplomacy (Koskenniemi 2004; Hathaway and Shapiro 2017). In a world where war was an acceptable means of settling disputes and collecting debts, threatening war was been a necessary tool of statecraft. In a world where offensive war is illegal (as it is under the United Nations charter), alternative arrangements have to be made for defusing conflict.

Finally, this law of investment operationalizes an eighteenth-century Enlightenment insight that courts help check popular excesses. The United States stood alone for most of modern history in elevating judicial review of legislation to a semi-constitutional status. Touring the young country in the early 1800s, Alexis De Tocqueville noted that "a more immense judicial power has never been constituted in any people [. . .] [T]here is almost no political question in the United States that is not resolved sooner or later into a judicial question" (quoted in Carrese 2010, xviii). By the late twentieth century, the arrangement had spread, with dozens of countries adopting US-style review. Indeed, the idea of democracy has become associated as much with the protection of minority rights as with majority rule—its original defining feature (Hirschl 2004).

Together, these three liberal projects elevate law above other means of resolving disputes, such as mediation, administration by bureaucrats, letting the market decide or fighting it out through politics or violence. Historically, however, today's rich countries did not use golden straitjackets. The politicization of their economies was the rule, not the exception. And judicial review (as just noted) only recently diffused beyond the United States. But even as neoliberal economics was tarred by the 2007–08 global financial crisis, the project's liberal underpinnings continue to be influential. There are not many calls for a shift of policy away from judicialization per se: rather, most calls are for moves between types of judicialization. For instance, the European Union has advocated for converting the system of ad hoc arbitration into a full-blown international investment court. More than 220 prominent economists and law professors wrote a letter to the US Congress asserting that investor–state dispute settlements should be replaced with domestic litigation (Sachs 2016). Critics of investment law may question neoliberal prescriptions to let the markets rip, but the system is resilient precisely because it plays into longstanding Western narratives about the rule of law.

Judge Knot takes a contrarian view. I argue in this book that investment arbitration is at its worst when closest to law and at its best when farthest away. National courts and legal scholars ask arbitrators to demonstrate neutrality and consistency as the conditions for judges deferring to arbitration awards. But neutrality is impossible and deference undesirable. Rather, the decisions of investment lawyers should ring out as one voice among many in the grand project of building a democratic political economy. Societies should not waste the most beneficial service these lawyers can offer—a capitalist-legal perspective on policymaking. But neither should this perspective be privileged above others, treating their decision making as final and relegating, to a second order, the resolution of disputes by politics, administrations and markets. A rightsized role allows international arbitrators to do what they do well, while complementary institutions check and balance them. *Global popular constitutionalism* is what I call this alternative, building off a complementary project in domestic law called *popular constitutionalism* (Kramer 2005). In my framework, structural change of economies and political engagement are not distractions from good governance—they *are* good governance. If this seems audacious, that is because it is. In an era where rising inequality is threatening the sustainability of democracy, a forward-looking agenda needs to be big and at scale.

To get to this alternative vision, I take the reader on an unprecedented look inside investor–state dispute-settlement tribunals. Because of the secrecy of these tribunals, current journalism and scholarship generally treat these bodies like black boxes. Over 3 years and 6 cities, I conducted 55 hours of interviews with arbitrators from 18 countries. I interviewed at least one arbitrator from almost every one of the nearly 350 finalized investment disputes from 1990 (the first case) to the middle of 2017. Over two additional years, I triangulated interview analysis with an original dataset containing over a hundred variables on the outcomes and characteristics of these disputes and performed close qualitative analysis of the legal decisions themselves.

While primarily aimed at a political science readership (both academic and general), *Judge Knot* is shamelessly interdisciplinary, drawing from law, development economics and sociology. As such, I will dedicate space to offering explainer-type introductions to concepts from each discipline—concepts familiar to specialists, but that may be confusing to outsiders. In particular, chapter 2 positions my approach within international relations theory, and chapter 3 does the same for economic development theory. Legal and sociological themes are scattered throughout. But this is not interdisciplinarity for its own sake. Rather, I aim to show the relevance of investment law for broader debates on the proper role of government and market in society writ large. The book also is definitively written from an American perspective, and many of the examples I explore and policy quandaries I pose come from the perspective of righting the distortions I see clouding the US ship of state.

At this point, a few words are in order about what this book is not. This is neither primarily a study of the rise of multinational corporations and their various strategies (arbitral and otherwise) for pressuring governments, nor an examination of the on-the-ground experiences of governments and social movements. These are vitally important questions and are explored in depth by political scientists and journalists such as Lauge Poulsen, Geoff Gertz, Julia Calvert, Haley Edwards and Chris Hanby. At the same time, this book is not an exhaustive survey of investment doctrine. Legal scholars such as Gus

Van Harten, Anthea Roberts, Mona Pinchis, Michael Waibel, Jonathan Bonnitcha, M. Sornarajah, Christoph Schreuer, Gary Born and a cottage industry of others have produced comprehensive works that fit that particular bill. Instead, my primary focus is on the judicial actors themselves and the broader issues their work raises. I build on the work of political scientists such as Lee Epstein, Mark Pollack and Karen Alter, who have produced detailed studies of the personalities and ideologies of adjudicators of the US Supreme Court, the World Trade Organization and the European Court of Justice. While Yves Dezalay, Bryant Garth and others have produced valuable socio-legal studies of commercial arbitrators, *Judge Knot* is the first volume to use qualitative political science methods and concepts for a close study of investment-treaty arbitrators. This struck me as an important gap worth filling, given how active these arbitrators are and how they have at least as much discretion in shaping rules as do their tenured counterparts. Throughout, I question the desirability or even achievability of so-called global "rule of law," echoing concerns raised in national security contexts by scholars such as Samuel Moyn and Ian Hurd.

Finally, a few notes on terminology.

Unless otherwise noted, I use ISDS, international investment law and investment-treaty law to refer to arbitration disputes launched by an investor against a state pursuant to a bilateral, plurilateral or multilateral treaty between states. This is distinct from private arbitration, disputes pursuant to investor–state contracts/concessions or litigation brought by an investor under national investment laws. These other variants of litigating can share many of the same features as treaty-based investor–state dispute settlement (and are even sometimes confusingly called ISDS), but they pose different policy challenges. Most importantly for present purposes, treaties are harder to get out of, often requiring difficult renegotiations—thus the title, *Judge Knot*. In contrast, states can change their own national investment laws or contracts with investors much more readily.

I use institutionalism in a variety of ways. Chapter 2 discusses rational-choice institutionalism, sociological institutionalism and historical institutionalism in international-relations literature, while chapter 3 turns to new institutional economics and institutionalist political economics derived from development studies. As can be seen from the nomenclature, there is consensus among many scholars that institutions matter, that society's rules and norms affect political and economic life. The point is obvious to the lay reader, but only makes sense by reference to the underlying disciplinary debates, where realists emphasize the balance of military power, and neoclassical economists emphasize the primacy of free markets. As will be clear from those two chapters in particular, I identify more closely with historical institutionalism as a research methodology and with institutionalist political economy as a substantive theory of how states and markets interact. But the precise lines between all of the various institutionalisms are blurry, and all schools will benefit from cross-fertilization with one another.

Wherever possible, I avoid acronyms—the alphabet soup that clutters up much writing on global economic issues. I make exceptions for a few frequently used proper names such as the primary focus of this book—the investor–state dispute-settlement system—as well as for terms such as the North American Free Trade Agreement, the World Trade Organization, fair and equitable treatment and most-favored nation.

References

Carrese, Paul O. 2010. *The Cloaking of Power: Montesquieu, Blackstone, and the Rise of Judicial Activism*. Chicago: University of Chicago Press.

Conahan, Amy. 2016. "Clinton and Sanders Get Specific on Trade Before PA Primary." Pittsburgh: Pennsylvania Fair Trade Coalition.

Edwards, Haley Sweetland. 2016. *Shadow Courts: The Tribunals That Rule Global Trade*. New York: Columbia Global Reports.

Friedman, Thomas L. 1999. *The Lexus and the Olive Tree*. London: Anchor Books.

Hanby, Chris. 2016a. "Secrets of a Global Super Court." *BuzzFeed*, August 28, 2016.

———. 2016b. "Elizabeth Warren Squares Off Against Global Super Court." *BuzzFeed*, October 9, 2016.

Hathaway, Oona A., and Scott J. Shapiro. 2017. *The Internationalists: How a Radical Plan to Outlaw War Remade the World*. New York: Simon and Schuster.

Hirschl, Ran. 2004. *Towards Juristocracy: The Origins and Consequences of the New Constitutionalism*. Cambridge, MA: Harvard University Press.

Koskenniemi, Martti. 2004. *The Gentle Civilizer of Nations: The Rise and Fall of International Law 1870–1960*. Cambridge: Cambridge University Press.

Kramer, Larry D. 2005. *The People Themselves: Popular Constitutionalism and Judicial Review*. Oxford: Oxford University Press.

Sachs, Lisa. 2016. "220+ Law and Economics Professors Sign Letter Opposing ISDS in the TPP." New York: Columbia Center on Sustainable Investment.

Sargent, Greg. 2015. "Is TPP Trade Deal a Massive Giveaway to Major Corporations? An Exchange between Obama and Sherrod Brown." *The Washington Post*, April 27, 2015.

Swanson, Ana. 2017. "A Nafta Battleground on the Shores of Canada." *New York Times*, October 16, 2017, sec. Politics.

Weisman, Jonathan. 2015. "Trans-Pacific Partnership Seen as Door for Foreign Suits Against U.S." *New York Times*, March 25, 2015.

Williamson, John. 1990. "What Washington Means by Policy Reform." In *Latin American Adjustment: How Much Has Happened*, 90–120. Washington, DC: Peterson Institute for International Economics.

Chapter One

ENTERING THE JUDGE KNOT

A company was able to sue a country over a public health measure through an international court. How the fuck is that possible? [. . .] You've got to give it to them. That's impressive. Someone should really give those lawyers a pat on the back. And, a punch in the face. But [. . .] a pat on the back first. Pat, then punch. Pat, punch. They need a pat, punch. Little pat, big punch. That's what they need.

—Comedian John Oliver (2015)

All Tangled Up

Did you hear the one about the billionaire, the nun and the lawyers? It is not a joke, but a story that reveals the enormous complexities of our international system for governing cross-border investment. The tale will take us from Manhattan to Missouri, from the Cayman Islands to Peru and back to the United States, showing us how any local investment dispute has the potential to go global.

Meet Ira Rennert. Once banned from the US securities brokerage business for taking excessive risks with his clients' money, the American financier went on to become one of the country's foremost buyers of distressed businesses. From smelters in Missouri to coal-pulverizing plants in Kentucky to magnesium pits in Utah, Rennert had an eye for finding floundering businesses and buying them up at bargain-basement prices. He financed the deals through junk bonds—loans in the newly acquired company's name (Thornton 2003). This brought cash in the door quickly but saddled the companies he acquired with heavy debt burdens for years to come. Rennert would gradually strip down and sell these companies' useable assets. Sooner or later, these businesses' stock prices would plummet or they would go into bankruptcy, and Rennert would jump ship and move onto the next deal (Elstein 2011; Shinkle and Lambrecht 2002).

His business acumen made him fabulously wealthy. According to *Forbes Magazine* (2017), he is worth more than $4 billion, making him one of the richest men in the world. His house in the Hamptons on Long Island is the largest private residence in the United States, valued at $500 million and taking up more than 100,000 square feet. The mansion boasts a dining room table the length of a baseball diamond, 21 bedrooms, and a Broadway-size theater (Crowe 2015). He gives generously to Jewish charities and Republican political candidates but avoids media attention and rarely gives interviews (Hiles 2007). From his vast influence, to his thick wallet, he is the perfect representative of the 0.01 percent upper crust of American society.

Few towns in America have experienced the good and bad of Ira Rennert like Herculaneum, Missouri, located 30 miles south of downtown Saint Louis. In the 1870s, the St. Joseph Lead Company began drilling for minerals in the area and gradually grew into a major regional smelting operation. The company was renamed Doe Run in the 1980s and acquired by Rennert's holding company in 1994 (Doe Run 2017). The smoke-stack is the most prominent sight in this company town, taller than even the Washington Monument. The massive structure casts a shadow over Main Street and Herculaneum High School, known for the Black Cats football team. Most of the city's 3,500 residents either worked at the smelter or knew someone who did before Rennert acquired the company and eventually shuttered it.

Doe Run gave to Herculaneum, but it also took away—before and after the acquisi-tion. The company's operations came at a huge cost to the local environment. Smelting produces substantial lead pollution, which can severely impair children's mental and phys-ical development. In 2001, a few years after Rennert purchased Doe Run, pollution had reached emergency levels. The US government considers 1,200 parts per million of lead in the air to require urgent remediation, dropping much lower if the area has residences with small children. Some parts of Herculaneum had lead levels of 300,000 parts per million—well over the urgency level. This environmental crisis forced the company to reach deep into its wallet and buy outright most of the uninhabitable homes that fell within a half mile radius of the smelter. Eventually, Doe Run would be forced to pay tens of millions of dollars to Missouri workers who claimed health damages (Thorsen 2014).

For years, Doe Run was hit with one government sanction after another. Herculaneum was declared a federal Superfund site, which gives the government special powers to push for companies to clean up communities on an expedited basis. On top of this, the Environmental Protection Agency (EPA) accused the company of violating the Clean Air Act, Clean Water Act and Missouri state law—charges that Doe Run settled for millions of dollars in fines (Nelson 2010). Finally, in 2010, rather than install pollution-control technologies demanded by the EPA, Rennert closed Doe Run. It was the last major lead smelter in the United States (Worstall 2013), and its shuttering delivered a major eco-nomic blow to a region that had long suffered the flight of industry and crippling job losses.

An almost identical showdown was happening more than 3,400 miles away at another Rennert company. In 1997, he bought up a privatized metal smelter in La Oroya, Peru. This town of 33,000 people, nestled in the highlands of the Andes mountains, is a four-and-a-half hours' drive northeast from the coastal capital of Lima. Founded by Spanish miners in the 1500s, the town's development trajectory began in earnest with the 1893 construction of the Lima–La Oroya railway. For nearly 100 years, this was the world's highest standard gauge railway.

Rennert had purchased La Oroya's smelter through a Cayman Islands shell company, which in turn was owned by a New York holding company, which in turn was owned by a Missouri company, which in turn was owned by The Renco Group, Inc., Rennert's per-sonal holding company in New York (Doe Run 1998). Despite this opaque financial own-ership web, he renamed the Peruvian smelter after his business back in Herculaneum: Doe Run Peru.

Like Herculaneum, La Oroya's economy is almost totally dependent on smelting jobs, with a giant smelter visible throughout the town. Like Herculaneum, La Oroya's environment is also badly damaged. The town was named one of the Top 10 worst polluted sites on Earth—right alongside the nuclear disaster site Chernobyl in Ukraine. In 1999, Peru's health ministry found that 99.1 percent of La Oroyan children had lead poisoning, with 20 percent in need of urgent medical attention. An in-depth scientific study from 2002 by the Inter-American Association for Environmental Defense noted several disturbing trends at La Oroya (Cederstav and Barandiaran 2002):

- Sulfur dioxide concentrations that exceeded World Health Organization (WHO) recommended limits by a factor of two or three on average, and by a factor of ten during the morning work hours. Sulfur dioxide "damages the respiratory system, aggravates existing respiratory illnesses (especially bronchitis), and diminishes the capacity of the lungs to expel foreign particles such as heavy metals," the report read. "It leads to a higher mortality rate, particularly when combined with the presence of elevated levels of particulate material." The study found that sulfur dioxide levels doubled in the years after Rennert's acquisition of the complex.
- Cadmium levels that exceeded WHO recommendations by as much as 40 times, which risks damage to the lungs, kidneys and digestive tract.
- Levels of arsenic, which has been associated with various types of cancer and reproductive problems, were many times greater than developed-country cities.
- Levels of lead above WHO standards, which can cause convulsions, comas, brain death, learning and behavioral disorders, memory loss, nausea, anemia, hearing loss, fatigue, colic, hypertension and myalgia.

Word of these horrors started making their way back to Missouri. Fernando Serrano, an Ecuadorian-born scientist, was conducting his doctoral work at Jesuit-affiliated Saint Louis University. One day, he received a call from a Presbyterian church group in Herculaneum that wanted him to hear missionaries' stories of Doe Run's impact on La Oroya. His academic focus was on the long-term effects of lead poisoning. He saw in the Peruvian saga an opportunity to both do good and do good research. Armed with a grant from the university's graduate program, he took a small team of scientists to La Oroya, where they confirmed many of the conclusions of the nonprofit group's earlier study. It was not an easy trip. La Oroyans feared the effects of lead poisoning, but they feared job losses from a publicity-driven smelter shutdown even more. A mob tried to prevent Serrano and his team from collecting soil samples. The protestors' efforts backfired, attracting even more attention to the research (Otto 2007).

Serrano wanted to help put La Oroya's economic and health future on sounder footing. He reached out to Sister Kate Reid, a nun with the Adorers of the Blood of Christ order in St. Louis. A longtime social justice activist who worked with immigrant women, Reid was outraged upon hearing about Serrano's findings. After looking into Missouri law with a local law firm, the two of them determined that La Oroyans could sue the Missouri-incorporated Doe Run in state courts. Having identified 137 young La Oroyans harmed by the smelter, they brought a claim in 2007 on the children's behalf, accusing the company of negligence and conspiracy, and demanding an award of punitive damages.

Rennert lawyered up fast. A local Missouri jury would be populated by people like the residents of Herculaneum, who were similarly in the throes of discovering how bad Doe Run's local operations were fouling their community and their health. These local workers and parents would probably have lots of sympathy for arguments against his company. Rennert's defense would live or die by his ability to get a different venue to hear the case. So, Renco twice sought to have the case moved to federal courts.

Enter Judge Catherine Perry. An Oklahoma native, she settled in Missouri for law school and developed a reputation as a fair but no-nonsense lawyer. When a federal judgeship opened up in 1994, then-US House Majority Leader Richard Gephardt put her name forward for consideration. The Clinton White House nominated her, and she was unanimously confirmed by the Senate (Bryant 1994; US Congress 1994). As the judge assigned to Renco's federal removal request, she found the company's approach untenable. The children's lawyers allege "only state law claims of negligence, civil conspiracy, and strict liability," she wrote. "I conclude that the plaintiffs' claims arise under state law and that this court lacks subject-matter jurisdiction [. . .] even if foreign relations are implicated by the defense in this case" (Perry 2008). She sent the case back to Missouri state court. Undeterred, Renco tried again. For a second time, Perry rejected them.

Doe Run was stuck. It looked like the company might have to answer in their own polluted US backyard for pollution it had dumped in patches of South America. Stuck, that is, until their lawyers chanced upon a brilliant legal strategy. Under a long string of case law, federal courts had jurisdiction on cases that related to international arbitration disputes. If Renco's legal team could turn their La Oroya problems into a formal arbitration, then they could force Judge Perry to take up their case.

As it happened, the United States had implemented a trade agreement with Peru just after Perry's rulings, in the final days of the George W. Bush administration in 2009. The pact provided for US investors to bring any disputes they had with the Peruvian government to international arbitration. Just days before New Year's Eve 2010—the same year Renco would close its Missouri smelting operations—the company became the first US firm to use this new pact's rights, arguing that the Peruvian government either owed them $800 million for not sharing in the clean-up or should let Doe Run Peru renege on the environmental obligations they took on in their 1997 contract (Tucker 2012).

The Missouri lawyer for the Oroyan children saw desperation. "The attempt by Doe Run to implicate the government of Peru is completely frivolous and is being done for this Hail Mary attempt to get federal jurisdiction and to perhaps see if there's some pressure that would be applied on us in pursuing this claim," he told a journalist (Wiese 2011).

But the Hail Mary pass worked. On January 7, 2011, just a week after filing its treaty claim with Peru, Doe Run again moved to have the children's cases removed to federal courts. After ruling against them twice, Judge Perry flipped. Even though the underlying facts and players had not changed, the case was now a matter of federal jurisdiction. Because of the parallel trade treaty arbitration, US law "creates original jurisdiction in federal courts," she wrote. "Because the arbitration panel's decision on the claims raised by Renco before that panel [. . .] could conceivably affect the issues in this case, these actions are removable." (Perry 2011). To be clear, the arbitration and the court case are not in the same universe. The DC-based arbitration would go on to deal with international law questions, and the potential liability of Peru to Doe Run. Perry, in contrast, would deal with domestic law, and the potential liability of Doe Run to La Oroya's children. Perry would not have to follow the arbitrators' lead, nor them hers. But the mere conceivability of the two forums dealing with some of the same facts was enough to shield Rennert from the least sympathetic jurors.

The removal killed the momentum in Sister Kate's case. Thanks to a tangled legal web in the global economy, an investment arbitration was now holding up the fate of 137 children with potential brain damage. It did not matter whether Doe Run's arbitration claim ultimately had any merit. Indeed, a trio of arbitrators terminated the case in Peru's favor in 2016, finding Rennert's legal filings had technical errors in them. Never shrinking violets, the corporation's lawyers immediately launched a second arbitration. This claim might also lack merit, but it does what it is supposed to do: stall Sister Kate and the children plaintiffs (whose ranks have swelled to 1,600 as of early 2018).

Welcome to the new world legal order, with lawyers paid by the hour while communities wait for justice.

From Jobs to Judges

Cadmium, clean-ups, cancer—these would seem to be classic matters for local health and safety regulators. Instead, justice for La Oroya's children was scuttled by an international trade agreement. The United States–Peru Trade Promotion Agreement was negotiated during the second term of President George W. Bush, passing Congress on a bipartisan basis in 2007. But the roots of the pact can be traced to his father's administration in 1991, when President George H. W. Bush unilaterally lowered tariffs for Peruvian exporters to access to US agricultural and textile markets. The hope was this step would help steer local farmers away from growing coca, the main ingredient in cocaine. For decades, the whole Andean region had provided fertile soil for major multinational criminal syndicates that dominated drug production in the Americas. While Bush Senior's strategy ultimately did not put a major dent in drug cultivation, it did set a precedent for deeper trade ties between the two countries.

By the time Bush Junior was elected, trade agreements had quietly come to encompass a lot more than just trade. Now hundreds of pages long, trade treaties included extensive rules on how national and even city governments had to treat foreign investors operating within their own territories. This was not how they were discussed in public. In the major trade debates of the 1990s, the focus was almost exclusively on jobs. The November 9, 1993 episode of *Larry King Live* captured the zeitgeist. On one side, Vice President Al Gore argued that trade integration would bring the jobs of the future. Meanwhile, businessman and one-time independent presidential candidate Ross Perot warned that the North American Free Trade Agreement (NAFTA) would amount to a "giant sucking sound" of US jobs to Mexico (King 1993).

Many Americans stood with the Texas businessman. The year before, Perot had received 20 percent of the popular vote in the presidential election, one of the best turnouts for a third-party candidate in US history. He had sound arguments to back up his opposition to NAFTA, highlighting the persistent lack of workers' bargaining power in Mexico. Even as the Latin country moved up the income ladder, its political structure kept its workers from benefiting from that climb. Perot asked whether US workers really wanted to be competing for factory work with a permanent exploited underclass abroad. He also recounted the difficulties even the European Union had experienced in integrating low-wage countries such as Portugal into the same economic union with richer nations such as Germany. Perot wondered aloud what made anyone think North America would do any better.

Yet the handsome vice president had something Perot lacked: props. "We've also had a test of his theory," Gore calmly stated. "I brought some pictures." He pulled out a photograph of two stodgy looking old men. "This is a picture of Mr. Smoot and Mr. Hawley. They look like pretty good fellas. They sounded reasonable at the time. A lot of people believed them." Gore looked up from the portrait, his eyes unsubtly drawing a line connecting his much older debating partner with these relics of history from the 1930s. "Then Congress passed the Smoot–Hawley Protection Bill. They raised tariffs, and it was one of the principal causes—many economists say the principal cause—of the Great Depression in this country and around the world," Gore told the nationwide audience. "Now, I framed this so you can put it on your wall if you want to."

The condescending attack was effective. The flustered Perot tried in vain to recover the upper hand, spitting out a flurry of denials and statistics. Gore volleyed each one, pitting forward-looking aspiration against Perot's backward-looking panic. "Will I be able to speak for a second or two? From time to time?" he pleaded with Larry King in his nasally Texas twang. But the debate was over, just minutes into the televised hour and a half. The North American Free Trade Agreement passed Congress a week later by a comfortable margin.

Trade proponents won the battle, but the war dragged on. Fast-forward to the 2016 election, when Perot's banner was taken up by candidates on both sides of the aisle. On the left, Democratic presidential aspirant Bernie Sanders claimed that the 25-year-old North American trade accord "cost us 800,000 jobs nationwide [. . .] I was on a picket line in early 1990's against NAFTA because you didn't need a PhD in economics to understand that American workers should not be forced to compete against people in Mexico making 25 cents an hour" (FNS 2016). Republican presidential candidate Donald Trump said much the same: "If you look at China, and you look Japan, and if you look at Mexico [. . .] they're killing us [. . .] we have to redo our trade deals 100 percent" (*Washington Post* 2016). Upon being elected, President Trump announced a range of initiatives to roll back North American economic integration.

Relatively lost in this long-running scuffle over international trade in the United States is the creation through trade deals of a global judiciary that can pass judgment on national laws. This secretive legal system was included in the North American Free Trade Agreement, but it was not widely discussed at the time. As a former member of Congress and eventual NAFTA judge told *New York Times* a decade after the pact's passage, "If Congress had known that there was anything like this in NAFTA, they would never have voted for it" (Liptak 2004). Under these new tribunals, complaining companies have the right to sue governments over many areas of policy, from bank bailouts to green energy to public health. The governments cannot sue back. Moreover, the companies (not just governments) have a hand in picking the judges, whom the contesting parties must pay for by the case. Under this system, companies have been paid billions of dollars from national treasuries.

Yet awareness of this treaty-enforced investor–state dispute-settlement (ISDS) system is on the rise. Both progressive Democrats such as Senator Elizabeth Warren of Massachusetts and Tea Party Republicans around the country have highlighted how trade pacts outsource the US justice system, including the dispute provisions within the Trans-Pacific Partnership trade deal that president Trump withdrew the country from upon his election.

Why the attention almost 25 years late? For one thing, governments of richer countries are now being sued (Barlow 2015). This legal regime was originally put in place to protect investments made by rich-country firms in poor developing nations. But as a sop to our trading partners' national pride, US negotiators agreed to let the lawsuits go against any of the signatory governments. Canada and the United States, for example, put these dispute-settlement provisions into NAFTA to protect their investors' assets in Mexico. Little did negotiators expect that Canadians and Americans with long histories of using each other's domestic courts would start suing each other outside of them. In just the past few years, Canadian companies have sued the US government over pharmaceutical safety testing and US companies have sued Canada over solar energy subsidies via ISDS tribunals.

Even the Canadian company behind the Keystone XL pipeline project has gotten in on the action. After President Obama refused to grant a permit for the operator to carry carbon-intensive tar sands oil from Alberta to the Gulf of Mexico, TransCanada sued the United States for $15 billion in taxpayer-funded compensation. With a rising number of cases against the United States and other rich nations, the original purpose of protecting their companies in less-developed nations was backfiring on them.

Global Institutions Meet Democracy

To the general public, these international investment rules seem surprising, even outrageous. But talk to an international lawyer—that rare species of professional you can find in Washington, DC, the Hague and a few other cities in the world—and they will tell you that the investor–state dispute settlement system is a rising part of law firms' business models—quietly transforming how governments and citizens are feeling the impact of globalization behind their respective national borders.

Consider rising cancer rates. Ever since it became clear decades ago that the big tobacco companies were intentionally turning citizens into nicotine addicts, governments have been ramping up their efforts to get people to stop smoking. In recent years, the World Health Organization determined that graphic labels documenting the damage to lungs, throats, and skin are among the most effective ways to stop potential smokers before they start. The industry is none too happy about these campaigns. After losing major legal disputes in courts in Australia and Uruguay, these companies turned to international investment treaties for a second legal vehicle to fight off government health regulations (Voon and Mitchell 2014). Recently, satirical news correspondent John Oliver documented just how far this had gone. Companies such as US tobacco giant Philip Morris International are not just using actual international litigation, but rather the mere threat of it, to chill common-sense tobacco warning labels in countries from New Zealand to Togo (Oliver 2015).

Or consider rising wealth and income inequality. The growing share of national income and wealth being accrued by the top 1 percent of society is sending shock waves through politics around the world. In the United States, the rise of the Tea Party, Bernie Sanders and Donald Trump can all be traced to anxieties about the rich taking more and more of the economic pie. Europe and Latin America have their own right- and left-wing variants of populism. The number-one way to address inequality is a fairer tax system, where those who can afford to pay more share more of the burden. Yet thousands of investment treaties have overlapping and conflicting rules laying out the limits of how countries can tax the rich (Zucman 2015; Lennard 2014).

The government of Panama demonstrates how this conflict could arise. The country created a finance industry that has perfected the art of inducing rich people around the globe and drug traffickers from across the Americas to stash their savings in secret bank accounts. Other governments have begun to wise up and have tried to make it harder for tax avoiders to transfer money to tax havens such as Panama. But Panama has a counterattack: using international trade and tax agreements to protect the flow of illicit money by challenging counties that attempt to crack down on tax havens (Eskelinen and Ylönen 2017).

Retirement security and financial regulations also are bound up in investment law. In the early 2000s, Argentina defaulted on its sovereign debt and had a financial crisis that tipped millions of people into poverty. To ease the burden and help the country get back on its feet, many of the country's bondholders (including American and European retirees) agreed to a debt-restructuring deal. But a few hedge funds and companies wanted preferential treatment. Their negotiating tactic? Get US and international judges to order the sovereign government of Argentina to pay them in full—even while most Argentines were broke, and pension funds holding the bonds had already accepted a lower return. This was only possible due to little-known international trade and investment treaties and an even lesser known alliances between domestic and international courts (Stevenson 2014; Roberts 2014).

Whether tobacco or taxes or sovereign debt, in each of these areas it is governments, not individuals or corporations, that are being put on the defensive. This leads to some key questions related to the basic functions of democracy. Can elected officials make promises and keep them, or will they be second-guessed by unelected international arbitrators? Will the public have to pay just once as taxpayers when policymakers build highways and parks, or twice when investors demand payment in investment courts? Will policies go into place quickly enough to solve national problems, or will they be held hostage to years or even decades of ISDS litigation and investment treaty obligations?

None of this happened as a result of some grand design. Instead of one giant investment treaty for the planet's nearly 200 nations, government officials have crafted thousands of overlapping bilateral and regional treaties. This multitude of legal instruments was not created with coherence in mind. Instead, treaty negotiators pursued these pacts piece by piece, as specific opportunities for collaboration arose. As the title of a recent article confirms, "diplomats want treaties" (Poulsen and Aisbett 2016). After all, foreign ministry officials do not get promoted for not signing them. If you are in the treaty business, you make treaties whether or not there is a master strategy.

Seen from the short-term perspective of the individual negotiator or government, this makes sense. But over the longer term, there are unintended consequences. For instance, the World Trade Organization (WTO) obliges governments to liberalize trade flows. At the same time, anti-tax-dodging and counterterrorism pacts require governments to put the brakes on financial flows when bad guys might be behind them. Environmental treaties command countries to dramatically lower carbon emissions, but investment treaties give polluters the right to sue governments that do so.

Political scientists have a name for such tangled webs: a "regime complex" (Raustiala and Victor 2004). Like the psychological diagnoses that this phrase echoes, regime complexes are hard to overcome. No one set of rules trumps another, and no single decider can fix the conflicts between them. In a regime complex, one set of judges can protect workers' rights while another can rule that such rights get in the way of business freedoms. One court can order the clean up the environment while another can slap penalties on governments that do so. And one treaty can cut off bank flows to terrorists, while another can keep capital as mobile as possible and not ask too many questions.

Adding to the confusion is this—treaty negotiators left the language of international agreements very imprecise. Instead of outright saying, for example, that governments must grant nuclear waste processing permits to companies whenever the companies want them, typical investment treaties say that governments must treat investors "fairly and equitably." Instead of barring officials from banning Internet gambling, a trade pact might simply say to not put numerical quotas on "Mode 1 service transactions,"—one of many obscure international trade terms. Hardly a model of clarity.

Such imprecision also makes sense in the short term because it is difficult to get negotiators from different political and legal cultures to agree on much of anything. Officials also know that it is costly to negotiate treaties, so it is convenient to build in some room to adapt the treaties to unanticipated future scenarios without having to renegotiate everything.

Over the long term, however, imprecision shifts power from elected officials to the lawyers and judges who must interpret what the treaties mean. Jeremy Bentham, the famous nineteenth-century English philosopher, famously quipped that, "The power of the lawyer is in the uncertainty of the law." And nowhere has uncertainty fueled more litigation than in today's global economic courts. More than 700 investor–state lawsuits have been launched—most of them in just the last few years. Nearly as many World Trade Organization cases have been filed. And taking into account the number of domestic court cases that touch on some part of this global regime complex, there are tens of thousands of globalization-related disputes.

Much as negotiating frenzies lead to regime complexes, imprecision leads to a legal practice known as "judicial supremacy." Long after negotiating teams and journalists have gone back home, new international courts put meat on the bones of governments' obligations, determine whether they are complying, and decide what the punishment should be. And judges have a number of peculiar ways of problem-solving, some of which are useful but all of which are best checked by legislatures with popular support and executives with subject-matter expertise. Judges are neither as responsive to social demands as elected politicians nor as systematic in their use of social and economic data. They may work mightily to obscure nonlegal influences on their decision making—a problem for transparency and accountability. They can misuse so-called "judicial economy," a term than means they decide too little of a case or decide too much. They think casuistically, which means focusing on the case at hand to try to get it off the docket rather than about how the case will influence future disputes. And while legislatures and markets can aggregate the wisdom and marginalize the individual failings of many actors, judges are few in number—raising the stakes when they get it wrong (Segal and Spaeth 2002; Slaughter 2004; E. A. Posner 2009; Vermeule 2012).

While taking new forms, this is a replay of an old governance problem. Political scientists Darren Hawkins and Wade Jacoby from Brigham Young University argue that judges as a general rule use incrementalism to steadily push out the edge of their power (Hawkins and Jacoby 2006). For instance, the Constitution did not give the US Supreme Court the power to review congressional statutes. Instead, the justices unilaterally asserted this power in an 1803 decision, *Marbury v. Madison*, in which they sided with the government. While the legal import of the case was momentous (relating to the relative power of the legislative and executive branches), the substance was low stakes. Namely, should a single justice of the peace for the District of Columbia get to keep his job?

Europe was much slower to embrace the idea of sweeping judicial review. As Yale University legal scholar Alec Stone Sweet notes in *Governing with Judges* (Stone Sweet 2000), the French Revolution in the eighteenth century prohibited court review of legislation, believing it was a tool of the Ancien Regime that hindered realization of the people's will. The nineteenth-century German constitution specified a similarly prescribed role for judges. Other countries (with the brief exception of Austria for a few years between the world wars) had similar arrangements. It was not until after the devastation of World War II that Germany and Italy (under US-occupation pressure) instituted judicial review—albeit through specialized constitutional courts rather than the normal judiciary. France followed suit after the Algerian crisis in the late 1950s, as did Greece, Spain and Portugal after the end of fascist rule in those countries in the 1970s, and Eastern European countries after the fall of Communism in the late 1980s. (The British followed a typically idiosyncratic trajectory that in 2009 culminated in a newly launched Supreme Court of the United Kingdom.)

Similarly, the 1957 Treaty of Rome created the European Court of Justice and empowered it to ensure that European Community officials would not exceed their mandate. Nonetheless, and mimicking the pattern set in *Marbury*, this court in 1964 unilaterally asserted the power to review European nations' laws in a case where they also sided with the government. In this seminal case, described by Northwestern University political scientist Karen Alter in her history of the court (Alter 2003), the Italian electricity service had recently been nationalized, a change that angered shareholder Flaminio Costa. As part of a one-man civil resistance, Costa stopped paying his $3 electricity bill. The public utility responded by hauling him into small-claims court. Costa pulled out every legal defense he could muster, including a fanciful argument that the nationaliza-tion was against EU rules. The claim puzzled the Milanese judges assigned to his case, who had never dealt with this new body of international law. They asked for advice from the European Court of Justice, which engaged in some clever baby splitting. No, Costa's argument was not correct, but, yes, national laws could in principle be overridden by European courts.

Indeed, the debate between democracy versus judges is central to long-running philosophical and theoretical quandaries. During the US constitutional debates in the late eighteenth century, the forerunners of today's Democratic Party (the Jeffersonian anti-Federalists) were concerned that judges would "be able to extend the limits of the general government gradually, and by insensible degrees." They feared constitutional interpretation would "commonly take place in cases which arise between individuals, with which the public will not be generally acquainted. One adjudication will form a precedent to the next, and this to a following one [even though] these cases will immediately affect individuals only" (Brutus 1788). Alexander Hamilton—the grand-father to today's Republican Party—did not contest the point, but argued only that the legislature's purse and executive's sword would rein in any danger from the judi-ciary: "It may truly be said to have neither FORCE nor WILL, but merely judgment; and must ultimately depend upon the aid of the executive arm even for the efficacy of its judgments" (Hamilton 1788). How these "mere judgments" would affect democracy were not explored.

More recently, the literature on accountability in global governance posits that courts are the way for citizens and other branches of government to hold political actors to account (Woods 2007; Borowiak 2011). The mid-twentieth century debates between Nazi apologist Carl Schmitt and Hans Kelsen, the godfather of Europe's constitutional courts, doubtlessly helped shape this conversation. Kelsen maintained that placing courts above politics were necessary because the courts would have no stake in legislation. Schmitt, in contrast, maintained that only the executive elected by the nation as a whole (unlike courts or representatives from smaller geographical units) could step in when normal pol-itics failed (Vinx 2015). Schmitt's unsavory ties made it complicated to question Kelsen's fundamental premise.

Some of these tensions are amplified in global courts. The periodic gatherings of trade negotiators form a weak parallel at best to executive and legislative branches in the domestic context. In contrast, the WTO's Appellate Body, which is the ultimate decider on trade disputes between countries, hears cases constantly and generates norms and rules much like powerful domestic judicial branches (Charnovitz 2011). Moreover, adjudicators in global courts are not typically required to follow precedent, although some choose to, which means there is uncertainty as to whether past cases will be reli-able guides to future decisions (Guillaume 2011). No national parliament can override or demand consistency in these decisions.

This global investment governance system has expanded its power in similarly unique lawyerly ways, where change comes gradually, at the margin, and flush with technical complexity. Indeed, investors lost some of the most dramatic cases, such as *Renco* and others I will discuss throughout the book. Nonetheless, arbitral awards (even and perhaps especially ones that side with states) present opportunities to insert pro-investor *dicta* (legalese for the parts of judicial writing other than the final disposition of the case). If you were looking only at win–loss statistics for evidence of an anti-democracy bias, you would miss the real story. Namely, in each case, arbitrators pushed outward their capacity to review democratic decisions even while siding with governments.

Two examples illustrate the institutional stickiness inherent in international investment law.

In 2000, a US toxic-waste company, Metalclad, sued Mexico over a Mexican municipality's ecological zoning restrictions, alleging various violations of NAFTA. The investment tribunal was made up of three leading legal lights: Elihu Lauterpacht (one of Britain's most prominent international law scholars), Benjamin Civiletti (former US president Jimmy Carter's attorney general), and Jose Luis Siquieros (a Mexican advisor to the Organization of American States). These men invented a new requirement (not found in NAFTA's text) that national governments should permit "no room for doubt or uncertainty" about their treatment by subnational governments such as local US or Mexican states. In other words, the tribunal determined that federalism (the division of government into national and subnational units) should not get in the way of multinational companies.

The case was controversial among investment law's critics. Mexico appealed the decision to British Columbia national courts, where Justice David Tysoe in 2001 determined that the tribunal had overstepped its mandate in making such findings. Tysoe's attempt to rein in arbitrators was in subsequent cases laughed off by arbitrators, who continue to accept Lauterpacht et al.'s version of events. In *Pope & Talbot, Inc v. Canada* (2002), arbitrators accused Tysoe of reaching his "conclusion without providing any analysis or reasoning," a failure that rendered his decision of "questionable precedential value." Judicial fighting words! Arbitrators in *Merrill Ring Forestry L. P. v. Canada* (2010) said that, even if Tysoe was right at the time, the weight of arbitration decisions in the years since effectively moved the customary international law standard.

More recently, as noted above, tobacco giant Philip Morris launched a claim against Uruguay's anti-smoking regulations. In 2016, the company-appointed ISDS arbitrator (Gary Born) on the tribunal issued a dissenting opinion in which he argued that the country's executive branch should have intervened in the independent judiciary to protect the company's interests. The dissenter did not convince his two arbitral colleagues, who were surely sensitive to the exposure given the case by the mass media. This included viral videos by the comic John Oliver that featured this and a parallel lawsuit against similar regulations in Australia. "A company was able to sue a country over a public health measure through an international court," said Oliver. "How the fuck is that possible?" (John Oliver 2015).

But in cases that received much less attention, investment tribunal majorities had been making similar government-branch–transgressing rulings for years (Tucker 2013). Indeed, in a 2017 ruling (*Eli Lilly v. Canada*), Born himself joined a unanimous tribunal in holding that the executive branches of government may be held accountable for even routine court judgments over pharmaceutical patents. This later ruling sets up an avenue for monopolists to challenge consumer cost-saving measures, even when affirmed by domestic courts.

I call this mixture of regime complex and judicial supremacy a "judge knot." The lawyers were let loose on globalization, and they tied it up. They wrote the rules, only they really understand the rules, and if anyone wants to change the rules then they're going to need a lawyer for that, too. In this judge knot, political accountability is virtually impossible. Because treaties require international coordination, they are harder to change than domestic legislation. If one treaty is criticized for being ineffective, then governments can shift blame to other treaties. If a WTO or other judicial ruling conflicts with the public interest, then elected officials can blame the judges. The judges can in turn blame the governments, which after all did negotiate imprecise trade pacts. And, as with the *Renco* case in Missouri, domestic judges can refuse to render justice when global judges step on their turf. Policy making by litigation, legalism instead of clarity, finger-pointing instead of taking responsibility. The title of this book, *Judge Knot*, is emblematic of this tangled mess.[1]

Outline of Remaining Chapters

In the chapters that follow, I will explore how international investment law came about, how the system works, what it means for economic development, and how to think about reforming the system.

In chapter 2, I will examine why investment arbitrations stayed beneath scholars' radar for so long. Investor–state dispute settlement is too international for many scholars of national politics, and too domestic and legal for international-relations scholarship. The buildup of the investment-law system was very slow-moving, with roots in the 1850s and observable consequences that only materialized in the 2000s. An integrated approach requires careful attention to history at the domestic and international level—a feat made easier by a new theoretical synthesis called historical institutionalism. Through an application of this framework and a series of historical case studies from around the globe, I will demonstrate how investment treaty law built on practices legal insiders were already comfortable with, but which non-insiders had little way of understanding.

Having shown how investment law was built up through gradual layering, I then move to exploring how the system works now. Building on ideas from law and economics that view litigation as a marketplace, chapters 3 and 4 explore how companies have reason to "demand" investment law, and arbitrators to "supply" it. This analysis is drawn from a unique source: the arbitrators themselves. In the first systematic social science study of the topic, I open up this particular black box of judicial deliberation and show how these specialized adjudicators make decisions, and I explore some of the unanticipated long-term consequences their decisions (often barely perceptible at present) will have

---

1. The title is also a play on the in-between role of investment arbitrators: like judges but not called judges. Judge not? Not judge?

for economic development policies. While parts of this narrative may read as salacious or undignified, that is not my intention. Arbitrators are not gods from the heavens, but people like you and me. They socialize with one another, compete with one another, and even occasionally snipe at one another. This, by the way, is also true of more traditional adjudicators, as qualitative studies of judges in other contexts have long shown. My hope is that this portrait humanizes arbitrators and clarifies some of the difficult constraints under which they labor.

The final two chapters of the book explore what to do going forward. Chapter 5 looks at how the international institutional framework in which the ISDS system works insulates it from meaningful accountability. Chapter 6 nonetheless imagines pathways of how reform could be made viable, drawing lessons from how judicialization was strengthened or weakened in the fields of labor, trade and tax. Unlike many critics, I see aspects of the system as salvageable and even laudable when compared with available alternative ideas like Europe's proposed international investment court. The chapter concludes with articulation of a global popular constitutionalist vision that can level the playing field between short-term business and long-term economic development interests.

References

Alter, Karen J. 2003. *Establishing the Supremacy of European Law*. Oxford: Oxford University Press.

Barlow, Maude. 2015. "NAFTA's ISDS: Why Canada Is One of the Most Sued Countries in the World." *Common Dreams*, October 23.

Borowiak, Craig T. 2011. *Accountability and Democracy: The Pitfalls and Promise of Popular Control*. Oxford: Oxford University Press.

Brutus. 1788. "The Power of the Judiciary, Part IV (Antifederalist Paper No. 82)." *New York Journal*, March 6.

Bryant, Tim. 1994. "Judgeship Pick Is Pride of Oklahoma Town." *Saint Louis Post Dispatch*, May 15.

Cederstav, Anna, and Alberto Barandiaran. 2002. "La Oroya Cannot Wait." San Francisco: AIDA.

Charnovitz, Steve. 2011. "A Post-Montesquieu Analysis of the WTO." In *Governing the World Trade Organization: Past, Present and Beyond Doha*, edited by Thomas Cottier and Manfred Elsig, 265–88. Cambridge: Cambridge University Press.

Crowe, Portia. 2015. "11 Crazy Facts about Junk Bond Billionaire Ira Rennert's $248 Million Hamptons Mansion." *Business Insider*, March 9.

Doe Run. 1998. "Form S-4—Registration of Securities, Business Combinations." Securities and Exchange Commission.

———. 2017. "Doe Run > Who We Are > Doe Run History."

Elstein, Aaron. 2011. "Inside Ira Rennert's Dirtiest Businesses." *Crain's New York Business*, November 27.

Eskelinen, Teppo, and Matti Ylönen. 2017. "Panama and the WTO: New Constitutionalism of Trade Policy and Global Tax Governance." *Review of International Political Economy* 24 (4): 629–56.

FNS. 2016. "Transcript of the Democratic Presidential Debate in Flint, Mich." *New York Times*, March 6, sec. Politics.

Forbes. 2017. "The World's Billionaires." *Forbes*, 2017.

Guillaume, Gilbert. 2011. "The Use of Precedent by International Judges and Arbitrators." *Journal of International Dispute Settlement* 2 (1): 5–23.

Hamilton, Alexander. 1788. *The Federalist: A Commentary on the Constitution of the United States*. New York: J. and A. McLean.

Hawkins, Darren G., and Wade Jacoby. 2006. "How Agents Matter." In *Delegation and Agency in International Organizations*, edited by Darren G. Hawkins, David A. Lake, Daniel L. Nielson, and Michael J. Tierney, 199–228. Cambridge: Cambridge University Press.

Hiles, Sara Shipley. 2007. "Religious Leaders Challenge a Polluter." *The Nation*, June 26.

King, Larry. 1993. "NAFTA Debate." *Larry King Live*. Atlanta: CNN.

Lennard, Michael. 2014. "Transfer Pricing Arbitration as an Option for Developing Countries." *Intertax* 42 (3): 179–88.

Liptak, Adam. 2004. "Review of U.S. Rulings by Nafta Tribunals Stirs Worries." *New York Times*, April 18, sec. U.S.

Nelson, Gabriel. 2010. "Lead Producer to Pay $7M Fine, Spend $65M on Cleanups." *New York Times*, October 11.

Oliver, John. 2015. "Tobacco." *Last Week Tonight with John Oliver*. New York: HBO.

Otto, Rachel. 2007. "Research Meets Mission in Peru." *Knowledge*.

Perry, Catherine D. 2008. AAZA v. Doe Run Resources Corp. (order granting plaintiff's motion to remand to state courts). Eastern District of Missouri.

———. 2011. A. O. A. v. Doe Run Resources Corp. (denial of plaintiffs' motion to remand to state courts). Eastern District of Missouri.

Posner, Eric A. 2009. *The Perils of Global Legalism*. Chicago: University of Chicago Press.

Poulsen, Lauge N. Skovgaard, and Emma Aisbett. 2016. "Diplomats Want Treaties: Diplomatic Agendas and Perks in the Investment Regime." *Journal of International Dispute Settlement* 7 (1): 72–91.

Raustiala, Kal, and David G. Victor. 2004. "The Regime Complex for Plant Genetic Resources." *International Organization* 58 (2): 277–309.

Roberts, John. 2014. BG Group PLC v. Republic of Argentina (Roberts, CJ, Dissenting). U.S. Supreme Court.

Segal, Jeffrey A., and Harold J. Spaeth. 2002. *The Supreme Court and the Attitudinal Model Revisited*. Cambridge: Cambridge University Press.

Shinkle, Peter, and Bill Lambrecht. 2002. "Doe Run Owner Built Empire on Junk Bonds Regulators Worry That Debt May Imperil Cleanup Effort." *Saint Louis Post Dispatch*, April 14.

Slaughter, Anne-Marie. 2004. *A New World Order*. Princeton, NJ: Princeton University Press.

Stevenson, Alexandra. 2014. "Judge Threatens Argentina With Contempt Over Its Statements." *New York Times*, August 8.

Stone Sweet, Alec. 2000. *Governing with Judges: Constitutional Politics in Europe*. Oxford: Oxford University Press.

Thornton, Emily. 2003. "Ira Rennert's House of Debt." *Bloomberg.Com*, February 17.

Thorsen, Leah. 2014. "Appellate Court Overturns $240 Million from Herculaneum Smelter Verdict." *Saint Louis Post Dispatch*, June 17.

Tucker, Todd. 2012. "Renco Group Uses Trade Pact Foreign Investor Provisions to Chill Peru's Environment and Health Policy, Undermine Justice." Washington, DC: Public Citizen.

———. 2013. "Investment Agreements versus the Rule of Law?" Discussion Paper 9. IPFSD-Forum. Geneva: UN Conference on Trade and Development.

U.S. Congress. 1994. *P.N1573 – Nomination of Catherine D. Perry for The Judiciary, 103rd Congress (1993–1994)*. Washington, DC.

Vermeule, Adrian. 2012. *Law and the Limits of Reason*. Oxford: Oxford University Press.

Vinx, Lars. 2015. *The Guardian of the Constitution: Hans Kelsen and Carl Schmitt on the Limits of Constitutional Law*. Cambridge: Cambridge University Press.

Voon, Tania S., and Andrew D. Mitchell, eds. 2014. *The Global Tobacco Epidemic and the Law*. London: Edward Elgar Publishing.

Washington Post. 2016. "The Fox News GOP Debate Transcript, Annotated." *Washington Post*, March 3.

Wiese, Kelly. 2011. "Threats Mar Doe Run Suit in Peru." *Missouri Lawyers Media* (blog). March 4.

Woods, Ngaire. 2007. "Multilateralism and Building Stronger International Institutions." In *Global Accountabilities: Participation, Pluralism, and Public Ethics*, edited by Alnoor Ebrahim and Edward Weisband. Cambridge: Cambridge University Press.

Worstall, Tim. 2013. "The Last Lead Smelter in the US Closes Because the Hippies Won." *Forbes*, December 23.

Zucman, Gabriel. 2015. *The Hidden Wealth of Nations: The Scourge of Tax Havens*. Chicago: University of Chicago Press.

Chapter Two

HISTORICIZING INVESTMENT LAW

The discovery of America [. . .] naturally gave rise to a vast number of disputes which the scanty International Code of the Middle Ages was quite unable to settle. That code [. . .] possessed no means of unraveling complications with regard to the character of the acts necessary in order to obtain dominion over newly discovered territory.
— British Foreign Secretary Charles Carmichael (1884) (quoted in China Mieville 2006)

Any scholarly consideration of international investment law faces an immediate hurdle: What theory or even what academic discipline is best suited to the task?

There are a few disciplines we can exclude from the outset, for instance economic development studies. From a pro-state *dirigiste* thinking of the postwar period to a market fundamentalist neoliberalism in more recent years, development scholars have thoroughly trod the terrain of the optimal balance between the state and the market in emerging economies. This happens to be much of the same subject matter that now consumes investor–state dispute settlement (ISDS) arbitrations, which are overwhelmingly brought against developing nations but increasingly against developed nations as well. The implications of this overlap are dealt with extensively in chapter 3. In this chapter, suffice it to say that economic development studies tell scholars and students a great deal about change within countries, but they say little about shifts in the international system such as investor arbitration.

Legal scholarship offers scarcely more help. The seeming legalese of investment arbitration awards—long and dense with Latin phraseology—suggests a tentative fit. Yet, as one prominent international law scholar told me, "The only trouble with teaching investment law is there is so little law in it." She did not mean lawyers were not involved. Indeed, lawyers run the law firms, arbitration centers and tribunals that make the system possible. Rather, she was making an observation well-known to practitioners—the decisions that the lawyers make are not particularly law-like. Take the 2014 award stemming from Russia's expropriation of fallen oligarch Mikhail Khodorkovsky's assets, collectively referred to as the *Yukos* cases. While taking up thousands of pages of text, these documents focused mostly on the recitation of a factual chronology of increasing state harassment of the once-favored billionaire, with legal interpretation taking up only a few pages (Fortier et al. 2014). Then there is the reality that tribunals hearing similar cases with nearly identical facts come to opposite legal conclusions, with no Supreme Court–like entity to bring uniformity.

Legal scholars have made admirable efforts to categorize dozens of different doctrinal approaches in investment law, and to assign ISDS to one of the branches or subbranches of law. Is investment law more like public international law between states

(Brabandere 2014)? More like private international law governing commerce (Cutler 2003; Born 2009; Park 2012)? Is it de facto constitutional or administrative law (Van Harten 2008; Schneiderman 2008)? There is much to learn from these efforts, yet they tend to black-box the things that most social scientists and observers of politics care about: What is the balance between structure and agency? Who decides who gets what, when, how? How do rulings change state behavior, or not? For those who suspect that law is not autonomous but rather embedded in and shaped by politics, complementary social science explanations are needed (as many of these authors would themselves acknowledge.)

But before we pooh-pooh the lawyers too much, its worth noting that arbitration may not be so much less legal than domestic law. After all, in the United States, where the Supreme Court chooses which inconsistencies in domestic law to resolve, so-called circuit splits (where courts in one part of the country rule differently than in other parts on the same question) can persist indefinitely. This is much like the inconsistencies so scorned in ISDS. And as political scientists Jeff Staton and Will Moore (2011) remind us, domestic court rulings against other branches of government require the latter's voluntary cooperation, just as international courts require state implementation. Whether domestic courts or international arbitrations, there are politics all the way down.

So what does political science tell us? Over the last decade, international-relations scholars have increasingly sought to apply lessons from the long-flowering domestic political science of courts to the international level (Dunoff and Pollack 2012). But until the last few years, much of the theorizing came from international relations' "isms," with realists emphasizing power, rational-choice institutionalists focusing on interests, and sociological institutionalists prioritizing norms.

These accounts (while valuable), leave key questions unanswered when it comes to investment law. If investment pacts are so great, why did more states not sign more of them before the 1990s? And if getting cash payments from governments is such a valuable remedy for corporations, why did more cases not get launched before the 2000s, a decade or longer after it was available? (See Figures 2.1 and 2.2.)

In this chapter, I argue that an emerging research framework called historical institutionalism provides the best leverage for understanding investment law. Its basic insight is that when things happen, and in what sequence, matters for what political actors do now and in the future. Its more recent applications to international relations explicitly theorize the interplay between the domestic sphere and the international sphere, researching how happenings at one level are contested or internalized at the other in a series of reactive- or path-dependent sequences (Rixen et al. 2016; Fioretos 2017).

The chapter unfolds as follows. First, I show how the dominant paradigmatic approaches in international relations—realism, rational-choice institutionalism, and sociological institutionalism—are poorly equipped to explain the emergence and staying power of international judicialization generally and investment law specifically. Second, I introduce the reader to the historical institutionalist project. Third, I apply this framework to interpret investment law's prehistory, using historical institutionalist concepts such as critical junctures and positive feedback. A final section sums up.

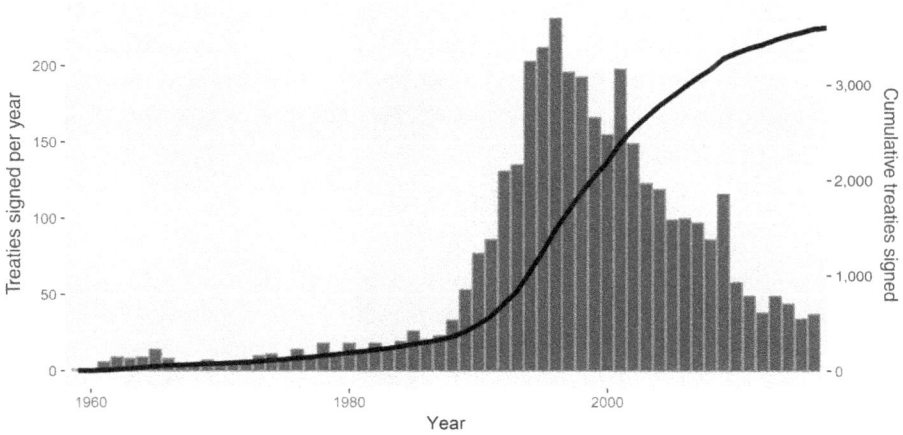

Figure 2.1 Investment treaty signings, 1959–2016
Source: Author's calculations using UNCTAD data.

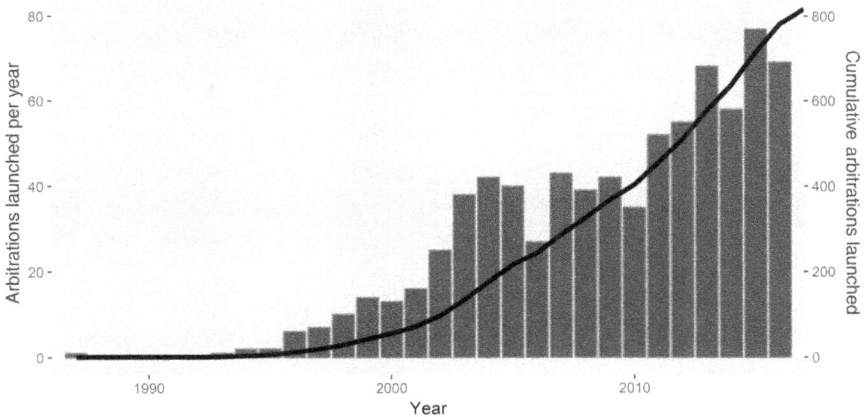

Figure 2.2 Investment treaty arbitrations launched, 1987–2016
Source: Author's calculations using UNCTAD data.

Strengths and Weaknesses of International Relations Paradigms

There are three broad paradigmatic approaches to understanding the dynamics of international relations. The first is realism, or the idea that power determines everything. The second is rational-choice institutionalism, or the belief that rules bind together the international system precisely because power dynamics do not result in constant displays of violent state actions. And the third is sociological institutionalism, or the concept that norms of behavior in international relations develop toward accepted rules of law. To understand the strengths and weaknesses of these approaches as they relate to the development of investment law, let us examine each of them in turn. To be clear, each paradigm is internally diverse, and individual scholars may deviate from the generalized typologies below. But making some generalizations allows for a more structured comparison between the paradigms.

Realism: Power Talks, Law Walks

For realists, the balance of power between states in anarchy determines international relations. In this theory, states are assumed to be rational and unitary actors capable of articulating and pursuing their own interests. The gaps between the haves and the have-nots are fundamental to understanding international order, while the niceties of international organizations are epiphenomenal. The function of international courts is not to restrain the powerful (as in rule-of-law ideologies), argues University of California, Los Angeles, law professor Richard H. Steinberg, but rather to be their instrument (Steinberg 2013). Rules—even seemingly neutral ones—reflect that power distribution. Steinberg, for example, argues that powerful states introduced rules to the World Trade Organization (WTO) that require consensus to change the charters of international organizations, thus ensuring no alterations are made without their consent (Steinberg 2002). Thus, even rules that seem to encourage participation are really tools of dominance.

In this paradigm, powerful states have the upper hand not only over weaker states but also over non-state actors such as adjudicators. Realists conceive of states' relationship with adjudicators as one between principals and agents. In this telling, powerful state principals gave international tribunals and tribunalists their power, and they can also take it back (Hawkins et al. 2006). Powerful countries will use their voices to bring agents into line with their preferences. Whenever these agents begin to get too full of themselves and rule against the powerful, the powerful exit. If the powerful have not exited, this is post hoc evidence of agents staying in line.

This framework gets many things right. Realism compellingly accounts for the withdrawal of the United States from the International Court of Justice's jurisdiction after rulings against President Ronald Reagan's anti-revolutionary Nicaragua policies and President George W. Bush's Mexican immigrant-detainee policies, as well as the United States staying in the WTO, where it loses many cases but also wins many and has significant informal influence over adjudicators (E. A. Posner and Yoo 2005). Moreover, the realist perspective could account for why powerful states such as the United States tolerate this dispute-settlement system even in the face of criticism. A realist might observe that the country has never actually lost an ISDS case, its investors have won many cases, doctrines in domestic US law get exported in its own treaties' text and such provisions in US treaties get cut-and-pasted into other countries' treaties (for evidence, see Allee and Elsig 2015). This system of international law imposes few if any observable costs on the United States and can be seen as an instrument to project US power.

Yet important questions of timing and content are black-boxed by a realist approach. If investment pacts are an instrument of the powerful—and given that the power asymmetries between developed and developing countries are centuries old—then why did rich nations not force treaties earlier? Decolonization offers one explanation: rich countries lost their direct rule over their former colonies throughout the 1950s and 1960s and needed indirect rule. But as Figure 2.1 shows, the real diffusion of signings did not happen until the 1990s and declined thereafter. And as Figure 2.2 shows, there was not even a single case until 1990—and not a significant number until the 2000s.

Moreover, realism has little to say about the influence of some legal norms and not others in the case law. A power-based explanation would expect that the treaty norms most consistent with US law (such as a ban on regulatory takings) would be the most utilized. As chapter 3 will show, this is emphatically not the case. Relatively untethered norms such as fair and equitable treatment are much more influential. Finally, realism tells us little about why powerful countries have reacted in the ways they have. For instance, some developed countries (among them Canada and Germany) are being successfully sued. But they have responded to domestic criticism by proposing reforms that would delegate even more power to investment adjudicators by a grant of tenure in an investment court system. This would make international judges even less reliant on states—a puzzling outcome for realists.

Rational-Choice Institutionalism: Rules That Bind

In the 1980s, cracks began to emerge in the realist consensus in international relations as a new generation of scholars puzzled over why modern inter-state relations are characterized by infrequent coercion and many instances of peaceful cooperation.

Political scientists, such as Stanford University's Stephen D. Krasner and Princeton University's Robert Keohane, borrowed extensively from neoclassical economics' explanation of a key puzzle: Why does all economic exchange not take place in spot markets? After all, in market institutions, inefficiencies quickly disappear as upstarts would innovate to displace incumbents with lower costs. But, instead, much economic activity takes place in nonmarket hierarchical organizations such as firms. Why? The economists' explanation: information gathering and resource mobilizing are costly, and rational actors want to minimize them. Writing separate contracts with a contractor for every day or hour's work would be an enormous hassle, while longer-term job offers and contracts thus save time and transaction costs. But there is a downside: with longer time horizons comes uncertainty. Market participants can contract for the known risks, such as nondelivery, but cannot enumerate every eventuality. This means participants will leave contracts somewhat vague and need legal institutions to help apply their original intent to new situations. In even more complex settings, government must step in to allocate extra-contractual legal responsibilities so that private actors internalize the externalities that their contractual dealings impose on third parties, such as pollution (Coase 1960; O. E. Williamson 1985).

If institutions matter in everyday economic exchanges between people, then rational-choice institutionalists argue that it also does between nations (Krasner 1982; Keohane 1984).[1] In a realist landscape, every state would constantly be testing other countries'

---

1. This school is sometimes called neoliberal or liberal institutionalism, but more recent work has settled on rational-choice institutionalism, which avoids unnecessary imputations of substantive political ideology.

resolve so as to expand its own power. But we do not see such perpetual contestation. As Northwestern University political scientist Ian Hurd notes, many of the world's most important borders are either undefended or indefensible, yet we see relatively few state "deaths" (Hurd 1999). Realism's coercion-based model has a difficult time explaining this, but rational-choice institutionalism does better. The growth of institutions such as the United Nations and trade agreements allow states to pursue mutual gain rather than zero-sum competition. International politics is thus about institutional rules as much as power.

If rules matter, then understanding their design is a key task for scholarship. For instance, some international treaties have dispute-settlement provisions and some do not. If states rationally design treaties then they will include such provisions for zero-sum subject areas where there are incentives to defect (say trade, where one country's gain might be another's loss) but omit such provisions for positive-sum areas where there is no downside to playing by the rules, such as certain types of technical cooperation (Koremenos 2007). Thus, international regimes can be understood by studying the functional problems treaty negotiators were trying to solve at the time of drafting.

A consequence of a legalized design, however, is that states must play by legalized rules. Signing treaties can be a way for states to appear more credible on the world stage. But this credibility only goes so far. States cannot throw their weight around, firing adjudicators who return unfavorable verdicts (as in the realist account). Rather, the adjudicators to whom they delegate decision-making power must be respected as independent trustees of a treaty regime's underlying objectives. Compliance—even and especially when it is painful—begets credibility. That is not to say that power is absent. States always retain ways of keeping adjudicators from mission drifting too far away. But both they and their trustees agree in advance to the rules of the game of how disapproval is expressed. Namely, states must express their interests through the prism of the law (Helfer and Slaughter 2005; Alter 2014).

Most political-science scholarship on investment law, and international political economy more broadly, come out of the rational-choice institutionalist paradigm (Lake 2009). Political scientists Sara Mitchell at the University of Iowa and Emilia Powell at the University of Notre Dame, for example, find that countries that ink deals first are more likely to face a global governance system that better reflects the rules they are used to at home, which enhances predictability (Mitchell and Powell 2011). In the case of courts involving non-state actors and states together, legal scholar Andrew Guzman argues that countries sign investment treaties to resolve a credible commitment problem vis-a-vis foreign investors. While countries can promise favorable treatment to investors ex ante, the state might be tempted to renege ex post when investors have sunk their costs and are thus "captive" (Guzman 1997; 2010).

The problem for states, then, is that multinational investors are not idiots. Knowing how states' incentive structures work, investors will not make their investments in the first place. This is a lose–lose situation, as the states do not get the investments and the investors do not get the returns. Guzman argues that investment treaties, with their prohibitions on expropriation (and delegation to third-party arbitrators), help solve the credible commitment problem. States that go back on their word will face financial penalties and reputational damage, so will be held to the bargain. The argument is compelling: nearly every contribution in the voluminous literature on the impact of treaties on foreign direct investment relies explicitly or implicitly on such credible commitment devices. The conclusions of this research are mixed. Some studies find little to no increase in foreign direct investment attributable to treaty signing, while others find substantial positive inflows. (For a recent contribution summing up the literature, see Kerner and Lawrence 2014.)

But, as with realism, much of what is interesting about international law is left obscure. While rational-choice institutionalism offers a plausible account of states' motivation to sign investment treaties, it explains little about the timing of treaty signing. If international law helps solve coordination problems then this would have been equally true at many points in history (Alter 2017), so why the boom in investment treaty signings in the 1990s and 2000s? Indeed, there is some evidence that developing countries were not engaging in strategic treaty signing, as per the Guzman theory. Instead, University College London political scientist Lauge Poulsen argues that developing countries did not understand the extent of the liability they were taking on until legal disputes started to emerge in the 2000s, at which point signings tapered off (Poulsen 2015). Moreover, in a system in which norms are fluid and invented and changeable by arbitrators (as we will see below), what substantive behavior states are credibly committing to is unknowable ex ante. In other words, we have more spot market than hierarchy.

Sociological Institutionalism: Doing What Is Right

While realists and rational-choice institutionalists take interests as given, sociological institutionalists examine how interests are discursively constructed. Far from serially calculating how to optimize power or economic gain, most social actors (states and people) behave by social convention, guided by a logic of appropriateness. These behavioral rules come about as the result of campaigning by so-called norm entrepreneurs, or those who attempt to persuade other intellectuals and eventually states to internalize these rules in what scholars have deemed a "norm life cycle" (Koh 1997; Finnemore and Sikkink 1998). This diffusion of rules of behavior can be observed through which words, concepts, and frames gain influence and which are banished from polite society (Barnett and Duvall 2005). Table 2.1 summarizes the three stages of norm development.

Laws are norms par excellence, with pride of place in the rightmost column in Table 2.1. Unlike communal norms, which may be irrational, law under the traditional sociological accounts is rational, non-retroactive, generally applicable, clear, accessible to the general public, knowable in advance, internally consistent and demonstrated through patterns of official conduct (Brunnee and Toope 2010). For sociological institutionalists, the formally anarchical nature of the international system makes law all the more important, which is very different from the realist view of international law as a misnomer or the rational-choice institutionalist view of it as credible commitments. Indeed, law (alongside the informal practices and beliefs of people in international institutions) is the repository of what interactions at the international level are all about (Farrell and Finnemore 2017). If nations invest energy in justifying their departures from the letter of the law, then this

Table 2.1 Norm evolution in sociological institutionalism

	Stage 1 Norm emergence	Stage 2 Norm diffusion	Stage 3 Norm internalizing
Who acts?	Norm entrepreneurs, activists	States, international organizations, networks	Lawyers, bureaucrats
Why do they act?	Ideological conviction	Desire to be seen as conforming	Conformity to professional norms
What tools do they use?	Persuasion	Demonstrating good behavior; socializing one another	Institutionalizing routines

Source: Author's adaptation of Finnermore and Sikkink (1998).

can be evidence of the law's normative pull because most states like to be seen as rule followers (Chayes and Chayes 1993).

Despite its more thoroughgoing engagement with the content and elaboration of law, the sociological institutionalist perspective is also not particularly well suited to my purposes in this book. ISDS rulings are unreviewable and reach contradictory interpretations across one another (Franck 2005). Moreover, the remedy for a state being found in violation is cash payment (not policy change). This is not a unique arrangement: various legal systems put a price on violation, which has the virtue of allowing for so-called breach and pay remedies when the benefits of rule breaking exceed the costs (Pauwelyn 2008). What is unique is that the range of behaviors that could constitute breach are not known in advance—a key sociological institutionalist criteria for law. As we will see in the chapters that follow, the lawyers in these tribunals show up at the "wrong" part of the norm cycle. Arbitrators do not help states internalize ISDS norms developed by activists. Instead, lawyers are the norm entrepreneurs, with states left guessing where a given tribunal may come down on any given policy area.[2]

Historical Institutionalism: Taking Temporality Seriously

It seems preposterous to argue that messy, real-world legislative battles are only about power interests. Indeed, Tufts University political scientist Dan Drezner cites such disciplinary shackles as one reason why international relations policy makers rarely seek out international-relations scholars for advice (Drezner 2017). Another reason: a discipline that (at its best) speaks truth to power may not always present the powerful with comfortable truths.

Yet theory has value, even for pragmatists. Without careful comparison of many cases and a search for regularities that distinguish probable outcomes from the merely

---

2. This complements a point made recently by Ian Hurd, whose work combines realism and sociological institutionalism. In *How to Do Things with International Law*, he argues that states use the flexibility in international law to justify their seeming deviations from humanitarian norms. In investment law, in contrast, the flexibility is used against states.

possible, policy devolves into a battle of competing spin. In my dozen years of close engagement with policy debates around international trade, I saw this firsthand. Labor and business groups would bludgeon one another with serial "myth versus fact" briefs, which highlighted helpful facts and suppressed inconvenient ones. But, without theory to assemble salient facts and point to falsifiable claims, it becomes difficult to discern and rank the large mass of facts out there. In policy areas where opponents cannot even agree on baseline realities, gridlock is inevitable (Sabatier et al. 1987).

Luckily, the gap between policy doers and policy theorizers can be bridged. Historical institutionalism, a moniker first coined in 1989, brings together political scientists interested in the study of outcomes in the real world, and in particular the way institutions (defined as formal rules and informal norms) shape and mediate those outcomes (Steinmo et al. 1992; Steinmo 2008). At its best, historical institutionalism uses thick, descriptive case studies from the past to assess probable future outcomes (Keohane 2017). This endeavor plays to what practitioners are likely to see as political scientists' value added: data-rich assessments of how policy makers' decisions today could have unintended consequences tomorrow.

This scholarship has yielded a threefold typology of temporal paths: change, non-change (stability), and resistance to change (stasis). Political scientists Thomas Rixen at the University of Bamberg and Lora Anne Viola at Freie Universität Berlin lay out pathways of change that vary by speed (the rate of change), scope (the number of features, issues or actors affected by a change), and depth (whether a change renders the institution more or less robust to later change) (Rixen and Viola 2016).

A common form of change explored in the literature of historical institutionalism is path dependence. This captures the notion that once a decision is made to adopt a technology or bureaucratic process it is often difficult to reverse. Social actors must invest energy to learn to use a new tool and will often get more out of it as their peers also do so. This means the process unleashed by the initial change has increasing returns, making alternative changes less attractive over time. The iconic example of path dependence is adoption of the QWERTY keyboard, which is suboptimal from an ergonomic perspective but so widely used that widespread switching is unlikely.

One type of path dependence is an unbendable, self-reinforcing lock-in of old rules. Here, no matter how much anyone tries, the weight of past decisions forecloses meaningful resistance or reform. The QWERTY keyboard fits this description. Another concept along the same lines is reactive sequences, whereby the order of events matters but remains contestable. As Northwestern University social scientist James Mahoney writes:

> Whereas self-reinforcing sequences are characterized by processes of reproduction that reinforce early events, reactive sequences are marked by backlash processes that transform and perhaps reverse early events. In a reactive sequence, early events trigger subsequent development not by reproducing a given pattern, but by setting in motion a chain of tightly linked reactions and counter-reactions. (Mahoney 2000, 526–27)

Mahoney argues that the failure of the United States to develop an economic bill of rights can be traced to a reactive sequence. In 1964, President Lyndon Johnson launched his War on Poverty. By 1968, this seemed like a failure, creating an opening for Martin Luther King Jr.'s Poor People's Campaign. King's assassination led to the implosion of that campaign, which led to urban riots, which shifted the focus of policy makers to providing welfare benefits to the very poorest—instead of enacting more broad-based social democratic policies.

Critical junctures comprise a third variant. At moments of social or institutional breakdown—think war, financial crisis, epidemics or declarations of national independence—the old rules may not apply. Much of social life is explained by the ordered regularities of path dependence or the tensions inherent in reactive sequences, yet critical junctures benefit from an institutional openness. In the formulation presented by Temple University political scientist Hillel David Soifer, these junctures are necessarily permissive—change is possible; change agents' decisions can matter—and be potentially productive, when one particular change is more likely than another (Soifer 2012). Seen from the perspective of an advocate of a favorite policy (say, limitations on the size of banks), a financial crisis can be a permissive condition without being a productive one. Indeed, this is precisely what happened with the 2008 Wall Street crash, where some change was inevitable, such as government fiscal and monetary stimulus measures, just not the ones more aggressive reformers had hoped for, such as a new financial system with smaller, less destabilizing financial institutions (Fioretos 2016).

Incremental change is a final trajectory positioned between the monotony of path dependence and the upheavals of critical junctures. Here, agency is at an intermediate level. In confronting extant institutions, reformers must consider whether it is more costly to eliminate, replace, or use them (Jupille et al. 2017). If the latter is the chosen course, then a number of more gradualist options are available. In the stickiest of institutions, the old ways of doing things may never be completely phased out. Here, reformers' best bet is to layer new elements on the old so that additional goals are added. In slightly more permeable settings, there are a number of logical possibilities, argue social scientists Wolfgang Streeck at the Max Planck Institute for the Study of Societies and Kathleen Thelen at the Massachusetts Institute of Technology. In their telling, the conversion of the old institution through a new purpose is one option, while the steady drift of the old institutional actors to new purposes, the exhaustion of the old actors through self-sabotage or the piecemeal displacement of the old actors by newer ones are other options (Streeck and Thelen 2005). They cite the US Congress as an example of a layered institution. Congressional budget committees, for example, were created in 1974 in response to concerns that legislators lacked an overall fiscal strategy. But these new panels did not displace the budget-authorizing, appropriations and revenue committees, which had powerful defenders. The result is a patchwork that no one would recommend if starting from scratch.

These dynamics of historical institutionalism are certainly applicable to the behavior of states on the international stage. But as a growing body of evidence suggests, incrementalism may be especially useful for understanding the behavior of non-state actors. Bureaucrats or judges at international organizations can reinterpret rules gradually so that any one change does not trigger states' attention. They can divide and conquer states by issuing rulings that split their interests and make states' collective response harder. Additionally, non-state actors can alter procedures (formal or informal), increase the influence of other non-state actors, obfuscate what they are actually doing to avoid detection, and even create their own second-generation "progeny" institutions to carry on their agenda under other guises (Hawkins and Jacoby 2006; T. Johnson 2014).

Taken together, the possibilities of path dependence, reactive sequences, critical junctures and incrementalism offer an important corrective to the three traditional paradigms in international relations. Specifically, they show that how an institution develops after it is set in motion can be as, or more, important as the original intent of its designers. Designers are not omniscient and could indeed have a very short time horizon. An institution designed for one purpose could end up furthering another, and the relevant environments and actors for the institution could change, generating substantial unpredictability. In short, subsequent history matters.

Historical institutionalism has at least two other benefits as a theoretical framework. First, it is highly compatible with the diverse "theories of change" studied in public-policy schools and philanthropy. Path dependence and reactive sequences have affinities with power-elite and regime-theory assumptions, which emphasize how incumbent actors can exert a stranglehold over their institutions. Critical junctures align with punctuated-equilibrium theory, which emphasizes the importance of exogenous events in producing big changes. Incrementalism overlaps with the more egalitarian agency of the advocacy-coalition framework, in which change is possible when core values of diverse actors align, and in multiple-streams frameworks, where change is possible when problem, solution and political framing are in sync (Sabatier and Weible 2014). Second, historical institutionalism also synchs with the professional-practice literature. This body of work provides rich insights into how judges and other policy makers actually conduct their day-to-day business in ways that matter for policy outcomes (Dunoff and Pollack 2015). In short, when combined with grounded-theory methods (see Appendix), historical institutionalism allows scholars to develop the types of greater situational sensitivity that allow for more fruitful exchange with policy makers and practitioners.

Judicialization of Investment Law: A Historical Institutionalist Account

Temporality matters greatly in judicialization—the process whereby institutional developments become mediated by judge-like actors. Once the power of judicial review of legislative and executive action is granted or successfully claimed, it is difficult to reverse. In certain countries, even constitutional amendments are judicially reviewable (Colón-Ríos 2014). By training, judicial actors reference what has come before, either formally as binding precedent in Anglo-Saxon or common law systems, or informally as reference points for past procedures in continental or civil law systems (Merryman and Pérez-Perdomo 2007). With an accumulation of citations to precedent, case law can take on a sticky quality that reinforces the weight of the past. Judicialization, once it takes hold, casts a shadow on pre-case bargaining, post-case law enforcing, and the political process more generally as nonjudicial actors frame their aspirations in the language of the law (Alter et al. 2017). In the parlance of historical institutionalism, the creation of judicial review is possible at critical junctures and, once established, will evince powerful path dependence from the perspective of would-be non-judge reformers. To judges themselves, the introduction of judicial review opens up a canvas on which to paint their own incremental changes in the fabric of the law.

In the domestic sphere, states over time have tried to de-commodify justice. English courts were initially funded by litigant fees, which incentivized judges to be generous finders of their own jurisdiction, so as to take business away from rival dispute settlers and secure their own pay. An aim of public-sector reform from the seventeenth through the twentieth century in developed countries was to eliminate practices such as tax farming and bureaucratic job selling, and reduce the incentives for judges to benefit directly from litigants' forum shopping (Strayer 2005; Shapiro 1986; Chang 2002).

But there is no necessary reason that adjudication could not have or retain market-like qualities. Indeed, merchants have long sought to settle disputes through private arbitration, where the adjudicators are paid and hired only for the case at hand. In the subsections that follow, I consider three waves of change that paved the way for the modern investor–state dispute settlement system to operate like a market. First, there was a critical juncture that allowed sovereign immunity to be peeled back in the nineteenth century, including through what I call "proto" ISDS cases. Second, we saw a reactive sequence between developed and developing countries from the 1920s to the 1990s that led to further trust being placed in judge-like actors. Finally, policy makers engaged in obfuscation and incrementalism of the management of this process on the homefront. This combination of factors helps explain why modern investment law seems like old and good news to legal insiders, while to outsiders resembling a covert build-up of global government.

Critical Juncture: Challenge to Sovereign Immunity in the Peripheries and Proto-ISDS

From the early years of modern states, suing the sovereign in the sovereign's courts was difficult. The prevailing Anglo-Saxon norm since the thirteenth century was that the "King Can Do No Wrong" (*rex non potest peccare*). This was less a moral statement than a conceptual one: if the state is the supreme authority that decides what is wrong and what is right in society, then there is no higher power above the state to rule on a state's crimes (Jaffe 1963). Yet as soon as early publicists such as Henry de Bracton could articulate a sovereign immunity rule in the thirteenth century, there was pressure for exceptions to it. The rebel barons who forced King John to issue the Magna Carta in 1215 wanted a check on arbitrary royal power. This led in time to the creation of a petition of right, which allowed private citizens to bring claims against the state.

But this right was often more theoretical than real: centuries later, it was still exceedingly difficult to collect on even a simple debt from the government. In the *Bankers' Case* (1697–1700), King Charles II had serially defaulted on money owed to a group of financiers, who then petitioned national courts for payment. The Court of the Exchequer found that treasury officials should not be able to authorize payment to the bankers, as the former "cannot, as such, be conusant of the [other] necessities of the state [such as] suppressing a rebellion, or resisting an invasion, or setting out a fleet [. . .] The law must remain as it is, till some new law hath changed it. And I should much doubt, whether a new law, for the more easy recovery of pensions granted by the crown, would be for the good either of king, or people" (Howell 1708).

This ambiguous relationship between the state judgers and the state judged persisted for centuries. The American Revolution was meant to create more accountable forms of government and correct some of the excessive protections that kings had enjoyed. Yet for nearly a hundred years after the Declaration of Independence, contractors who were owed money by the federal government had to appeal to Congress for so-called "private bills" on a case-by-case basis. This cumbersome process taxed both the private citizens who demanded legal and financial relief, and the legislators tasked with supplying it. Accordingly, one of President Abraham Lincoln's first acts in office in 1861 was to call for a Court of Federal Claims empowered to render final judgments against the government without the need for special legislation.

Yet, even today, despite steps toward greater liability with the 1946 Federal Tort Claims Act, there are many barriers for private parties in the United States to attain compensation for torts and takings. For instance, bureaucrats executing their official duties cannot be held liable for torts to private citizens, and US courts have been reluctant to see even aggressive regulation as takings (Schuck 1983; V. C. Jackson 2003).

If matters were difficult for local capitalists at the dawn of the modern nation-state, life was even harder for foreigners. Under the original Roman law, which was the model for much of law after the Dark Ages, access to courts was a right of citizenship that foreigners did not enjoy. In a bow to pragmatism and the imperatives of the classical world's multinational business class, the Roman Empire created pilgrim magistrate courts (*prateor peregrinus*). In these proceedings, plaintiffs and defendants were temporarily given pseudo-citizenship status as a formalistic solution (Tigar 2000).

Similar institutional bifurcation characterized England, dating to the late Middle Ages. English communities gave merchants some limited power to self-police, which gradually became absorbed into specialized state-led merchant and admiralty courts (Pollock and Maitland 1898; Sachs 2006). Across the Atlantic, it was not until 1931 that the US Supreme Court clarified that "alien friends" could sue the government for violations of property rights (Pepe 2013).

Such workarounds were sufficient for the core of Western civilization, but what about farther from home? Early trading empires were reluctant to impose their own home institutions on overseas areas under their influence. This was largely due to the higher administrative burden involved in wholesale importing of institutions (Mann 1986). Yet, by the sixteenth century, the Spanish Empire changed the template for a more fulsome imposition of external legal systems by force. Imperial jurists initially justified this through a crude division of the world into Christians and nonbelievers such as the Amerindians, who were not protected by Christian notions of just war. Sixteenth-century Spanish legal philosopher Francisco de Vitoria developed a more sophisticated argument, maintaining that even though the Amerindians had certain rights under the law of nations, they did not include the right to wage just wars of resistance against Spanish invaders. This was because the justness of war was defined by its contribution to advancing God's will; nonbelievers did not seek to advance this will so could not fight just wars and were thus only partially sovereign (Anghie 2007). This paralleled the legal justifications for enslaving foreign peoples offered by the Catholic Church in the fifteenth and sixteenth centuries in a series of papal bulls.

With the Protestant Reformation, justifications for Europe's imperial projections became less religious and more commercial. At the turn of the seventeenth century, the Dutch government chartered the East India Company, a novel combination of early shareholder capitalism with state militarism. The company successfully raised private funds to finance overseas operations, including attacks on Portuguese trading posts in East Africa, India and modern-day Indonesia. Just as the Spaniard Vitoria sought to give a legal underpinning to his nation's policies a century earlier, legal scholar and East India Company shareholder Hugo Grotius argued that the Dutch were helping to maintain freedom of commerce on the high seas. Despite this commercial rhetoric, the company conquered Jakarta in 1619 and put the locals under the supervision of its courts, which enforced property rights through torture and other forms of harsh justice (Miles 2013).

Colonial adventures led to a number of legal institutional developments. By 1756, the British East India Company began ruling parts of India—until the British Crown directly assumed control a century later. Even in regions never directly administered by Europeans, the colonial powers found ways to create extraterritorial courts that would hear disputes involving their own nationals. Beginning in the 1820s and stretching into the 1840s, Western powers established consular courts in China, Japan and the Ottoman Empire—sometimes creating these institutions *de novo* and in other instances through nationalizing functions previously filled by private merchant bodies. Instead of Qing, Meiji or Ottoman law, Western officials at these institutions would apply home-country law (Kayaoglu 2010). The integration of these legal systems into home-country institutions was extensive by the twentieth century. In 1906, the US Congress went so far as to create a US court for China that was under the supervision of the Ninth District federal courts (Ruskola 2008).

Two critical junctures in the mid-nineteenth century introduced greater state liability to private foreign actors, both in contested geopolitical settings. The first dispute was nominally an inter-state one but was carried out at the behest of foreign investors. In 1816, the Kingdom of the Two Sicilies in modern-day southern Italy had promised British merchants certain privileges in the sulphur export business. These privileges, however, were later undercut by an 1837 deal with French merchants. As the British began seizing Italian ships, the Neapolitans beseeched the Austro-Hungarian Empire (nominally the Great Power entrusted with overseeing Italian affairs) for support. Chancellor Metternich (the leading Austrian statesman of the era) did not wish to be dragged into an affair that could threaten the peace with the other major powers, especially when they were all competing for influence in the Middle East. Metternich's offer of mediation was rebuffed in favor of one by Adolphe Thiers, the prime minister of France. The result: a French determination in 1840 that the Sicilians owed *both* the British and French merchants (Sedivy 2011).

The second dispute a few years later had the investor in a more prominent role. In 1855, French businessman Ferdinand de Lesseps had made arrangements with his student Muhammad Sa'id Pasha (Muhammad Ali's son and the *de facto* ruler of Egypt) to finance the building of the Suez Canal. Yet local Egyptian leaders did not have full sovereignty over their own territory, as they were nominally under the control of Ottoman overseers in Istanbul, themselves under the influence of the British. With such divided rule and unclear lines of authority, contractual conflicts were bound to occur. For instance, Sa'id had agreed to provide Lesseps with *corvee*, indentured labor. Yet Britain wanted to stamp out new trade channels to Asia and prevailed upon the Ottomans to use objections to the labor practice to frustrate construction after it had already begun. In 1864, Lesseps' Suez company appealed to Napoleon III to arbitrate the dispute. The French emperor in turn appointed a five-member commission of French politicians and lawyers to render a decision. They determined that Sa'id had agreed to supply labor (forced or otherwise). For backtracking on this promise, Lesseps deserved indemnification for the difference between using local labor and being forced to instead import foreign professionals. For this and other obstacles identified by the commission, the emperor awarded damages of 84 million francs (Yackee 2016).

These two cases indicate that a turn to legal dispute resolution is more likely when lines of authority are unclear and contested. Sovereign immunity from lawsuits was a core feature of Western legal systems, where it is still partially intact. Exceptions to it were easier to push on the periphery, where local dispute-settlement authorities were displaced (in early colonialism), layered on top of local jurisprudence (in later colonialism through extraterritorial courts) or placed alongside these extraterritorial courts (as happened in the proto-ISDS cases noted above (in the mid-nineteenth century). Had the French or British business groups in those two legal cases had clear dominance over their Egyptian and Italian-state counterparties, they would not have needed to resort to the more neutral-seeming ad hoc bodies assembled by Thiers and Napoleon III. But such authority was not present. Instead of the total dominance of early colonialism, rich countries competed for influence—leaving a void filled by novel legal processes.

Reactive Sequence: The Rights of Business After Social Upheavals

While the early breakthroughs toward peeling back sovereign immunity came at critical junctures during the colonial era, the drive toward further institutionalization of private rights against foreign governments occurred over more than a hundred years, beginning in the nineteenth century in a series of fits and starts.

Alongside the novelty of the early Sicilian and Egyptian dispute settlements, a much more common arrangement for dispute settlements arose—ad hoc arbitration between states. From the late 1700s through the beginning of World War I, there were 310 recorded inter-state arbitrations. Arbitrators in these cases were often leaders from a non-disputing country. Among the earliest cases, 35 percent of which related to disputes between great powers, nearly half of all the cases over that period involved a dispute between a great power and what would now be considered a developing country.[3] According to scholars of the period, great powers often pressured lesser ones into accepting the arbitration procedure (Ralston 1929).

These extraterritorial semi-courts provoked nationalist reaction. In 1868, Argentine jurist Carlos Calvo announced a legal doctrine that Europeans investing in developing countries should only have access to national courts and should not get better treatment than what the latter afforded their own nationals. After Western powers blockaded Venezuela in 1902–3 over a debt dispute, Luis Drago (another Argentine lawyer) advanced a corollary argument against the use of military intervention. Both Calvo and Drago charged Europeans with using legal and military might to bully newly independent nations over mere commercial concerns, while they intervened in intra-European affairs only for important balance-of-power or moral reasons (Hershey 1907).

The backlash became increasingly codified in national laws and practice. The 1917 Mexican Constitution gave the government expansive rights to push land reform and energy nationalization through expropriating the property of foreigners and nationals (Dwyer 2009). A world away, Soviet Russia was taking similar steps, with communist jurists such as Evgeny Pashukanis arguing that contracts (despite their seeming legal sanctity) were but a paper manifestation of exploitative class relations (Mieville 2006). Even in Europe itself, the territorial realignments after World War I had made property ownership less secure (Macmillan 2003).

The backlash was met in kind by the more powerful countries. US administrations created international legal yardsticks against which to measure Mexican post-revolution law. If its southern neighbor did not provide "prompt, adequate, and effective" compensation for expropriated American investors, then the United States would compel Mexico to submit to binding international arbitration. In these proceedings, State Department officials represented US business interests in a so-called Mixed Claim Commission and attained lump-sum settlements to distribute back home (Koppes 1982). From 1926 through 1931, this commission published 168 awards for US investors against Mexico. Following the US lead, France and Great Britain pushed for their own commissions with Mexico in 1928 and 1929, winning 40 and 126 awards, respectively.[4]

Around the same time, Western business interests also sued the Soviet Union and other peripheral countries through private international arbitration panels located in Paris and London. These cases forced various institutional innovations, including in the Western countries themselves. For instance, British common law governing a court's oversight of arbitration once required tribunals of arbitrators to arrive at consensus before their award could be recognized by national courts. Yet the 1930 arbitration case *Lena Goldfields Co., Ltd v. the Soviet Union* set a different precedent. In this important case litigated at the Royal Courts of Justice in London, it was the Soviets who abandoned their

---

3. This calculation is by the author, as derived from data collected in Stuyt (1990) and Posner and Yoo (2005).
4. Based on author's calculations, as derived from data from the United Nations' Reports of International Arbitration Awards at http://legal.un.org/riaa/states/mexico.shtml.

defense against British capitalists' arbitration claim, instructing their appointed arbitrator S. B. Chlenov to step down as well. The remaining two arbitrators (the German chairman and geologist Otto Stutzer and the company-appointed British solicitor, Sir Leslie Scott) issued a majority award, inaugurating a majority-rules practice that was picked up by arbitrators again in the latter half of the century (Wetter and Schwebel 1964; Veeder 1998).

This vision of law as international order became increasingly popular in elite circles. While Great Power–diplomacy of the seventeenth through early twentieth centuries left little role for international lawyers, both progressive and conservative elements in the United States and Europe envisioned a much greater one (Koskenniemi 2004). In his famous January 1918 "Fourteen Points" speech to the US Congress, President Woodrow Wilson argued for settling international disputes in the public view and for a league of nations to protect nations' ability to govern domestically as they saw fit. Yet, later that year the president's Democratic Party lost its majority in the Senate. To have a shot at gaining Republican approval, Wilson softened his general skepticism toward law-oriented dispute settlements. The international law cause was also popular with his immediate Republican predecessor in the White House, President William Howard Taft (Knock 1995).[5]

Despite its social democratic roots, the Permanent Court of International Justice established under the auspices of the post–World War I League of Nations set international precedents for a business-friendly judicializing of international relations. An early case, the *S.S. Wimbledon, Britain et al v. Germany* (1923), established that an attribute of sovereignty is the ability to give it up via a treaty. This argument formed the basis for aggressive interpretations of a state's consent to arbitral jurisdiction in cases to come. A later case, *The Factory at Chorzow, Germany v. Poland* (1928), dealt with Poland's 1922 seizure of a German-owned nitrate factory in Upper Silesia. The jurists determined that not only must Poland pay the value of whatever the German investors had sunk into the property, but also "must, as far as possible, wipe out all the consequences of the [. . .] act and reestablish the situation which would, in all probability, have existed if that act had not been committed" (Anzilotti 1928, 47).

In practical terms, this meant putting a dollar figure on the state of the world pre-expropriation, and handing over that amount from the public purse to the private investor. This is more generous than what home courts typically order their executives to pay to domestic private interests in similar expropriations, even today (Clagett and Poneman 1988). The imprimatur of the Permanent Court of International Justice—the precursor to the United Nations' International Court of Justice today—has ensured the lasting influence of both of these century-old cases, which are among the most cited

---

5. As it turned out, inclusion of the resulting Permanent Court of International Justice (PCIJ) helped kill the bill. America First conservatives wanted no PCIJ review of US decision making. Progressives had already grown cold to the bill, given its more punitive elements. In the end, even President Taft reversed his position. The Senate ultimately voted down the proposal, and the United States never joined the League (Fleming 1945).

authorities in international law generally and modern investor–state dispute settlement decisions specifically.

Notably, legal advocacy for investors during these precursor years of the ISDS system was still generally carried out by their home governments (rather than by investors directly). According to one tally, there were only a few dozen ad hoc investor–state awards for the century after the 1864 Suez Canal case, mostly under contracts (Stuyt 1990). The number of standing bodies that allowed such suits by private actors against governments was almost nil. The leading example is the Central American Court of Justice (1908–18), which entertained only five such suits, dismissing all five in governments' favor (Hudson 1932).

After World War II, decolonization increased the number of sovereign developing countries. Accompanying their political agenda was an economic one. In 1952, the Egyptian Revolution led to a taking of the Suez Canal—nearly a hundred years after the arbitration over its construction had begun. A few years later, the 1955 Bandung Conference of Asian and African nations in Indonesia stridently condemned colonialism and called for national sovereignty over natural resources. This was soon followed by similar moves by developing nations within the official structure of the United Nations: the 1962 Declaration for the Permanent Sovereignty Over Natural Resources and the 1974 Declaration of a New International Economic Order.

European governments and investors grew nervous, demanding a government response. From 1957 to 1959, a commission led by Deutsche Bank AG chairman Hermann Abs and former UK attorney general Hartley Shawcross developed a draft international convention (never formally adopted) that gave investors various substantive and procedural protections for their overseas investments, including direct standing to sue host-state governments. Notably, Germany and the United Kingdom were not the first instituters of ISDS clauses in bilateral investment treaties, despite Abs and Shawcross' respective nationalities. Indeed, Germany discussed and then rejected the possibility in its 1959 treaty with Pakistan. Instead, the Netherlands and Italy were the first movers in treaties with Indonesia in 1968 and with Chad in 1969. France, the United Kingdom, the United States and other Western powers would institute their own programs throughout the 1970s (Bonnitcha et al. 2017; Parra 2012; Vandevelde 1988).[6]

This new model for governing foreign direct investment had strengths and weaknesses. On the one hand, it created the prospect of a more institutionalized dispute-settlement system. On the other, international arbitrators serving in contract-based cases were well aware of the novelty and possible controversy of the procedures and so tended to defer to states (Lalive 1981). Moreover, early contract arbitrators disappointed some businesses when they ordered payments rather than policy reversals, struggled with how to assess damages, and made rulings that were hard to compel sovereign nations to respect.

---

6. According to University of Wisconsin legal scholar Jason Yackee, the UN data analyzed in my Figure 2.1 does not separate out these investment treaties without ISDS from other investment treaties. Nonetheless, he finds that the vast majority of modern treaties (around 80 percent) include investor access to dispute settlement (Yackee 2007).

The Iranian Revolution in 1979 presented an unexpected opportunity to resolve these challenges. After Iran's revolutionaries expropriated the properties of US citizens and dual nationals, the country was hit by waves of claims in US courts. In order to stop the onslaught of litigation, Iran agreed to the Algiers Accords, which established a US–Iran Claims Tribunal.

The new tribunal had several features that made it a particularly suitable laboratory for pro-business norm entrepreneurship. First, it was equally divided between US judges and Iranian judges, and judges from third countries (many Western European). While the Iranian judges argued early on that three-way consensus was necessary, they made a practice of voting the pro-Iranian position in all cases. This was bad strategy. The bulk of the cases that the tribunal heard were US business interests against a revolutionary government—cases in which the other two jurists were unlikely to hold either Iran's position or that of the Iranian jurist's in high esteem. Out of necessity comes invention—the non-Iranian judges responded to the gridlock by making two-on-one majority votes, as had happened previously in the *Lena Goldfields* case in 1930 (Aldrich 1996). As we will see in the chapters that follow, this endorsement of the obscure practice of two-on-one arbitration awards by the tribunal became particularly important in facilitating arbitrators' incremental expansionist strategies in subsequent investment treaty disputes.

The establishment of the tribunal also affirmed a goal of libertarian law-and-economics scholars: that public interest regulation could amount to a regulatory taking. While this notion had not found receptive audiences among domestic judges (liberal and conservative alike) in cases against the US government, the Reagan administration appointees to the UICT were able to advance the notion against a much less sympathetic defendant. In the 1984 case *Tippetts, Abbett, McCarthy, Stratton v. TAMS AFFA Consulting Engineers of Iran*, for example, a two-to-one majority found that an Iranian government action did not have to amount to a takeover that benefited the government itself to be considered an expropriation. This decision opened up legal minds to the possibility that governments could be held liable for a much wider range of government action than previously thought.

The tribunal also allowed for a clarification of the potential levels of government-to-investor compensation in international law. The *Chorzow Factory* case noted above had inspired distinct interpretations in the years since it was handed down. Under one interpretation, "wiping out the consequences" of an expropriation were limited to damages directly suffered as a result of government action (*damnum emergens*). But a more expansive reading of the same decision could include lost future profits (*lucrum cesaans*), a projection of business success into a hypothetical future. In the 1987 *Amoco International Finance Corp. v. The Government of the Islamic Republic of Iran* case, Reagan administration tribunal appointee Charles Brower hewed to the latter standard, calling any other conclusion "a misreading of *Chorzow Factory* and a misunderstanding of economics" (Aldrich 1996, 236). While he was not able to convince his co-judges at the time, he has since become one of the most active arbitrators in ISDS tribunals, where his arguments are more widely accepted (Abdala and Spiller 2008).

Finally, and crucially, Iran had left itself with no choice but to comply. Enforceability was a non-issue because Iran deposited a lump sum in escrow in Algeria from which arbitrators could order pay outs to be made. Had the money been located in Iran then the government could have dragged its feet. (The enforcement in ISDS rulings, which occurs in third-country courts where respondent governments' assets are located, benefits from a similar model.) Had Iran had a mechanism to appeal the ruling, then the arbitrators' decisions might have been more difficult to sell in the future as "good law." This is because states that persistently object to a nascent international norm are not bound by it, according to the International Court of Justice and other legal authorities (Dumberry 2010).

No way to object, no way to not be bound: third-party dispute settlements are powerful, and third-party enforcement more powerful still. But from the perspective of overhauling the relationship between foreign capital and host states, there was only one problem: Iran was just a single country. How to generalize these procedures?

Luckily for investors, a parallel enforcement apparatus was available. When the World Bank balked at becoming the arbiter of investment treaties in the 1960s, its general counsel, Aron Broches, came upon a way to be even more useful to states (at a time when the international financial institution was still securing its place in global governance). Instead of an investment treaty, the World Bank would make a treaty to govern the treaties: The so-called 1965 Washington Convention, which provided for an arbitration center—the International Centre for the Settlement of Investment Disputes (ICSID)—and rules for national courts to help enforce its decisions.

Parallel to the Washington Convention, discussions at the United Nations in the 1950s had produced the New York Convention, or (as it is known by its formal title) the Convention on the Recognition and Enforcement of Foreign Arbitral Awards. This pact obligated national courts to help enforce private arbitration decisions. Even though the United States joined the Convention in 1970, lawyers were unsure how the obligation would be interpreted by the Supreme Court. The opportunity to settle the matter came with *Mitsubishi Motors Corp. v. Soler Chrysler-Plymouth, Inc.* This 1985 case concerned whether the Japanese carmaker could compel its business partner, a Puerto Rican car dealer, to settle an antitrust dispute in Tokyo arbitration rather than in US courts. Private arbitration associations put their full weight behind the case, submitting *amicus* (friend of the court) briefs that none too subtly advertised that a viable arbitration system could provide gainful post-bench income opportunities for Supreme Court justices.

The *amicus*, for example, listed the recently retired Supreme Court justice Potter Stewart (an Eisenhower administration appointee) alongside other US judges who had served in business arbitrations in Paris and elsewhere. According to informants interviewed by legal sociologists Yves Dezalay and Bryant Garth, Supreme Court Chief Justice Warren Burger had recently removed any barriers that would have prevented Stewart from making the transition—so the judge-to-arbitrator pipeline was known to the justices (Dezalay and Garth 1996, 158). A 5-to-3 majority of the court sided with Mitsubishi, ruling that the New York Convention required courts to defer to arbitrators when two businesses sign an arbitration agreement. The majority took pains to emphasize the narrowness of their ruling, and that "the national courts of the United States will have the opportunity at the award-enforcement stage to ensure that the legitimate interest" of the public is served. Even so, Justice William Brennan wrote a scathing dissent, arguing that

> the Court's repeated incantation of the high ideals of "international arbitration" creates the impression that this case involves the fate of an institution designed to implement a formula for world peace [. . . I]nternational arbitration will only succeed if it is realistically limited to tasks it is capable of performing well—the prompt and inexpensive resolution of essentially contractual disputes between commercial partners. As for matters involving the political passions and the fundamental interests of nations, even the multilateral convention adopted under the auspices of the United Nations recognizes that private international arbitration is incapable of achieving satisfactory results [. . .] Consideration of a fully developed record by a jury, instructed in the law by a federal judge, and subject to appellate review, is a surer guide to the competitive character of a commercial practice than the practically unreviewable judgment of a private arbitrator. (Blackmun 1985)

In short, both the majority and minority saw courts as superior to arbitration—either as supervisor or eliminator of the latter.

A reluctant opening is still an opening. The next step forward came when a young cadre of private lawyers showed how to bring a wider suite of legal actions against governments in a series of cases between 1987 and 1990. Up to that point, international lawyers were uncertain whether claims could be brought against governments outside of a specific contractual undertaking or specialized treaty such as the Algiers Accords. Then came the case *Southern Pacific Partners v. Egypt* (knowns as "the Pyramids case"), which fell under a third type of instrument: a domestic investment promotion law. Southern Pacific Partners, a Canadian–Hong Kong company, had sought to develop a tourism infrastructure project in Egypt. Initially, the government was supportive, but then it forced a local partner on the company, and later revoked the investment authorization. At the recommendation of Boston-based lawyer William Park, Jan Paulsson from the law firm Coudert Freres represented the company in a contract-based claim against Egypt at the International Chamber of Commerce (Paulsson 2012). Representing Egypt was Ahmed El-Kosheri. (All three men—Park, Paulsson, and El-Kosheri—would go on to become prominent ISDS arbitrators.)

What happened next changed the face of international law forever. When Paulsson prevailed at the International Chamber of Commerce, El-Kosheri pushed for review in French courts. Because the Egyptian government was not technically a contractual counterparty (a state-owned company was), the French courts annulled the ICC award. Paulsson then took a closer look at Egypt's investment law, which he read as a standing offer to arbitrate for any alleged wrongdoing. At his counsel, Southern Pacific Partners took their claim to the World Bank's International Centre for the Settlement of Investment Disputes. Egypt appointed an Egyptian chair, while Paulsson pushed for the appointment of Robert Pietrowski, a US corporate lawyer. The ICSID put forward Eduardo Jimenez de Arechaga, the Uruguayan head of the International Court of Justice, as chair. Just as the imprimatur of the former Permanent Court of International Justice helped institutionalize its decisions in the *S.S. Wimbledon* and *Chorzow Factory* cases, the appointment of such distinguished lawyers made all the difference in terms of the legitimacy of the groundbreaking jurisdictional decision in 1988. As one interviewee told me:

> If Jimenez de Arechaga [. . .] says, "this can't be done," I think we would never have had any more. There was a real chance that he could have said, "this has been thought about, this is nonsense [. . .] there is not such a thing as unilateral arbitration." Whatever. He might have said that. And the fact that he did say that this was possible, coming from, not only from the former president of the ICJ [International Court of Justice], but a Latin American, who is going to argue with it? It was really a, you talk about a seminal case, that was right there. It was 2 to 1, and I think they could have gone either way.

Meanwhile, El-Kosheri had been attacked in Egypt for conceding to colleagues that Egypt (his client) might have been in the wrong in the *Southern Pacific Partners v. Egypt* case. He withdrew, which freed him up to chair another case: *AAPL v. Sri Lanka*. It was the first case for the International Centre for the Settlement of Investment Disputes under a bilateral investment treaty rather than a contract or domestic investment law. It was brought in 1987 by British–Hong Kong shrimp farmers claiming damage from Sri Lanka's long-running civil war. The country argued that the investor should have first exhausted remedies in national courts. Samuel Asante, the Ghanaian arbitrator appointed by the Sri Lankan government, agreed in a dissenting opinion. But El-Kosheri and the investor appointee, in another pivotal 2-to-1 decision rendered in 1990, disagreed and sided with the investor.

Paulsson and El-Kosheri went on to become evangelists for the system and practices they had almost single-handedly birthed. In a now-famous law journal article, Paulsson argued that arbitration no longer required privity, the common law term for bilateralism in contractual relationships where a party and counterparty sit down and sign a compact (Paulsson 1995). Rather, any investor from a home country could sue a host country, even if company representatives had never received a direct specific governmental commitment of any kind (to be supportive of the investment, for example, or to agree to arbitration). As one interviewee commented on these cases, they "opened the Pandora's box for all the cases that you are having now." As another put it:

> I was doing very large-scale commercial arbitration just at about the time when people woke up to bilateral investment treaties. So round about the time that Jan Paulsson published his 1995 article [exploring the strategy used in the cases], which was kind of the threshold, really. Then a lot of us, it started to transform our practice [. . . A] lot of commercial work then turned up as treaty work [. . . W]hen I think about life before Jan Paulsson's article, I think about some major cases that I was involved in which really should have been treaty cases, except nobody woke up to that fact.

In short, innovators such as Paulsson and Brower helped get the key elements of investor–state dispute settlement in place by the early 1990s. This included innovations such as advance state consent to whole classes of investors, a peel-back of sovereign immunity so states could pay damages, the basic procedural elements of arbitration—some of which drew on practices from earlier in the twentieth century. By the beginning of this century, investors benefited from the path dependence of practices that these innovators had birthed, and arbitrators had a canvas on which to incrementally push out the edge of the law.

Incrementalism and Obfuscation: Congress as Frog in Boiling Water

International lawyers' steady norm entrepreneurship—their internalization through novel arbitration rules in dispute-settlement cases—is only a piece of the puzzle of the emergence of the ISDS system. The other side is how the citizens of rich countries—through their elected representatives—were pressured or convinced to assent to these initiatives. The political dynamics were slightly different in each European country and has been canvased elsewhere (Bonnitcha et al. 2017); here, I focus on just the United States.

US politicians have had a longstanding allergy to international law, dropping out of designs for the League of Nations in the 1920s (partly over its court provisions), the International Trade Organization in the 1940s and varied international courts in the decades since. In this context, how was domestic sign-off for ISDS arbitration and case law even possible? The answer: incrementalism and obfuscation. At any given decision point, executive agencies limited the scope and depth of their requests of Congress. This enabled a system to be built up gradually that would have never been agreed in one fell swoop. At every turn, officials discounted foreseeable future implications of present decisions.[7]

Consider the first floating of investor–state arbitration in the 1960s. In 1966, the US Senate considered whether or not to approve the Washington Convention, which created the International Centre for the Settlement of Investment Disputes. Senator Frank Church (D-Idaho) expressed concerns about potential impacts on the United States:

> I am not quite sure that I am entirely clear on how this convention would affect the domestic law. Suppose, for example, that a foreign investor having an investment in this country were to encounter some problem with respect to the application of a federal or a state law, and the government of the United States gives consent to an arbitration procedure under this convention and, as a result of the arbitration award, the foreign business concern would be relieved of some burden under domestic law otherwise application as we normally construe the law. Would this mean that through the device of arbitration the domestic law would be lifted or changed as it affected the particular foreign investor? (Fulbright 1966, 54–55)

The State Department representative Leonard Meeker responded:

> We should not anticipate arbitral awards given against the United States which would have the effect of altering any provision of United States law. The reason I say that is that when

---

7. In preparing this section, I retrieved and analyzed the texts of dozens of congressional hearings on investment policy from 1966 through the present.

a foreign investor invests in this country he most often does it not pursuant to some special contract or agreement with the United States. There is no concession, contract or agreement the terms of which would be expected to govern the investment. Instead when an investor comes here he does so understanding that the United States laws are going to apply to him just as to any other entrepreneur [. . .] This is different from, say, an investment, perhaps, in an underdeveloped country, where the foreign investor may make a specific contract or agreement with the host government. (Fulbright 1966, 54–55)

In this telling, the United States would not be sued because the Washington Convention was a mere enforcement device for dealing with expropriations that happened elsewhere. It is true that the United States had not yet signed a treaty that would have opened it up to liability. But across the Atlantic, European countries had been contemplating doing so since 1959—a fact Meeker would have known as it is what gave impetus to the World Bank to develop the Washington Convention. Yet he did not acknowledge this foreseeable implication, even though senators raised the possibility.

A similar obfuscating script was used in the 1968–70 campaign to get the Senate to ratify the New York Convention (the treaty at issue in the *Mitsubishi* case discussed in the previous section). In a 1968 hearing, senators asked why the United States had backed away from the agreement when it was negotiated in 1958. The State Department's Richard Kearney blamed the traditional hostility of US judges to arbitration, but argued that this was changing in recent decisions in US district courts. Moreover, he said the US "failure to be a party has caused our businessmen trouble in trying to obtain enforcement of arbitration awards in foreign countries which are parties to the convention" and apply it only reciprocally vis-à-vis businessmen whose home countries are also members (Sparkman 1968, 6).

Finally, in what is becoming a familiar play for lawyers who are gradually expanding some new regime, Kearney argued that the treaty was limited in scope, applying "only when parties to a dispute have agreed in writing to submit to arbitration any or all differences arising out of their legal relationship. This means that there is nothing in the convention which imposes any burden on an individual which he had not voluntarily agreed to assume" (ibid., 3). Yet, as the executive branch conceded just a couple of years prior, it was not only private individuals but also states that could be hauled into arbitration. The scope was not as limited as executive-branch officials now made the convention appear.

A few short years later (while the aforementioned Senator Church was still in office) the Carter administration and then the Reagan administration did begin considering such treaties. At a 1981 hearing canvassing the issues involved in setting up a new treaty program, Assistant US Trade Representative Harvey Bale framed the issue as one of US outward policy, not domestic policy: "By agreeing to a bilateral investment treaty, a country which desires to attract US investment will agree to general and specific commitments which will be welcome by US investors" (Mathias 1981, 188). In a follow-up hearing in 1986, Bale maintained the same line saying, "stability, fairness and transparency—are already available to foreign investors operating in the United States. What the BITs [bilateral investment treaties] will now accomplish is to make these assurances reciprocal" (D. J. Evans 1986, 5–7). Under this telling, foreign investors in the United States could be expected to simply go to national courts.

Again, would the US government have any liability under a legal system outside of national courts? At the time of the 1986 hearings, the United States had just lost a case at the International Court of Justice, to tiny Sandinista-led Nicaragua. The State Department's William Milam conceded that "since the treaties are fully reciprocal [. . .] we offer to investors form the partner countries" the same procedural rights to sue the US government. He added, however, that "the United States Government preserves its right to protect its essential security interests" in any arbitration proceeding, which (he argued) should help the US government avoid a repeat of its loss at the International Court of Justice.

But the Reagan administration soon reverted back to implying national law and courts would be controlling. In 1988 hearings, the State Department's Eugene McAllister elaborated that bilateral investment treaties "are compatible with both international and US domestic law. Each provision was carefully crafted to ensure that a foreign company operating here could not claim additional rights than those it already receives under U.S. law" (Pell 1988, 5–7).[8] This interpretation placed emphasis on treaty makers as controlling designers, without acknowledging that interpretation would be outsourced to arbitrators beyond state control.

It was not until the enactment of the North American Free Trade Agreement that Congress began seeking out experts outside of the executive branch (from unions and academia) to explain the investor–state dispute settlement system. But the debate was still never fully joined. From 1991 to 1993, there were more than a hundred congressional hearings, the published records for which totaled 20,843 pages. If laid out lengthwise, they would stretch to 19,106 feet, the length of 53 football fields. Yet within this mass of information, mentions of investor–state issues numbered in the mere dozens. Moreover, the issue was not presented in a way that raised the most salient concerns. Among NAFTA's critics, the investment provisions were invoked as evidence of a double standard vis à vis labor and environmental interests. The prospect of the United States losing a case was not a focus.

As for those who testified from the executive branch, NAFTA's advocates in the George H. W. Bush administration and Clinton administration made the rules seem like a race-to-the-top or alternatively as a lock-in device for other countries. President Bush's US Trade Representative, Carla Hills, for example, said, "The investment chapter enables each country to impose environmental conditions as a condition of new investment, and it renounces the lowering of standards in order to attract new investment [. . .] The dispute settlement mechanism has been applauded" (Rostenkowski 1992, 34). Hills emphasized that trade accord would help lock in the liberalizing changes made by

---

8. McAllister also put the matter as one of rivalry with "other developed countries, such as West Germany and Japan, [that] have over 300 BITs in force. These countries are using their BITs to increase their ability to penetrate new markets. I believe we should protect our companies in the same manner" (ibid., 7).

the Mexican government in the 1980s (a period when leftist political leader Cuahtemoc Cardenas nearly won the presidential race after decades of one-party rule). The US Treasury Department's Barry Newman assured Congress that

> as I understand it, and again, I am not a lawyer, I am an economist, there is an international definition or standard of unreasonable expropriation that has been used for many years to deal with cases like this [. . .] You said that future Mexican governments may change, and they may not have the same attitudes as the current government. The benefit of NAFTA is that it will lock into an international legally binding and enforceable agreement the kinds of changes that the present government is seeking and that we are strongly encouraging so that it will be very much more difficult for future governments to pull back from what is now being developed in the context of the NAFTA. (Gonzalez 1993, 44)

Would the current state of the investor–state dispute settlement system around the world today have been different had executive branch officials been candid about NAFTA from the beginning? There is no way of knowing for certain. But, as noted above, a former member of Congress and eventual investment arbitrator Abner Mikva told *New York Times* a decade after the pact's passage, "If Congress had known that there was anything like this in NAFTA, they would never have voted for it" (Liptak 2004). In 2002, shortly before his presidential run, Senator John Kerry (D-Massachusetts) said, "When we debated NAFTA, not a single word was uttered in discussing Chapter 11. Why? Because we didn't know how this provision would play out. No one really knew just how high the stakes would get" (ibid.).

   In light of the long-standing aversion among US policy makers to being second-guessed by international adjudicators, it seems unlikely that they would have supported any treaty provisions that elevated their power relative to US courts were this possibility made clear. If the Johnson administration in 1965 had noted the possibility that US treaties could be docked onto the Washington Convention enforcement apparatus, if the Reagan administration in the 1980s had noted bilateral investment treaties with developed countries could follow those with developing countries and if policy makers from the Bush and Clinton administrations more thoroughly conceded NAFTA's reciprocity and delegation to adjudicators, then all of these administrations would have certainly had a harder time getting legislative sign-off than in the piecemeal, incremental manner in which they doled out this information.

   There may be another answer for the State Department's lack of candor. Had the department been candid, it would have admitted that it had long maintained that dealing with foreign claims against the United States or by US citizens against other countries was a foreign-affairs matter that did not require legislative approval. Taking stock of US practice in the nineteenth and early twentieth centuries in 1943, State Department legal advisor G. H. Hackworth noted that Congress had no formal role unless an appropriation for payment of a claim was required—and even then, the money could come out of departmental funds without congressional authorization (Hackworth 1943, 404). In 1909, for instance, State Department officials wrote that "the arbitration of private claims against foreign governments is merely a step in diplomatic procedure in which the United States uses its good offices in aid of its citizens" and as such "the action of the

Senate was not necessary to the validity of the protocol." In contrast, when the United States might be on the hook for money, Hackworth said that it is a "question of policy for the Secretary to determine as to whether [arbitration agreements] should be submitted to the Senate either for its information or for its formal advice and consent" (ibid.). Over the years, US courts have tended to hold that certain powers (including claims settlement) are inherent to nationality, and the executive branch as the nation's representative gets to wield them. In other words, the executive gets to choose if and how to bring in Congress.

The same working assumption seems true today. There is nothing in the implementing legislation for the North American Free Trade Agreement that specifically authorizes the United States to be sued in arbitration. Rather, it is only in the agreement itself—as agreed to by the executive. The United States could stop responding to NAFTA claims or simply give in on all of them: they would not be in violation of any express provision of statute. So one answer to Sen. Kerry's entreaty above is that Congress never did vote explicitly on the merits of investor–state dispute settlement. Even implementing legislation in later agreements, such as in the recently signed US–South Korea trade agreement that mention arbitration provisions, only do so for a subset of potential contractual claims against the US government. Nonetheless, the political question is different than the legal one, and had Congress forced a political resolution, history might have been different.

Summing Up

This chapter argues that history matters for considering how investment law emerged, and showed how. From an initial condition of state sovereign immunity, colonialism represented a critical juncture where the idea of states sacrificing sovereignty was imaginable. After that moment, developed and developing countries were on different paths, with incrementalism reining in the former and a series of brutal and surprising reactive sequences dominating the latter. By the 1930s, the most important doctrinal innovations were in place, serving as resources to generations of international lawyers.

By the 1990s, lawyers could invoke the weight of past and precedent to complete the finishing touches. *AAPL* (the first ISDS case) was decided on a 2-to-1 vote, an outcome made thinkable by the 2-to-1 *Tippets* vote in the US-Iran Claims Tribunal, itself made possible by the 2-to-1 1930 precedent of the *Lena* case against the Soviet Union. Iran and the Soviets were unsympathetic actors on the international stage, but the lawsuits against them would not have been possible without the selective scaling back of sovereign immunity in suits going back to the nineteenth century. Figure 2.3 offers a historical institutionalist account of investment law's emergence from the initial conditions in 1500 to the path dependence of the present. And, fair warning: this and some of the other graphics you will see in this book are intentionally knotty and gnarly. They are meant to model the complexity of the judge knot, which frameworks like historical institutionalism and regime complexity help illuminate.

Indeed, seen through the light of history, there is little about investor–state dispute settlement that is truly new. Many of the features that are most controversial—among them lawsuits against sovereign nations outside of national courts, arbitrators selected by the case, the recouping of unlimited future profits and whole classes of investors able

Initial condition:
States largely have monopoly on rendering justice, and largely avoid suits against themselves (sovereign immunity)

Critical juncture

Sovereign immunity of core countries is sticky (1500–)

Colonialism or war opens up peripheral countries to suit (1500–). Example: Suez Canal arbitration

INCREMENTALISM IN DEVELOPED COUNTRIES

REACTIVE SEQUENCE FOR DEVELOPING, TRANSITIONAL COUNTRIES

US example: US executive branch quietly approves US participation in investment conventions (1968–70); lessens judicial review of arbitration awards (1985); begins building an investment treaty program that opens up governments to suit (1979–89)

Reaction: Soviet Revolution and postwar territorial shifts threaten property rights (1917–22)

Counter-reaction: Western investors turn to arbitration and international courts (1924–30)

Reaction: Latin America demands more respect (~1917)

Counter-reaction: Latin America forced into claims courts (~1926–31)

Reaction: Developing countries demand more respect (~1955–74)

Counter-reaction: Developed countries sign investment treaties and conventions (~1959–80)

Reaction: Iranian Revolution, Mexican leftists nearly take power (~1979–88)

Important precedents:
- Sovereignty can be surrendered by treaty (SS Wimbledon)
- Governments liable for lost future profits after expropriation (Factory at Chorzow)
- Split courts and tribunals render consequential decisions (Lena Goldfields, Mitsubishi)

Counter-reaction: US-Iran Claims Tribunal, early investment treaty arbitrations (~1980–90)

Investors launch more complaints Arbitrators add to case law (Chapter 3)

Self-reinforcing path dependence of investment law today / map of book

Arbitrators gain experience and know-how (Chapter 4)

States' backlash managed through the regime's complexity (Chapter 5)

Important Precedents:
- Governments liable for lost future profits even without expropriation (Tippets)
- Enforcement of awards happens in third countries (US claims on Iran)
- Investors do not need a government contract to sue government (AAPL)

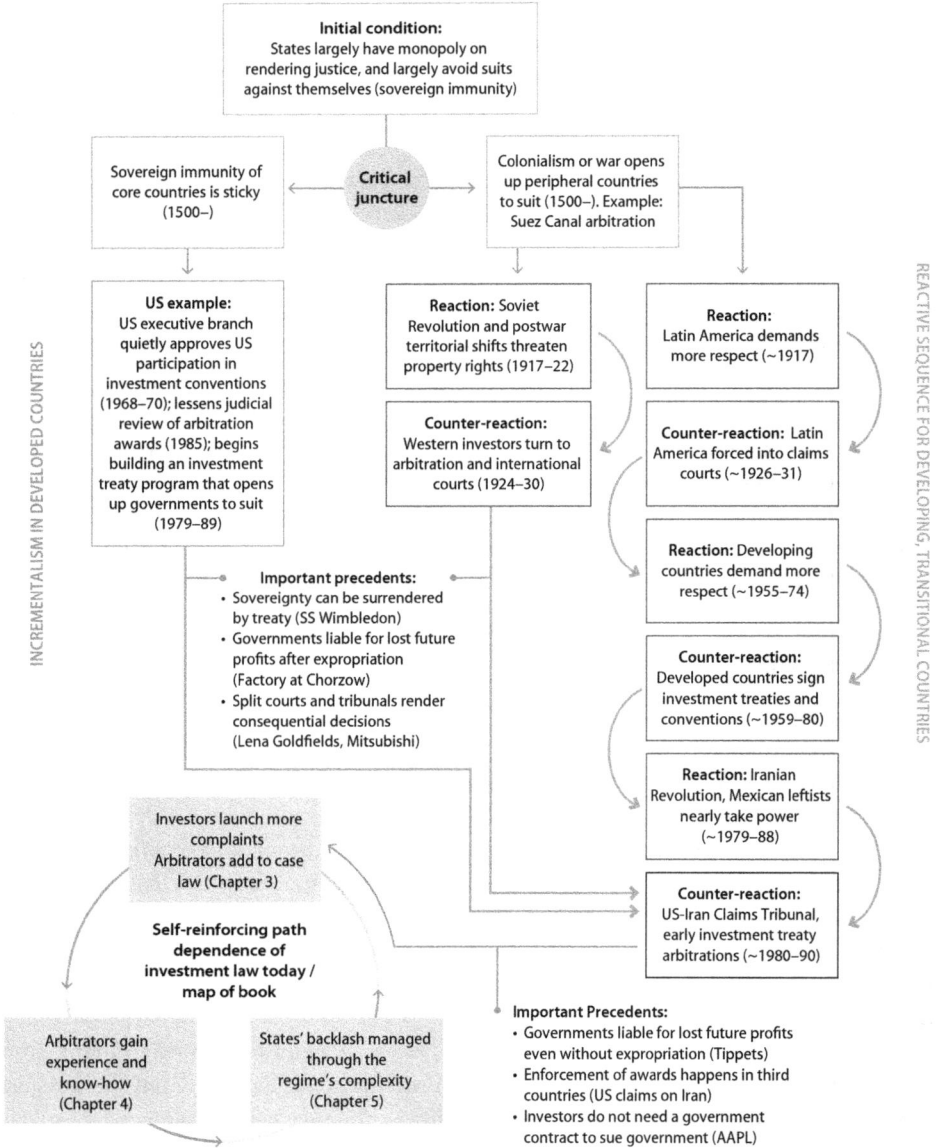

Figure 2.3 Investment law's development: A historical institutionalist account
Source: Author's analysis.

to bring cases (rather than just those with a state contract—were in place before the first modern ISDS case ever happened. This vintage is of clear benefit to practitioners, who can emphasize continuity with the past. Practitioner manuals reach for precedent to an almost comical degree, linking "The origins of international arbitration [. . .] to ancient mythology. Early instances of dispute resolution among the Greek gods, in matters at least arguably international by then-prevailing standards, involved disputes between

Poseidon and Helios over the ownership of Corinth (which was reportedly split between them by Briareus, a giant)" (Greenberg et al. 2010, 2).

But the last subsection above illustrates why it is equally understandable that non-practitioners see the system as unanticipated. From the 1960s through the 1980s, various investment treaties opened up the possibility of arbitrator review of national decisions—a possibility that executive-branch agencies must have realized was real but which they dismissed out of hand. Thus, the perception could persist as recently as 2001. By the time the US Congress began to focus on the possibility of actual lawsuits, the path had already been set. Thus, major political-science studies of commercial arbitration could wonder as recently as 2001 whether we would ever see a significant investor–state case, due to the perception that states had jealously foreclosed their sovereignty (Mattli 2001). With the benefit of hindsight (and historical institutionalism), the path to the present is clearer.

References

Abdala, Manuel A., and Pablo T. Spiller. 2008. "Chorzow's Standard Rejuvenated: Assessing Damages in Investment Treaty Arbitrations." *Journal of International Arbitration* 25 (1): 103–20.

Aldrich, George H. 1996. *The Jurisprudence of the Iran-United States Claims Tribunal.* Oxford: Oxford University Press.

Allee, Todd, and Manfred Elsig. 2015. "Why Do Some International Institutions Contain Strong Dispute Settlement Provisions? New Evidence from Preferential Trade Agreements." *Review of International Organizations,* May, 1–32.

Alter, Karen J. 2014. *The New Terrain of International Law: Courts, Politics, Rights.* Princeton, NJ: Princeton University Press.

———. 2017. "The Evolution of International Law and Courts." In *International Politics and Institutions in Time,* edited by Orfeo Fioretos. Oxford: Oxford University Press.

Alter, Karen J., Emilie M. Hafner-Burton and Laurence R. Helfer. 2017. "Judicializing International Relations."

Anghie, Antony. 2007. *Imperialism, Sovereignty and the Making of International Law.* Cambridge: Cambridge University Press.

Anzilotti, Dionisio. 1928. Case Concerning the Factory at Chorzow (Claim for Indemnity) (Merits) (Germany v. Poland). Permanent Court of International Justice.

Barnett, Michael N., and Raymond Duvall. 2005. *Power in Global Governance.* Cambridge: Cambridge University Press.

Blackmun, Harry. 1985. Mitsubishi Motors Corp. v. Soler Chrysler-Plymouth, Inc., 473 US 614. U.S. Supreme Court.

Bonnitcha, Jonathan, Lauge N. Skovgaard Poulsen and Michael Waibel. 2017. *The Political Economy of the Investment Treaty Regime.* Oxford: Oxford University Press.

Born, Gary. 2009. *International Commercial Arbitration.* Alphen aan den Rijn, the Netherlands: Kluwer Law International.

Brabandere, Eric De. 2014. *Investment Treaty Arbitration as Public International Law: Procedural Aspects and Implications.* Cambridge: Cambridge University Press.

Brunnee, Jutta, and Stephen J. Toope. 2010. *Legitimacy and Legality in International Law: An Interactional Account.* Cambridge: Cambridge University Press.

Chang, Ha-Joon. 2002. *Kicking Away the Ladder: Development Strategy in Historical Perspective.* London: Anthem Press.

Chayes, Abram, and Antonia Handler Chayes. 1993. "On Compliance." *International Organization* 47 (02): 175–205.

Clagett, Brice M., and Daniel B. Poneman. 1988. "The Treatment of Economic Injury to Aliens in the Revised Restatement of Foreign Relations Law." *The International Lawyer* 22 (1): 35–68.

Coase, Ronald H. 1960. "The Problem of Social Cost." *Journal of Law and Economics* 3: 1–69.

Colón-Ríos, Joel I. 2014. "A New Typology of Judicial Review of Legislation." *Global Constitutionalism* 3 (02): 143–69.

Cutler, A. Claire. 2003. *Private Power and Global Authority: Transnational Merchant Law in the Global Political Economy*. Cambridge: Cambridge University Press.

Dezalay, Yves, and Bryant G. Garth. 1996. *Dealing in Virtue: International Commercial Arbitration and the Construction of a Transnational Legal Order*. Chicago: University of Chicago Press.

Drezner, Daniel W. 2017. *The Ideas Industry: How Pessimists, Partisans, and Plutocrats Are Transforming the Marketplace of Ideas*. Oxford: Oxford University Press.

Dumberry, Patrick. 2010. "The Last Citadel! Can a State Claim the Status of Persistent Objector to Prevent the Application of a Rule of Customary International Law in Investor–State Arbitration?" *Leiden Journal of International Law* 23 (2): 379–400.

Dunoff, Jeffrey L., and Mark A. Pollack, eds. 2012. *Interdisciplinary Perspectives on International Law and International Relations*. Cambridge: Cambridge University Press.

———. 2015. "Comparative International Judicial Practices: A Manifesto." In *APSA Annual Meetings 2015*. San Francisco.

Dwyer, John. 2009. *The Agrarian Dispute: The Expropriation of American-Owned Rural Land in Postrevolutionary Mexico*. Durham, NC: Duke University Press.

Evans, Donald J. 1986. *Bilateral Investment Treaties*. Washington, DC: Alderson Reporting.

Farrell, Henry, and Martha Finnemore. 2017. "Global Institutions without a Global State." In *International Politics and Institutions in Time*, edited by Orfeo Fioretos. Oxford: Oxford University Press.

Finnemore, Martha, and Kathryn Sikkink. 1998. "International Norm Dynamics and Political Change." *International Organization* 52 (4): 887–917.

Fioretos, Orfeo. 2016. "Retrofitting Financial Globalization: The Politics of Intense Incrementalism After 2008." In *Historical Institutionalism and International Relations: Explaining Institutional Development in World Politics*, edited by Thomas Rixen, Lora Anne Viola and Michael Zurn. Oxford: Oxford University Press.

———, ed. 2017. *International Politics and Institutions in Time*. Oxford: Oxford University Press.

Fleming, Denna Frank. 1945. *The United States and the World Court*. New York: Doubleday, Doran & Company.

Fortier, L. Yves, Charles Poncet and Stephen M. Schwebel. 2014. Hulley Entreprises Ltd., Yukos Universal Ltd., and Veteran Petroleum Ltd. v. the Russian Federation (Award). PCA.

Franck, Susan D. 2005. "The Legitimacy Crisis in Investment Treaty Arbitration: Privatizing Public International Law through Inconsistent Decisions." *Fordham Law Review* 73: 1521–1626.

Fulbright, J. William. 1966. *Convention on the Settlement of Investment Disputes*. US Senate: Ward & Paul.

Gonzalez, Henry B. 1993. *Financial Services Chapter of NAFTA*. Washington, DC.

Greenberg, Simon, Christopher Kee and J. Romesh Weeramantry. 2010. *International Commercial Arbitration: An Asia-Pacific Perspective*. Cambridge: Cambridge University Press.

Guzman, Andrew T. 1997. "Why LDCs Sign Treaties That Hurt Them: Explaining the Popularity of Bilateral Investment Treaties." *Virginia Journal of International Law* 38: 639–88.

———. 2010. *How International Law Works: A Rational Choice Theory*. Oxford: Oxford University Press.

Hackworth, Green Haywood. 1943. "Treaties Chapter XVI." *Digest of International Law* 5: 1–434.

Hawkins, Darren G., and Wade Jacoby. 2006. "How Agents Matter." In *Delegation and Agency in International Organizations*, edited by Darren G. Hawkins, David A. Lake, Daniel L. Nielson, and Michael J. Tierney, 199–228. Cambridge: Cambridge University Press.

Hawkins, Darren G., David A. Lake, Daniel L. Nielson and Michael J. Tierney. 2006. "Delegation under Anarchy: States, International Organizations, and Principal-Agent Theory." In *Delegation and Agency in International Organizations*, 3–38. Cambridge: Cambridge University Press.

Helfer, Laurence R., and Anne-Marie Slaughter. 2005. "Why States Create International Tribunals: A Response to Professors Posner and Yoo." *California Law Review* 93 (3): 899–956.

Hershey, Amos S. 1907. "The Calvo and Drago Doctrines." *The American Journal of International Law* 1 (1): 26–45.

Howell, T. B. 1708. *A Complete Collection of State Trials and Proceedings for High Treason and Other Crimes and Misdemeanors from the Earliest Period to the Year 1783.* T. C. Hansard for Longman, Hurst, Rees, Orme, and Brown.

Hudson, Manley O. 1932. "The Central American Court of Justice." *American Journal of International Law* 26 (4): 759–86.

Hurd, Ian. 1999. "Legitimacy and Authority in International Politics." *International Organization* 53 (02): 379–408.

Jackson, Vicki C. 2003. "Suing the Federal Government: Sovereignty, Immunity, and Judicial Independence." *George Washington International Law Review* 35: 521.

Jaffe, Louis L. 1963. "Suits Against Governments and Officers: Sovereign Immunity." *Harvard Law Review* 77 (1): 1–39.

Johnson, Tana. 2014. *Organizational Progeny: Why Governments Are Losing Control over the Proliferating Structures of Global Governance.* Transformations in Governance. Oxford: Oxford University Press.

Jupille, Joseph, Walter Mattli and Duncan Snidal. 2017. "Dynamics of Institutional Choice." In *International Politics and Institutions in Time*, edited by Orfeo Fioretos. Oxford: Oxford University Press.

Kayaoglu, Turan. 2010. *Legal Imperialism: Sovereignty and Extraterritoriality in Japan, the Ottoman Empire, and China.* Cambridge: Cambridge University Press.

Keohane, Robert O. 2017. "Observations on the Promise and Pitfalls of Historical Institutionalism in International Relations." In *International Politics and Institutions in Time*, edited by Orfeo Fioretos. Oxford: Oxford University Press.

Kerner, Andrew, and Jane Lawrence. 2014. "What's the Risk? Bilateral Investment Treaties, Political Risk and Fixed Capital Accumulation." *British Journal of Political Science* 44 (1): 107–21.

Knock, Thomas J. 1995. *To End All Wars: Woodrow Wilson and the Quest for a New World Order.* Revised edition. Princeton, NJ: Princeton University Press.

Koh, Harold Hongju. 1997. "Why Do Nations Obey International Law?" *The Yale Law Journal* 106 (8): 2599–2659.

Koppes, Clayton R. 1982. "The Good Neighbor Policy and the Nationalization of Mexican Oil: A Reinterpretation." *The Journal of American History* 69 (1): 62–81.

Koremenos, Barbara. 2007. "If Only Half of International Agreements Have Dispute Resolution Provisions, Which Half Needs Explaining?" *Journal of Legal Studies* 36 (1): 189–212.

Koskenniemi, Martti. 2004. *The Gentle Civilizer of Nations: The Rise and Fall of International Law 1870– 1960.* Cambridge: Cambridge University Press.

Krasner, Stephen D. 1982. "Regimes and the Limits of Realism: Regimes as Autonomous Variables." *International Organization* 36 (02): 497–510.

Lake, David A. 2009. "Open Economy Politics: A Critical Review." *Review of International Organizations* 4 (3).

Lalive, Pierre. 1981. "The First 'World Bank' Arbitration (Holiday Inns v. Morocco)—Some Legal Problems." *British Yearbook of International Law* 51 (1): 123–62.

Liptak, Adam. 2004. "Review of U.S. Rulings by Nafta Tribunals Stirs Worries." *New York Times*, April 18, sec. U.S.

MacMillan, Margaret. 2003. *Paris 1919: Six Months That Changed the World.* New York: Random House Trade Paperbacks.

Mahoney, James. 2000. "Path Dependence in Historical Sociology." *Theory and Society* 29 (4): 507–48.

Mann, Michael. 1986. *The Sources of Social Power, vol. 1: A History of Power from the Beginning to AD 1760.* Cambridge: Cambridge University Press.

Mathias, Charles McC. 1981. *U.S. Policy Toward International Investment*. Washington, DC: Government Printing Office.

Mattli, Walter. 2001. "Private Justice in a Global Economy: From Litigation to Arbitration." *International Organization* 55 (04): 919–47.

Merryman, John Henry and Rogelio Pérez-Perdomo. 2007. *The Civil Law Tradition: An Introduction to the Legal Systems of Europe and Latin America*. Redwood City, CA: Stanford University Press.

Mieville, China. 2006. *Between Equal Rights: A Marxist Theory of International Law*. Chicago: Haymarket Books.

Miles, Kate. 2013. *The Origins of International Investment Law: Empire, Environment and the Safeguarding of Capital*. Cambridge: Cambridge University Press.

Mitchell, Sara McLaughlin, and Emilia Justyna Powell. 2011. *Domestic Law Goes Global: Legal Traditions and International Courts*. Cambridge: Cambridge University Press.

Park, William W. 2012. *Arbitration of International Business Disputes: Studies in Law and Practice*. Oxford: Oxford University Press.

Parra, Antonio R. 2012. *The History of ICSID*. Oxford: Oxford University Press.

Paulsson, Jan. 1995. "Arbitration Without Privity." *ICSID Review* 10 (2): 232–57.

———. 2012. "The Pyramids Case." *Collected Courses of the International Academy for Arbitration Law* 1 (1).

Pauwelyn, Joost. 2008. *Optimal Protection of International Law: Navigating between European Absolutism and American Voluntarism*. Cambridge: Cambridge University Press.

Pell, Claiborne. 1988. *Bilateral Investment and Tax Treaties*. Washington, DC: Alderson Reporting.

Pepe, Douglas J. 2013. "Foreign Affairs Takings: The Question of Foreign Plaintiff Standing." In *Foreign Affairs Litigation in United States Courts*, edited by John N. Moore, 129–46. Netherlands: Martinus Nijhoff Publishers.

Pollock, Frederick, and Frederic W. Maitland. 1898. *The History of English Law before the Time of Edward I*. Cambridge: Cambridge University Press.

Posner, Eric A., and John C. Yoo. 2005. "Judicial Independence in International Tribunals." *California Law Review* 93 (1): 1–74.

Poulsen, Lauge N. Skovgaard. 2015. *Bounded Rationality and Economic Diplomacy: The Politics of Investment Treaties in Developing Countries*. Cambridge: Cambridge University Press.

Ralston, Jackson Harvey. 1929. *International Arbitration, from Athens to Locarno*. Redwood City, CA: Stanford University Press.

Rixen, Thomas, and Lora Anne Viola. 2016. "Historical Institutionalism and International Relations: Towards Explaining Change and Stability in International Institutions." In *Historical Institutionalism and International Relations: Explaining Institutional Development in World Politics*, edited by Thomas Rixen, Lora Anne Viola and Michael Zurn. Oxford: Oxford University Press.

Rixen, Thomas, Lora Anne Viola and Michael Zurn, eds. 2016. *Historical Institutionalism and International Relations: Explaining Institutional Development in World Politics*. Oxford: Oxford University Press.

Rostenkowski, Dan. 1992. *North American Free Trade Agreement*. Washington, DC.

Ruskola, Teemu. 2008. "Colonialism Without Colonies: On the Extraterritorial Jurisprudence of the U.S. Court for China." *Law and Contemporary Problems* 71 (October).

Sabatier, Paul A., Susan Hunter and Susan McLaughlin. 1987. "The Devil Shift: Perceptions and Misperceptions of Opponents." *The Western Political Quarterly* 40 (3): 449–76.

Sabatier, Paul A., and Christopher M. Weible, eds. 2014. *Theories of the Policy Process*. 3rd ed. Westview Press.

Sachs, Stephen E. 2006. "From St. Ives to Cyberspace: The Modern Distortion of the Medieval 'Law Merchant.'" *American University International Law Review* 21 (5): 685–812.

Schneiderman, David. 2008. *Constitutionalizing Economic Globalization: Investment Rules and Democracy's Promise*. Cambridge: Cambridge University Press.

Schuck, Peter H. 1983. *Suing Government: Citizen Remedies for Official Wrongs*. New Haven: Yale University Press.

Sedivy, Miroslav. 2011. "Metternich and the Anglo-Neapolitan Sulphur Crisis of 1840." *Journal of Modern Italian Studies* 16 (1): 1–18.

Shapiro, Martin M. 1986. *Courts: A Comparative and Political Analysis.* Chicago: University of Chicago Press.

Soifer, Hillel David. 2012. "The Causal Logic of Critical Junctures." *Comparative Political Studies* 45 (12): 1572–97.

Sparkman, John. 1968. *Convention on Foreign Arbitral Awards.* Washington, DC: US Senate.

Staton, Jeffrey K., and Will H. Moore. 2011. "Judicial Power in Domestic and International Politics." *International Organization* 65 (3): 553–87.

Steinberg, Richard H. 2002. "In the Shadow of Law or Power? Consensus-Based Bargaining and Outcomes in the GATT/WTO." *International Organization* 56 (02): 339–74.

———. 2013. "Wanted—Dead or Alive: Realism in International Law." In *Interdisciplinary Perspectives on International Law and International Relations: The State of the Art*, edited by Jeffrey L. Dunoff and Mark A. Pollack, 146–72. Cambridge: Cambridge University Press.

Steinmo, Sven. 2008. "What Is Historical Institutionalism?" In *Approaches and Methodologies in the Social Sciences: A Pluralist Perspective*, edited by Donatella Della Porta and Michael Keating, 118–38. Cambridge: Cambridge University Press.

Steinmo, Sven, Kathleen Thelen and Frank Longstreth, eds. 1992. *Structuring Politics: Historical Institutionalism in Comparative Analysis.* Cambridge and New York: Cambridge University Press.

Strayer, Joseph R. 1970. *On the Medieval Origins of the Modern State.* Princeton, NJ: Princeton University Press.

Streeck, Wolfgang, and Kathleen Ann Thelen. 2005. *Beyond Continuity: Institutional Change in Advanced Political Economies.* Oxford University Press.

Stuyt, Alexander Marie. 1990. *Survey of International Arbitrations: 1794–1989.* Netherlands: Martinus Nijhoff Publishers.

Tigar, Michael. 2000. *Law and the Rise of Capitalism.* New York: Monthly Review Press.

Van Harten, Gus. 2008. *Investment Treaty Arbitration and Public Law.* Oxford: Oxford University Press.

Vandevelde, Kenneth J. 1988. "The Bilateral Investment Treaty Program of the United States." *Cornell International Law Journal* 21: 201–76.

Veeder, V. V. 1998. "The Lena Goldfields Arbitration: The Historical Roots of Three Ideas." *International and Comparative Law Quarterly* 47 (4): 747–92.

Wetter, J. Gillis, and Stephen M. Schwebel. 1964. "Some Little-Known Cases on Concessions." *British Year Book of International Law* 40: 183.

Williamson, Oliver E. 1985. *The Economic Institutions of Capitalism.* New York: Free Press.

Yackee, Jason Webb. 2007. "Conceptual Difficulties in the Empirical Study of Bilateral Investment Treaties." *Brooklyn Journal of International Law* 33: 405.

———. 2016. "The First Investor-State Arbitration: The Suez Canal Company v Egypt (1864)." *Journal of World Investment & Trade* 17 (3): 401–62.

Chapter Three

WHY INVESTORS DEMAND
INVESTMENT LAW

If you are a country that is up and coming and trying to attract foreign direct investment, you do not want a feature on the website of the International Centre for the Settlement of Investment Disputes. Principally, for me, apart from the political clout of the process (which is different from being in a court) [. . .] is what is known as the Washington factor. The Washington factor is important [for investors] to actually be able to bring your claim at the international level, where people in Washington corridors will be waking up to it, and noticing it.
—Investment arbitrator interviewed for *Judge Knot*

To invert the slogan from the 1980s movie *Field of Dreams*, just because you build it, does not mean they will come. The twentieth century is full of examples of ambitious international courts that were dreamed up, built, but then never utilized. Duke University political scientist Suzanne Katzenstein recounts stillborn proposals such as the 1907 Court of Arbitral Justice, the 1920 Criminal Court and the 1949 Human Rights Court (Katzenstein 2014). In each case, enterprising legal scholars and practitioners identified a theoretical need for international dispute resolution. But due to a lack of uptake by states and non-state actors, none of these forums ever got off the ground.

One example from the period shows why an enthusiasm gap emerged. In 1908, Pedro Diaz of Nicaragua challenged the government of Guatemala in the Central American Court of Justice over unjust imprisonment. By a 3-to-2 vote, the judges on this then-novel panel voted against admitting his claim. Their argument: the treaty establishing the court required Diaz to go first through national courts. The doctor for his part claimed that he was unlikely to get justice from the state that had imprisoned him in the first place. After that, not many cases by individuals were brought to this particular court, none were successful and the forum disbanded a few years later (Hudson 1932).

International investment arbitration could have faced a similar challenge. It is true, all else being equal, an international court that allows access by non-state actors is more likely to get used when compared to courts where only governments get standing. With governments, there is a range of diplomatic considerations that can get in the way of legally challenging one another (Keohane et al. 2000). One need look no further than the Trump administration's slow-walking in 2017 of a World Trade Organization (WTO) challenge to China over aluminum subsidies in hopes that the latter would help US goals with North Korea. But, even for non-state actors, launching claims is not costless, which is why it is incumbent on investors with skin in the game to actually see it as useful.

Indeed, this is part of a generalizable problem with courts. As an early scholarly contribution to the law-and-economics literature put it (Landes and Posner 1979), adjudication can be thought of as a market where there is both demand and supply for judicial services. On the demand side, plaintiffs incur the costs of making their argument, the risks of alienating the defendant and the potential payout from a judicial decision. At the same time, they must always decide whether the payout they expect exceeds what they would be able to obtain in an out-of-court settlement where they would not pay for the adjudicators' services. On the supply side, adjudicators can provide a low- or a high-quality decision, work slowly or fast, and provide reasoning aimed only at the parties to the dispute or to a broader universe of potential future buyers of their services. In the past, domestic judges were paid out of litigant fees; they were literal market players instead of the figurative ones they are today. Arbitrators—both domestically and internationally—lack tenure, so they can be thought of more clearly as market actors. As such, the arbitration market can suffer from the types of failures we see in other markets: incentives toward overproduction of case law if paid by the case; possible monopolization and anti-competitive behavior; excessive expenditure on advertising; problems of economies of scale, such as the rules that adjudicators create are only valuable if a powerful state will enforce them; and a temptation to use information asymmetry to arbitrators' own advantage by, say, writing vague opinions so litigants will not know how you will decide until they have been paid.

If there was any doubt of its viability in the early days, the market for investment law has heated up over the past 17 years. According to the data I presented in Figure 2.2, more than 50 new cases have been launched every year since 2011, with 70 new cases in 2015 alone. And these are not merely trial balloons floated by an overly eager investor class. Arbitrators have taken up many of these claims, finalizing dozens of awards per year for a grand total of nearly 350 over the last quarter century. (Figure 3.1 graphically demonstrates these trends.) This is a respectable tally, especially considering that the World Trade Organization—called the "most important and most powerful of international law tribunals" as recently as a decade ago (J. H. Jackson 2006, 203)—has only adopted around 200 rulings over its two decades in existence.

I attribute this growth to two factors, both related to the benefits to the system's users. First, while the average investor loses their claims, the average outcome leaves them better off than they would be absent the remedy. Second, litigating helps define a global normative floor for acceptable state behavior. While this does not necessarily lead states to change their ways (after all, they retain their sovereignty), it helps reinforce the default market and the legal values that the system of golden straitjackets was designed to encourage. This is the more subtle effect, but it also is the more consequential one over the long haul.

To be sure, investment arbitration is no carbon copy of neoliberal structural adjustment policies. Indeed, according to my interviewees, while early ISDS cases saw arbitrators pushing strongly anti-state norms, self-restraint kicked in over time, with arbitrators being more cautious in their pronouncements. As one frequent arbitrator told me:

> It is increasingly accepted that you should give bigger room, larger room to policy making things. Because in the beginning, the arbitrators were too enthusiastic about this. "Oh, look at what we can say!" I think we should be more modest as arbitrators.

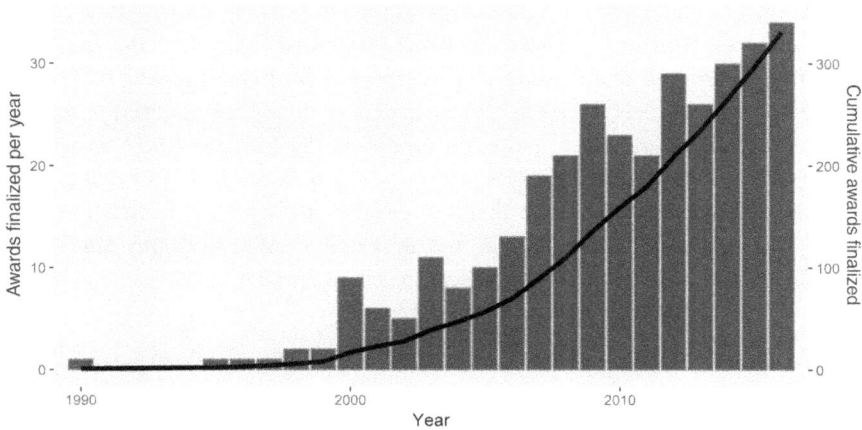

Figure 3.1 Investment awards finalized, 1990–2016
Source: Author's calculations using original data. Finality defined as decision on merits or rejecting jurisdiction.

Nonetheless, I will show in this chapter that even when arbitrators side with states on all or most of the outcome of a case—for example by letting the state win or awarding low damages—the reasoning is used incrementally to push outward the extent of states' possible international liabilities. Echoing a conceptualization from Henry Sumner Maine's nineteenth-century treatise *Ancient Law* (1861), I argue that states' liability under investment law has generally moved from one based on status to one based on contract. In early cases, arbitrators treated states as inferior and untrustworthy entities that should be subjugated to market forces. This is akin to how the law treated peasants under feudalism: their lot in life would be primarily dictated by their lord. In later ISDS cases, states' regulatory prerogatives were given greater weight, but they were balanced against their contractual and semi-contractual commitments. This is akin to workers under capitalism, who on paper are given the right whether to freely sell their labor. Pro-labor voices look skeptically at this formal equality of arms, noting that "between equal rights, force prevails" (Mieville 2006). That international law would push and pull between states' freedom of maneuver is unsurprising. As legal theorist Martti Koskenniemi has argued, the whole professional enterprise is based on restraining states but requires their consent (Koskenniemi 2005). Thus, international adjudicators must constantly make reference to states' will, even as the adjudicators shrink states' policy space.

This chapter proceeds as follows. First, I offer some descriptive statistics of how investors have fared in the nearly 350 cases that reached finalization between 1990 (the first case, *AAPL v. Sri Lanka*, discussed in chapter 2) and mid-2017 (when research for the book was completed). This is the complete known universe of cases, five-sixths of which have publicly available awards that have reached the public domain. Second, I review some of the central paradigms influential in development economics, namely new institutional economics and institutionalist political economy. This digression offers comparative grist for the third section, where I analyze the ideologies that arbitrators bring to their case work, which I derived (as elsewhere in the book) from extensive interviews with a cross-section of arbitrators. These ideologies can be thought of as the raw material that arbitrators bring to deliberation and interpretation of the law, which then shapes the results of cases. Finally, I look for evidence of these ideologies mattering in the case law. Namely, I look at both best- and worst-case scenarios for investors in terms of legal reasoning across a number of ISDS standards. As I show, both the inputs that arbitrators put into the case law and the outputs that they produce are attractive from a business perspective. Throughout the chapter, I will look for evidence of temporality mattering: Do arbitrators change their emphases over time, and if so, how?

Investor–State Dispute Settlement: The Mixed Empirical Track Record

Investment law regularly comes in for beatings in the public square. At a meeting of Latin American leaders in 2007, Bolivian president Evo Morales declared that "Governments in Latin America and I think all over the world never win the cases. The transnationals always win" (AP 2007). A 2012 advocacy report deemed the system "neither fair, nor independent, but deeply flawed and business-biased" (Eberhardt and Olivet 2012, 7). According to another piece, investment rulings "overthrow the sovereignty of parliaments and the rulings of supreme courts" (Monbiot 2013).

Advocates of investment law are quick to point out that the investment regime has been kinder to states than these claims would indicate. Stephen Schwebel, a prominent arbitrator, has written that

> these criticisms are more colorful than they are cogent [. . . ;] states [at the time of writing] won 87 cases when arbitrators resolved a dispute arising under a treaty, while investors won 57 [. . . ;] even when investors were awarded damages, they won significantly less than the amount claimed, and [. . .] about a quarter of investment claims were dismissed at the jurisdictional stage [meaning the stage where arbitrators determine whether the investor has standing and cause to bring the case]. These findings hardly suggest bias against states. (Schwebel 2014)

Earlier work revealed that arbitrators from developed countries were no more biased against states than their developing-country brethren (Franck 2009).

Critics and proponents each have some sound arguments. As Figure 3.2 shows, states did initially lose more than they won.[1] The early investment treaty cases raised alarm bells with progressive critics, who saw a string of state losses over sensitive questions like how to regulate toxic waste dumps. But after nearly fifteen years of tentative international law experimentation, states' lots began to change. Between 1990 and 2003, arbitrators finalized 39 cases, finding that states had violated investment standards in

---

1. My case statistics run from 1990 (the first known case) to encompass all known treaty-based ISDS cases that produced a final award on the merits or jurisdiction at any arbitration center as of August 2017.

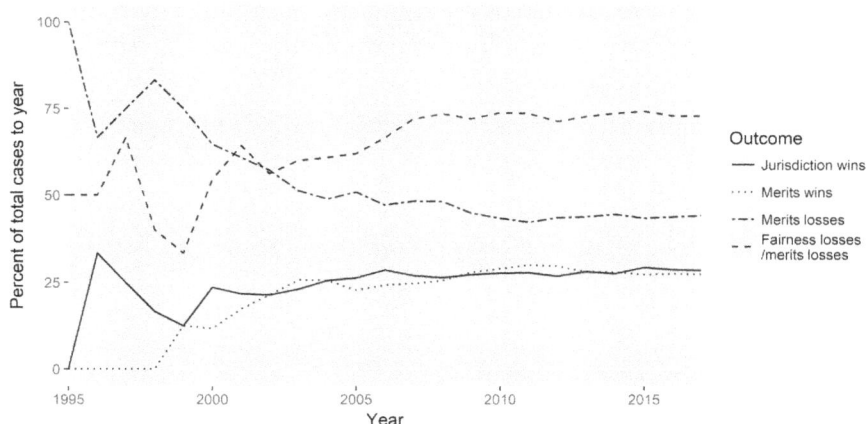

Figure 3.2 Do states win or lose investment arbitrations (and how)?
Source: Author's original data analysis.

20 disputes (the dash-dotted line) and not violated the standards in 10 disputes (the dotted line). In an additional nine disputes, arbitrators hit the stop button at the jurisdictional stage, finding that investors lacked standing to advance their cases or had made other errors in their submissions (the solid line). Adding these two ways in which states dodged bullets together (merits and jurisdictional wins), we learn that investors won about 51 percent of the time, a slight edge.

By the next year, the tables had turned. Of the total 47 cases brought up until 2004, states had a slight edge—winning 24 and losing 23. After a quick seesaw back to an investor lead in 2005, that basic pattern would hold up to the present. Over the lifetime of investment arbitration (nearly 350 cases), states have won about 54 percent of the cases where arbitrators rendered a final legal decision.[2] This supports the view of the arbitrator quoted earlier in the chapter, who suggested that arbitrators made a course correction over time from radicalism to modesty.

While this would contradict the views of President Morales and other critics of ISDS, it is not the end of the story. The two regions with the lowest gross domestic product, Latin America and sub-Saharan Africa, lose more than they win, while all richer regions win more than they lose. Maybe the Bolivian leader was partly right, from his local vantage point. As shown in Table 3.1, the overall win rate masks some important regional variance.

These mixed results also are evident in the raw dollar amounts at stake. Unlike some other areas of international law, the remedy for violating investment rules is not policy change but financial compensation.[3] As Figure 3.3 shows, investors' financial demands of

---

2. As opposed to cases that were settled, where arbitrators were not running the show.
3. In recent years, arbitrators have experimented with ordering states to change policies instead of or in addition to making payment. However, these orders cannot be enforced, unlike cash claims that can be taken to third-country courts.

Table 3.1 Investment arbitration outcomes by region, 1990–2017

Region	Investor Wins	State Wins	Total	Percent Investor Wins
Advanced Economies	7	24	31	22.6
Middle East/North Africa	9	25	34	26.5
Developing Asia	8	12	20	40.0
Former Soviet/Eastern Bloc	57	79	136	41.9
Latin America and Caribbean	60	46	106	56.6
Sub-Saharan Africa	11	8	19	57.9
Grand Total	*152*	*194*	*346*	*43.9*

Source: Author's calculations based on original dataset.

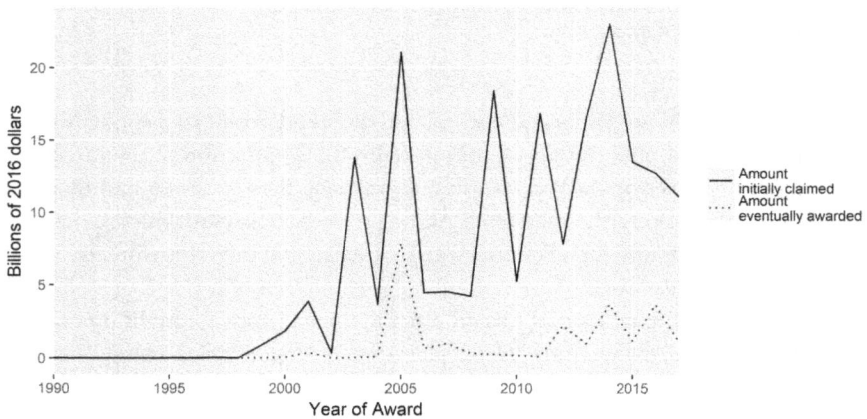

Figure 3.3 How much do investors demand and get in investment arbitrations?
Source: Author's original data analysis of all 342 final cases; four outlier claims above $20b omitted.

states have risen steadily over time, with the total amount of damages claimed seesawing between $10 and $20 billion in recent years. Nonetheless, arbitrators have been fairly consistent in awarding investors only a fraction of what they demand. Figure 3.4 zooms in similar numbers, presented in percentage form. On the positive side from the state perspective, investors in an average year attained only 17 percent of their claimed damages. The average claimant obtained a quarter of their claim in only two years, 2007 and 2012.

Are these numbers high or low? It depends on the point of comparison. A commonly cited alternative to investment claims is political risk insurance, which typically will reimburse investors for about 80 percent of the value of an expropriated investment (Bekker and Ogawa 2013). A 17 percent average reimbursement on the claim in ISDS cases is of course far below that figure. At the same time, the grounds for claims in these

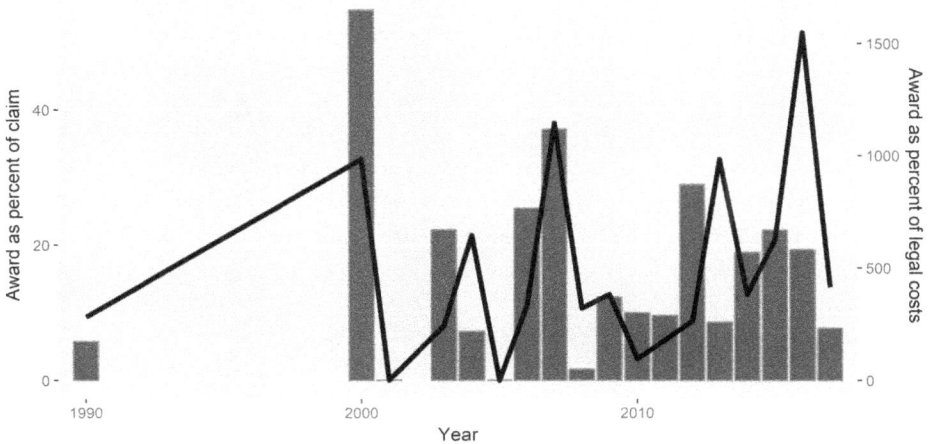

Figure 3.4 How well do investors and their lawyers make out in investment arbitration? *Source:* Author's original data analysis of 138 final cases for which comparable data available.

dispute-settlement cases go far beyond expropriation. To return to Figure 3.2, the black line shows the percentage of successful claims where investors claimed they had been treated unfairly and inequitably, an amorphous standard known as "fair and equitable treatment" that has become a catch-all term for a wider suite of disliked government actions. By 2007, investors successfully invoked this standard in more than 70 percent of their wins, a reliance that continues to this day. In other words, investment law is providing protection above and beyond what investors can access through other avenues—at a reputational and financial cost to states.

The data is murkier still. The right-hand axis in Figure 3.4 shows that for the 138 cases from which we have complete data, investors were typically awarded more than 5.5 times their legal expenditures. The average award of $52.7 million was secured on an average legal expenditure of $6.3 million. In 2007 and then in 2017, the average return to legal costs was more than tenfold. Notably, this average for the period as a whole holds even though investors were awarded zero damages in the majority of cases (55 percent). Putting the damage award in the context of the legal costs is a valid comparison. At the moment investors make the decision to invest, they must decide between the risk-adjusted return they could make if all goes well versus the risk that they will lose everything. But at the moment investors make the decision to launch the case, whatever damage they allege has already happened. If they do nothing, they will get nothing. Their choice at that moment is whether to spend money to litigate the case. At the margin, what they are out is their legal expenditure, and what they stand to gain is some amount up to the value of their claim. Seen in this light, it is rational to make the legal expenditure.

Indeed, the outcomes in investment cases seem consistent with a system experiencing excessive litigation. While an efficient legal system encourages settlement, McGill University political scientist Krzysztof Pelc finds that claims over less-precise rules "are

52 percent more likely to persist to the ruling stage, in a manner consistent with the belief that investors bringing such cases may be more interested in the benefits of litigation itself than in securing a favorable early settlement" (Pelc 2016, 32). As the quote that opens this chapter notes, for companies there is an inherent benefit in the case generating negative publicity for the regulating government. For the lawyers, arbitrators and other specialists, the average of fees per case is $10 million, while median fees are $6 million (Hodgson 2014). And with returns well in excess of legal fees, a market for this specific kind of litigation finance has emerged, where hedge funds and other third-party funders bankroll cases in exchange for a portion of the award, as much as tripling their investment in the process (Smith 2012).

This book does not look at such bargaining in the shadow of the law or at the law firms and third-party funders themselves, huge topics better suited for a separate study. But, in the sections below, I argue that the inputs and outputs of arbitration are sufficiently appealing to business interests that they would be foolish not to demand as much creation of investment law as the system can manage and they can afford.

What Do We Know about the Role of the State in Development?

Before we delve into how arbitrators see states and their role in promoting economic development, let us first review how social scientists and historians do. The simplest definition of economic development—one often used by international agencies—is little more than a binary coding of countries as above or below a given income threshold. Some development economists prefer a broader conception. University of Cambridge economist Ha-Joon Chang invokes a structural definition: "Development is largely about the transformation of the productive structure (and the capabilities that support it) and the resulting transformation of social structure—urbanization, dissolution of the traditional family, changes in gender relationships, rise of labor movements, the advent of the welfare state, and so on" (Chang 2010). As he argues, this conceptualization of development allows us to sidestep the absurd implication under the now-standard definitions that rich oil states are fully developed just because they passed an income threshold, or that Western European countries temporarily devastated by war or economic crisis are somehow undeveloped just because they dropped below the same income thresholds. Chang goes on to note that many factors combine to influence development, including institutions, politics, technology, the environment and human capacities (ibid.).

Yet one institution, the state, influences all others. Its laws protect, promote or regulate industry, incentivize technology through intellectual property enforcement, define the appropriate protection and use of environmental resources and make provision for the education and training of individual humans. Few states have achieved the broad metric of development outlined above. But those that have done so (in Western Europe, North America, Oceania and Japan) have relied heavily on institutions of the state in one form or another (Chang 2002b). Even scholars who are not as sympathetic to states put them at the core of their analysis, as we see below. When these scholars say "institutions matter" for development, they are mostly talking about institutions of the state (Acemoglu and Johnson 2005).

Interest in the state has fallen in and out of intellectual fashion. For several decades in the postwar period, many social scientists conceived of states as fairly colorless entities. For international relations realists, a state's power was determined by other states' military strategies in a world of anarchy (Krasner 1982). For Marxists, states were arenas, or instruments, of class rule (Clarke 1991). Traditional development economics scholars put nearly unlimited faith in states' abilities to lead economic transformation. Such approaches tended to see the state in relatively unproblematic terms: the state could drive capital accumulation (Gerschenkron 1962), promote backward and forward linkages in the economy (Hirschman 1958) and serve as the guardian of the social welfare and creator of markets (Polanyi 1944).

These views began to change in the 1970s and 1980s, when social scientists began revisiting state theory. The development successes of states in East Asia that intervened directly in their economies (Rueschemeyer and Evans 1985), coupled with the failures of states in Africa that also did so (Bates 1981), led a diverse range of scholars to pay greater attention to the conditions under which states could be expected to facilitate development. I will review two of these revisionist approaches here: new institutional economics and institutionalist political economy.

New Institutional Economics and Theories of State Development

New institutional economics overlaps considerably with the rational-choice institutionalism explored in the previous chapter, but it focuses on domestic economics more than international relations. An early contribution to the field departed from the assumption that "in the beginning, there were markets" (O. E. Williamson 1975, 20), and then sought to explain how states deviated from that norm in sometimes-perverse ways driven by politics. Subsequent works in the subfield theorized that states are unable to neutrally guide the process of economic development because their political and bureaucratic personnel have incentives to "grasp" national wealth instead of allow the market's "invisible hand" to efficiently allocate resources, and therefore constraints should check policy making discretion (North 1990; Olson 1993). Even if institutions of state helped Western countries' development, similar strategies would not work for today's poor countries, according to University College London economist Deepak Lal, because developing countries have particularly "rapacious and inefficient" governments (Lal 1997 [1983]).

States thus had the capacity to retard development. Prices, not interventions, are what can alter individuals' incentives in developing nations (Krueger 1990). Attempts at state intervention to override informal norms through formal laws are unlikely to work, as informal norms such as culture are harder to legislate out of existence (North 1990). New institutional economics encourages minimalism—states should only correct market failures that cannot be resolved by private actors. This means paving roads, combatting fraud, running monetary policy, providing law and order and protecting the commons. The goal for all of these policies is to help private actors get the prices right, not to shape the price structure through political decision making.

These early contributions in institutional economics spawned a generation of empirical literature and data collection. For example, in a widely cited string of papers and books, economists Daron Acemoglu and Simon Johnson at the Massachusetts Institute of Technology and James Robinson at the University of Chicago studied dozens of countries over centuries of development, finding that states need to be strong enough to tax their populace efficiently, but simultaneously need to be constrained by institutions such as constitutions that ensure property rights (Acemoglu et al. 2001; 2012). The separate Polity IV "good governance" indicators coded by the Political Instability Task Force (a research project funded by the US government) relate almost exclusively to constraints on states, such as the existence of multiple veto points (courts, legislatures, ombudsmen) on executive decisions (Marshall et al. 2013). The International Country Risk Guide published by the PRS Group contains similar indicators (Howell 2013). Finally, the Worldwide Governance Indicators developed by the World Bank—another widely used dataset—relies on the subjective views of international businesspeople who favor constraints on states (Arndt and Oman 2006). All these indicators reveal that most developing-country regions fall short of ideals. For instance, every developing-country region ranks 15 to 50 percentage points lower on average than the Polity IV indicator on executive constraints for developed nations.

Summing up a generation of new institutional economics thinking, political theorist Francis Fukuyama wrote, "Everyone is interested in studying political institutions that limit or check power—democratic accountability and rule of law—but very few people pay attention to the institution that accumulates and uses power, the state" (Fukuyama 2013, 347).

The Institutionalist Political Economy Alternative

Outside the mainstream, heterodox thinkers have tried to push the pendulum back toward a more active role for the state. This body of scholarship, which Ha-Joon Chang labeled "institutionalist political economy," takes seriously the possibility that state intervention can go wrong—that it is not sufficient for development (Chang 2002a). But these thinkers diverge from new institutional economics in arguing that intervention is nonetheless necessary, and so attempt to identify the conditions under which more robust interventionist development policies might work.

According to this school of thought, states intervene in subtle but pervasive ways. For instance, states determine who is allowed to participate in markets, what can be legitimately traded, and how to balance overlapping rights claims. Compared to the dark view of humanity that inheres in much economics research, institutionalist political economy notes that humans have diverse motivations: selfishness, certainly, but also altruism and solidarity. States are not passive actors here: by cultivating esprit de corps, government agencies can train bureaucrats to value national achievement over personal gain. Finally, institutionalist political economy accepts politics' pervasiveness. There is no neat dividing line separating disputes that are political from those that are economic, because the distinction itself is a product of political contests by previous generations. Trade in humans, the sale of public office, and child labor were all once legitimate market activities; now they are not. Peoples' perceptions of their own interests and of appropriate targets of political action are all shaped by their institutional environment and history.

Institutionalist political economists rest their theory on deep case studies that disentangle what multi-country regression analysis might miss. University of California, San Diego, political scientist Chalmers Johnson studied Japan's Ministry of International Trade and Industry, finding that government engineers eschewed markets (and economists' advice) and instead made state plans indicating which industries would be developed and when (Johnson 1982). Against mainstream perspectives that South Korea developed by liberalizing tariff rates, interest rates and currency rates in the 1960s—essentially "getting the prices right" by removing government distortions and letting private actors make their own decisions—Alice Amsden of the Massachusetts Institute of Technology documented the extensive and deliberate efforts of the Korean government to get the "prices wrong" so that steel and shipbuilding could be protected, then subsidized them until they became globally competitive (Amsden 1989). Political economy and development scholar Robert Wade identified similar strategies in Taiwan (Wade 1990). University of California, Berkeley, sociologist Peter Evans studied how South Korea, India and Brazil jumpstarted information technology industries through close but autonomous collaboration with private capitalists (Evans 1995). And more recently, Boston University economist Kevin Gallagher documented how China's development model involved extensive state coordination of the industrial and financial sectors (Gallagher 2016). Turning toward today's rich nations, Cambridge University's Chang shows that the US and European governments intervened extensively in markets during their period of economic takeoff, utilizing trade protection, theft of intellectual property, and subsidization of national firms. In these cases, states more than market actors set the prices (Chang 2002b).

For these scholars, a successful development strategy may also entail getting the process of institutional development "wrong." Against the World Bank's good governance, pro-property rights agenda, Robert Wade argues that private property holdings may hold back development and need to be redistributed when overly concentrated in elite hands (Wade 2010). And bad governance (through the political manipulation and distribution of rents to agents capable of blocking economic change) may be a necessary part of managing developmental transition costs. When dominant classes would otherwise have the power to block economic change, it may be better to buy them off through otherwise inefficient payments than to not develop. Economists Mushtaq Khan at the University of London and K. S. Jomo at the University of Malaya describe how these types of patron–client networks helped ensure political stability in Indonesia, Thailand and Malaysia without hurting (and sometimes helping) development (Khan and Jomo 2000). In sum, shaking up markets and property rights might lead to lower scores on good governance indices, but actually may be a prerequisite for dynamic growth.

Role Reversal on Courts

There is one non-pathological part of the state for new institutional economists: courts. By enforcing private contracts, courts underpin markets (North 1990). By restraining the exercise of executive power, courts limit the state and maximize private freedom and efficiency (R. A. Posner 1998; Zywicki and Sanders 2008). This tension between rolling back the state in some contexts and employing it in others can make it difficult to categorize. In a critical assessment by Yale University's David Grewal and Duke University's Jedediah Purdy, it is noted that neoliberalism (a political term that overlaps with new institutionalism) is not about "more market, less state," but about a particular kind of state where the law is used to aggressively promote certain interests and displace others (Grewal and Purdy 2015). In short, among the institutions that matter to new institutional and neoliberal scholars, courts are among the most important.

Yet not all courts are created equal. Developing-country courts are not as good as developed-country courts, according to Nobel Prize winner Douglass North, who argued that developed-country judges have more integrity, honesty and morality than their developing-country counterparts (North 1990, 60). The founder of the "law and economics" school of thought, former US federal court judge and University of Chicago economist Richard Posner argues for a more institutional rather than psycho-cultural explanation, saying that developed-country courts are superior because of better judicial compensation practices and administrative support (Posner 2010, 333). Getting developing-country governments to strengthen the role of courts is a key part of rich countries' "rule of law" agenda for foreign aid (Dam 2007; Haggard and Tiede 2011).

For some scholars, not even all developed-countries courts are equal. Common-law countries such as the United Kingdom and the United States are said to be superior to civil-law countries such as France and Germany. Dartmouth University economist Rafael La Porta and his colleagues assert that common-law countries' adherence to case-law precedents creates an additional check on executives attempting to influence the judiciary (La Porta et al. 2004). Precedent gives judges an additional tool to resist pressure to go along with governments' (usually misguided and inefficiency-promoting) proposals. Because potential litigants can refer to case law, there is more certainty of how legal disputes will be decided, thus incentivizing efficient out-of-court settlements (Posner 1998: 589).

Institutionalist political economy scholars are more skeptical of this judicial love fest. Summarizing the work of Chang, Wade and others, political scientist Meredith Woo-Cumings points to the usage of informal administrative guidance by executive branch officials in Japan, South Korea and Malaysia (Woo-Cumings 2006). Far from recourse to adversarial litigation, she documents how officials pressured businesses to keep disputes out of courts, while for their part, she found that judges were passive and deferred to executive branch decisions. It was only after these nations' economies became more developed that their courts took on a more state-constraining role. Similarly, Germany and other continental European countries (both in their earlier development and today) emphasized macroeconomic planning, top-down regulation and informal bargaining over legalized dispute settlement (Kagan 2003; Rogers 2016).

Attractive Inputs: Arbitral Development Ideologies

With this scholarship in mind, how do investment arbitrators stack up? Since few of them are development experts, their ideology matters. I do not use this term pejoratively. Rather, it denotes the mental models all of us use to manage cognitively the informational complexities of the world and to orient both descriptive and normative understandings (North 1990, 23). In other words, to say these arbitrators have ideologies is another way of saying they are normal human beings. What makes their ideologies matter is that, unlike development scholars, arbitrators are given virtually unchecked interpretative discretion to decide the international legality of domestic public policy. Given that investment arbitration is an asymmetric system focused on the obligations the public sector owes the private sector (or at least the foreign-owned, treaty-protected section of it), it is not surprising that arbitrators' basic political economy ideologies have an opportunity to surface, do good, and/or make mischief.

Categorizing ideology is a fraught exercise, especially across national contexts. Since University of Chicago's Anthony Downs formalized spatial modeling of politics in the 1950s, it has been common for political scientists to attempt to place politicians or voters as scatterplots on a left–right axis. Two observations close in space indicate two political actors close in ideology. In studying US judges, political scientists have often used a proxy for ideology: judges appointed by Republicans are deemed right-leaning, while those appointed by Democrats are left-leaning. But this does especially poorly for cross-national comparisons. For instance, in their study of the Canadian Supreme Court, University of South Carolina political scientist Donald Songer and his colleagues used an axis that encompassed judges' conceptions of the "scope and purpose of government's role in society" (Songer et al. 2012, 6). At the transnational level, matters are still more complicated. University of Gothenburg political scientists Olof Larsson and Daniel Naurin argue for a four-quadrant adjudicatory ideological space, with views sortable along a spectrum of liberal to social market economies on one axis and national to transnational control along the other (Larsson and Naurin 2015).

Not wanting to presume which dimensions of investment arbitrators' ideology would be the most salient, I used qualitative grounded theory methods (described in the Appendix) to elaborate four dimensions. First, what types of state behavior are investment treaties meant to root out? Second, how should government policy change? Third, what role, if any, should arbitration play in this process? Finally, what discretionary sensitivity should arbitrators grant to states? I describe each of these axes in the subsections that follow. For ease of exposition, I describe the dozens of interviewees' perspectives in narrative form, with quotes from differing respondents alongside one another. The purpose of this exercise is to identify qualitative categories, not show any category's incidence. But to give a sense of their preponderance in my sample, I also show respondents' often overlapping responses through a series of Venn diagrams. (See the Appendix for further description of the methodology I used.)

What Types of State Behavior Are Investment Treaties Meant to Constrain?

How do arbitrators conceptualize what states are all about? What are their pathologies that investment treaties help contain, or virtues that treaties can help unlock? The standard argument for investment law is that it constrains rapacious state bureaucrats. The US Trade Representative's office, for instance, argues: "Investment protections are intended to prevent discrimination, repudiation of contracts, and expropriation of property without due process of law and appropriate compensation" (USTR 2014). Or as *The Economist* editorial board wrote, "the only power governments are giving up [through investment treaties] is the right to behave badly" (*Economist* 2014).

To ascertain whether arbitrators were similarly minimalist in their assessments, I asked my interviewees a hypothetical question: What would their advice be to a developing-country government that wanted to enact a new environmental policy but also wanted to avoid violating treaty claims? My aim with this question was simple: get arbitrators to flesh out their views of where a state (particularly the less-developed kind often in the crosshairs of multinational investors) goes wrong or right on the substance of policy. I then posed a follow-up question: Are investment treaties necessary between rich countries themselves? This was salient, given that so-called "mega-regional" trade deals such as the Trans-Pacific Partnership and Trans-Atlantic Trade and Investment Partnership were then very much in the news, and would have placed investor–state dispute settlement at the core of these countries' economic relationships. If ISDS were mainly a tool to constrain behavior characteristic of poor nations, then it would be pointless to include it in pacts between rich ones. But if there were some residual pathology that states retained even as they scaled the developmental ladder, then an argument could be made for making investment arbitration available against all states. In short, these questions were a way to prompt arbitrators to reveal their inner political theorist, without my having to introduce an alienating abstractness to the conversation.

Their answers were telling. In passing remarks, in aggressive tirades, and in mocking exasperation, my interviewees abhorred just the kind of predatory states USTR and *The Economist* warned about. These states violate contracts. Their officials, said various interviewees, are "corrupt" and "greedy." More specifically, the interviewees said these officials are personalistic, handing out favors to their friends and relatives. Unlike private individuals helping out friends, however, these predatory bureaucrats were described as working across branches and organizations of government to ensure that "the whole system collaborates" to help allies and punish rivals. More pejoratively, they are described as "smart" but "consciously over clever," concocting "bogus schemes" that disguise arbitrary action under the veil of regulation. They are petty, agreeing to support investors, but then they "play tricks" by plotting to "get this guy as soon as" they can.

Justice does not work in predatory states, where "funny things happen in courts," said one interviewee. Judiciaries and administrations in predatory states, he said, take

> specific acts against a specific foreign investor. The typical example is a foreign investor has an asset, an investment. The state comes and takes it away. Expropriation. It is, you know, a decision that, 'Todd will be expropriated.' It can be an expropriation decree. It can be a taking away of your licenses. It can be a court judgment which says that you are driven into bankruptcy.

When arbitrators inveighed against predatory states, many reached for metaphors of underdeveloped countries. "If you take Africa for example," said one, "the governments are so corrupt! [. . .] It is so common in Africa to have this kind of abusive conduct." Another said an investor who alleged harmed from a US measure "was treated like if he had been dealing with one of the worst African countries by the Mississippi system" in a case involving the United States. Others said matter-of-factly, "developing countries have corrupt people" or "of course Bulgarians will misbehave." As for the claim by some observers that states no longer take the kind of predatory actions they did in the mid-twentieth century, one interview observed, "then along come the Venezuelans! [Laughter] Make no bones about it, by God, we are going to send in the troops and unfurl the banners with a picture of the glorious leader. We've got us an old-fashioned Stalinist expropriation!" It is easy to see why arbitrators would dislike blatantly abusive conduct and appropriation by states, and why they paint arbitration as a guard against it. There are few scholarly or other defenders of such arbitrary action.

It is treading into slightly more contested waters, however, to argue that states should not favor national champions. This contradicts the classic "infant-industry" argument, which avers that industrialization in late-developing countries requires that national firms be temporarily protected with tariffs from lower unit-cost overseas producers until these national champions can attain sufficient scale and expertise to lower their own costs (Chang 2002b). Still, anti-protectionism is a popular position in many economic circles and rhetorically favored by policy elites advocating trade and investment agreements (Bergsten 1996). It is thus also ultimately unsurprising that arbitrators would express anti-protectionist views.

While predatory states transfer wealth to government officials, arbitrators see protectionist states as transferring wealth from foreigners to nationals through an altering of competitive conditions. The discrimination could be *de jure* ("there is the problem that a law can be entirely constitutional but nonetheless be discriminatory, so the courts are obliged to apply that law but nevertheless it is discriminatory", said one). It could also be *de facto* ("are laws uniform in theory and in practice? It is easy to design a regulation that is uniform as to the one person you apply it to," said another.) Several arbitrators variously bemoaned Polish governments that designed beer taxes that only applied to foreign-owned breweries, Canadian governments that imposed environmental restrictions just to protect national waste-processing facilities, and other countries that refused to pass laws of general application.

Investment treaties were seen as prohibiting protectionism, with arbitrators claiming that such a claim would be "easy" to decide against the state. While this certainly would curtail states' cultivation of infant industries, it can also be seen as evidence of a limited scope in treaties. As one arbitrator put it, some countries "do not treat their own investors as well, for example, as the United States does." In such a case, the arbitrator said the foreign investor is not "entitled to be treated any better than domestic investor would be treated." In this view, states can mete out regulatory mandates or even abuse so long as it is evenhanded.

Anti-predation viewpoints and anti-protectionism are natural ideologies for arbitrator lawyers to embrace. They are consonant with sociologist Max Weber's classic concept of the rationality of modern law, where legal mandates are phrased as abstract obligations that apply generally to all like-situated parties, not as commands directed at specific named groups or individuals (Weber 1978, 656). But arbitrators I interviewed

went considerably farther, articulating a view that government policy should affirma-
tively privilege foreign investors. As one told me:

> You cannot just treat foreigners in an arbitrary fashion. You cannot even treat foreigners
> the way you treat your own people. They are protected more than your citizens. Do not get
> shocked. You signed the treaty! International law protects foreigners in ways that it does not
> others.

One basis arbitrators cite for this proposition is *SS Wimbledon*, the Permanent Court of
International Justice case discussed in chapter 2. This international law text is required
reading for lawyers in training and has diffused far outside its original application to
inter-state relations.

What were the contours of this pro-foreign treatment expressed by the arbitrators in
interviews? For some, it could mean faster adjudication than that available to nationals in
the local courts. For others, it could mean providing less-onerous adjudication in terms
of not having to provide the type of disclosure of private company documents that
would come out in a national court proceeding. It could mean the right to raise bases for
complaints (such as an appeal of Supreme Court decisions) that would not be available
in national courts or under national laws, where the top court is, well, the top court.
Foreign investors could get all of that and more through the arbitration channel whereas
local courts would not be legally capable of reviewing their own conduct or that of the
executive in cases brought by national investors, Indeed, foreign investors could in some
cases use both the local courts and international arbitration to complain about the same
or closely related state actions, leveraging legal rights in both systems in parallel fashion.

All countries are fair game for critique under this ideology, not just the least developed among them. One arbitrator bemoaned how French courts could adjust government contracts in the name of fairness and balance to the state's own interests. Another
lamented how certain European countries pass laws (perfectly democratically) that are
"excessive" by international standards. One thought it was "a joke" to go to "Chinese
courts" rather than investment arbitration. When I asked whether Canadian and US
investors get something in the North American Free Trade Agreement that they could
not get through the national-level legal system, one arbitrator said:

> All you are doing [in local courts] is checking to see if the Canadian courts or the US courts
> applied their own administrative laws reasonably, fairly and reasonably. So you are applying
> US law, and you are giving a significant degree of deference to their application of US law
> [. . .] It is completely different in ISDS [. . .] If you believe *in efficiency* and a broader equal
> treatment, then I think there is a good argument to be made for investment treaty arbitration.
> [Emphasis added.]

In other words, investment treaties are not only about ensuring that investors have the
procedural right to judicial review, but also that the outcomes of the reviews would
achieve specific economic outcomes.

The preferential option for foreigners was not a mere legal matter, but also financial
and political. There was a frequent refrain among my interviewees that states should pay

foreign investors compensation when they change policies (even if national law does not allow it for domestic firms). One interviewee lauded Venezuela for going outside its own courts to pay off aggrieved foreign investors. And as the quote that opened this chapter noted, investors who launch litigation rev up the "Washington factor" in ways that reinforce preferential treatment of foreigners.

Just how preferentially foreign investors should be treated could vary even within the same interview with one arbitrator. When I asked an arbitrator what a state might do to avoid arbitration, he initially responded, "just avoid any kind of abuse of powers, because, you know, what we see in general, is that the conduct of the states when they lose is terribly appalling [. . .] it is really abuse of power. It is really improper conduct." This is in line with the anti-predatory ideologies noted above.

But the arbitrator rapidly contradicted himself, arguing that not only predatory behaviors but also protectionist policies are undesirable. "Sometimes the state is condemned because they acted in a certain way, they have enacted legislation which is not in accordance with international law or their obligations under the bilateral investment treaty, and they did it probably in good faith," he explained. "But in the end we still reached the conclusion that it was not proper conduct, even if when they enacted the law they did it with good intentions. For example, they favor local manufacturers. They did not realize. Or maybe they did realize they were favoring local manufacturers, but they did not realize it was contrary to the [international] law. I have seen that." In a final revision and elaboration of his views, this arbitrator argued that foreign investors would only invest in poor countries if they had recourse to international arbitration rather than national courts—an option not available to local firms.

In sum, in a few short minutes over coffee, the arbitrator had shifted from a minimalist anti-predatory or anti-protectionist stance to a much more demanding concept of desirable state behavior. And he was far from the only arbitrator that expressed contradictory viewpoints. Another interviewee praised a state for passing laws of "general application" that applied to foreign and domestic gold miners, a view in line with standard anti-protectionist sentiment. But he then noted that "if you only have one gold miner and he happens to be a foreigner in your country, do not pass legislation that will affect only gold mines." In other words, a country with the misfortune of having only one foreign firm in a sector might not be able to regulate that sector at all without risking a legal claim should a dispute arise with that investor.

Figure 3.5 shows that views about the most pertinent states' vices and virtues were all over the map, and certainly would not lend themselves to the neat spatial models favored by many political scientists. Is this a disturbing indication of erratic thinking, or a to-be-expected bundle of hunches about political economy from people who are (after all) not development specialists? As a student of theories of the state, I found many of their viewpoints well within the mainstream of the types of state-skeptical views ceded by the economics and legal professions over the last few decades. Since at least the 1960s, the conservative law-and-economics movement has seeded the notion that government bureaucrats are bumbling at best and wealth-grasping at worst (MacLean 2017). For an area of practice like investment law (where only states can be sued and only by grievance-toting foreign investors armed with imprecise standards), it is unsurprising that

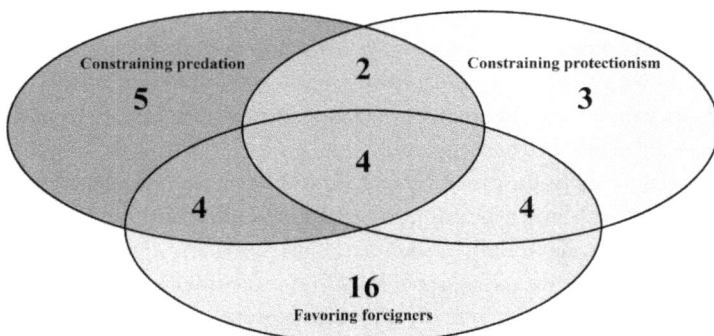

Figure 3.5 What state vice or virtue does investment law address?
Source: Author's grounded theory analysis of pertinent arbitrator responses (38).

my interviewees would find a wide range of government behavior potentially objection-able. Nonetheless, nearly half of my entreaties for arbitrators to play mock counselor-to-states ended with them advising some version of "treat foreigners better than your own people." If these ideologies are accurate reflections of the broader pool of arbitrators' predispositions, then it would not be enough for states to ban protection for national champions and curtail corruption—goals that would be difficult enough for developing nations to meet and still overcome political and economic hurdles to industrialization. Instead, nations at all levels of development would have to overhaul fundamental tenets of equality before the law by privileging the interests of foreign investors.

How Should Policy Change?

Arbitrators were not only concerned with what state behaviors to encourage or to tamp down, but also how states should go about changing their behaviors. All my interviewees were lawyers and, unsurprisingly, many expressed proceduralist ideologies. These interviewees like states that "diligently" follow set procedures, conduct "good record-keeping," and substantiate policy goals with paper trails. Such states "go slowly," do not "take hasty decisions," and do not enact "a policy on the fly" or "short-circuit things by passing the regulations without fairly considering all the steps that need to be considered in its own regulation." When celebrating proceduralism, arbitrators relied strongly on metaphors of individual human intelligence and ageing. States were characterized as "sensible," "grown up" and "mature" when they followed set procedures.

   The proceduralist state also is one that takes itself out of the picture as much as possible. Such states, said various interviewees, "let go" and get "independent determinations" by scientists and economists not in their employ before launching new regulations. Arbitrators did not describe these experts' value in terms of the correctness of their views. Instead, their value is about optics. Evidence of science in policy making would be if a govern-ment regulates the same sectors in the same way as arbitrators see other governments regulating. "There was enough evidence around the world that countries were getting rid

of this," suggested one interviewee about procedural decision making. "There was international activity on it." Said another, science cannot be produced by some "kangaroo
court or an inquiry by some commission that you appointed that nobody believes." The
test of good policy, said another, is one that passes "the Washington Post test [. . .] never
write anything you wouldn't want to see on the front page of the Washington Post."
Arbitrators will not second-guess proceduralist states: they do not want to because they
do not see themselves as "environmental experts," said another. In other words, a scientif-
ically based policy in an arbitrator's view does not have to match the scientific discipline's
definition of science (testable hypotheses that are confirmed through scientific method).
Rather, it has to conform to widespread social practice.

Proceduralism was how states should go about making change, but actually existing
states fell far short of that ideal and were motivated instead by "politics." What counted
as political was not fixed, but was always distasteful. It could be kowtowing to electoral
interests and constituencies, because politicians want votes, or bureaucrats want to service their constituencies. It could be putting the short term ahead of the long term. It
could be moving too fast. "The problem with many politicians is that they want to take
decisions which will be applauded by people all around, that it has to be done very rapidly to please the media," explained one interviewee. It could be decision making through
"tremendous unthinking fear" rather than reason, "like so many things in political life,"
he added. Or it could be chasing the "sex appeal" of opportunistic criticism of investment arbitration to rile up voters, or refusing to settle a losing treaty case, or complaining
about the outcome of a case. "Politically speaking," said another arbitrator, "it is convenient [for states] to be able to blame the tribunal [. . .] and the previous government,
which signed the treaty." Politics, another said, could be "the aggrandizement" of the
state, such as when European politicians urge reforms to treaties that would require foreign investors to exhaust their claims in national courts before launching international
arbitration claims. He described this proposal as "bullshit political games."

The inherent fuzziness of arbitrators' conception of politics can be found in this
arbitrator's piece of advice for states:

> Try to spot the conflict before parties take rigid political positions. It's commonsense. Often,
> the origin of the conflict is not some action done by the president in the presidential chambers.
> It is often by some mid-level political bureaucrat. And it grows. It would be useful for the gov-
> ernment to realize, to keep aware of the problems, and try to deal with the problems, try to
> negotiate the problems, negotiate a solution, rather than wait until they become full-blown
> problems, full-blown conflicts, where individual political groups take positions on the conflict,
> and therefore really inhibit the ability to search for a solution. What we are trying to do is
> give confidence to investors that the state will treat them fairly. And if they are not treated
> fairly, that they do not have to just rely on political agreements, that there will be some legal
> process.

Yet four mentions later of forms of the word "political" and it is not clear what the
concept demarcates for the interviewee. To him, it is simultaneously an absence of flexibility motivated by group interests and ideologies outside the state, bumbling unelected

personnel within the state, and an agreement so flexible it can be broken at will—in contrast to the lawyers' vision of the stabilizing force of law. In sum, "procedure" is good; "politics" are bad.

After a love of proceduralism and a distaste for politics, a final ideology about the ideal change path was austere: states are better off not changing. Multiple interviewees described with disgust how politicians would campaign on changing environmental rules or "past privatizations," win the elections on that basis, and then try to fulfill their campaign pledges. These officials think they are "the top of the heap [. . .] They are shaping their country's future, and if they think it is good for the country, they are going to do it, no matter what. They do not understand the consequences." Said another arbitrator: "You have to define policies not for this government but somehow you have to agree with the opposition or with the other political parties for the future."

These arbitrators acknowledged the role that elections play in changing states' policy orientation. Others did not, talking of a state as if it were functionally the same personnel across time. Several commented on the circumstances related to Argentina's 1990s pegging of its currency to the US dollar and the 2000s unpegging of its currency, which made it a leading target of investment law claims. The state "overdid it" in the 1990s and "play[ed] games with all these people" only to reverse course "because of a crisis," said one interviewee. Left unremarked or considered unimportant was that the Latin American country seesawed during the period from the neoliberalism of Carlos Menem to the populism of Nestor and Cristina Kirchner, politicians who could not be more different in their style and priorities for governing. For other arbitrators, Eastern European countries created "a lot of expectations" with their "dramatic" transition to market economies, expectations that their policy makers have not met, said another. Regardless of whether inconsistency came from shifting electoral mandates or from other unspecified mechanisms, investment treaties were a way around states' inconsistencies. These treaties are "straitjackets" so that "nobody can move" and thus avoid "a legal environment which is [. . .] changing continuously," concluded one interviewee.

While straitjacket-type metaphors were widely used by my interviewees, they differed in terms of when the obligation to be consistent is triggered. For some, it was not time-bounded: absolute consistency was required for all time ("Nobody can move," said one interviewee). Others bounded the obligation to the time when the treaty was signed, when a specific pledge was made to an investor, or simply when an investment was made. States should not take actions that "are going to run contrary to the milieu, the environment, the landscape, in which the investor has come," said one arbitrator. "I think it is quite simple. Do not spring any surprise." For the more lenient interviewees, the moment after which states must "leave no room for surprise" came the moment a new policy was announced. "Come up with a coherent program, saying you know 'these are our policies, from now on everything we do is going to be consistent with this program,'" explained one of these arbitrators.

There were also those interviewees that argued states should not only be consistent across time, but also across the domestic space. Federal and sub-federal agencies and governments need to behave consistently with one another. "For us, it is all the same

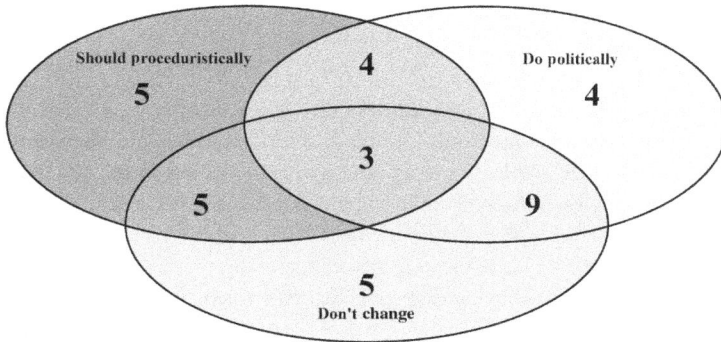

Figure 3.6 How should/do states go about changing?
Source: Author's grounded theory analysis of pertinent arbitrator responses (35).

country," said one arbitrator. "Whether it is the customs official or the government or the courts or the administrative courts," even if these agencies have differing objectives that they pursue legally and in good faith. For instance, if an investment official allows a foreign investor to open up a paper recycling operation, then the country's environmental ministry cannot later impose limits on what types of waste paper can be processed—even if both agencies are following the law, and even if the company has the option to use other types of paper. When an issue is regulated at the national and provincial level, there is a greater risk that policies will "have a change and then a change back" across time and between the levels of government, warned one interviewee. While foreign and trade ministries are seen as typically "literate" about their treaty obligations, other agencies "have no concept of what the country's obligation is" and, consequently, "some mid-level political bureaucrat" is often to blame for violations, he added.

Arbitrators were hard pressed to find solutions to inconsistency. One noted that federal governments could trigger liability if they "wash their hands away" of treaty-violating actions of sub-federal officials, but could do so equally if they "wanted to handle the whole thing" for the lower-level governments. Other arbitrators thought the only way to change policy would be to pay off foreign investors for the privilege of doing so. Interestingly, none of the interviewees explicitly advocated getting rid of elections or sub-federal governments—the only surefire way to avoid this type of inconsistency.

As Figure 3.6 shows, arbitrators were fairly evenly distributed around these three different ideological approaches to change. Out of 35 interviewees that made relevant comments, 17 liked proceduralism, 19 chided states for politicization and 22 said no change was the safest option. In other words, even if they bashed politics or celebrated legal procedure, nearly two-thirds of the interviewees simply thought stasis was advisable.

Intriguingly, even the most state-skeptical arbitrators thought there was one part of the state that worked: the agencies that negotiate treaties and that attempt to chill or preempt any policy action that is inconsistent with treaties or likely to anger investors. Arbitrators' discussion of these agencies wove together critiques of politics and praises of proceduralist agencies that have mandates to render state policy static and consistent.

One arbitrator spoke glowingly of such states, using evolutionary biology metaphors that likened state behavior to human ageing:

> The Canadians I think have dealt with this in a very *mature* manner [. . .] I understand that they have created their own little office in Trade and External Affairs that handles these things. They have created a little subgroup, it is an interagency subgroup, that looks at each case and makes a fairly early determination whether it is meritorious or not, and if they think they've got a problem, they will go out and settle. Which is why, a lot of governments would be better off if they did that. I give them great credit, and they have settled some things. Was this because they were bludgeoned or coerced? No. It is because they are *grown up*. (Emphasis added.)

Another made a similar point:

> I think we do not probably put enough emphasis on negotiation and conciliation, and having somebody in the government who is not so tied to the position that is being challenged that he is going to say, 'we cannot do this, because it will create political problems with my career or other reasons why I cannot possibly compromise.' You get governments like Canada, the DFAIT [the Department of Foreign Affairs and International Trade], which has enough backing of the Justice Department, and the Foreign Ministry and the Prime Minister's office [. . .] Where they can look at that and say 'we do not wish to go to arbitration,' and so they settled [a dispute], for a huge amount of money, like $140 million. It takes a lot of guts for a bunch of government lawyers to do something like that. But they got backed up! [. . .] How do you develop that type of confidence and that type of backup when these issues become frequently political footballs?

In sum, for many arbitrators, simply being a part of a government (with its representative and bureaucratic imperatives) was seen to convert most government officials into unreliable actors—so much so that straitjackets were needed to bind them across time and space. Investment-responsible agencies, though part of states, somehow avoided being crippled by the same burdens.

What Role Do Treaties Play in National Development?

If investment treaties hold the potential to keep states from pursuing the wrong things in the wrong ways, what is their actual track record in the eyes of arbitrators? Do they help the countries that submitted to the bindings? For many, the answer was clear and clearly positive.

The "sales pitch is true" said one interviewee: in a point echoed by others, treaties are a prerequisite for foreign direct investment. Rather than point to specific evidence to support this claim, arbitrators more often used parables. In a country where investors do not "trust the courts," where there is high "political risk," or where slum dwellers "steal the electricity," investors either would not invest or would require a much higher rate of return, said one interviewee. Arbitration reassures these investors that "they are not going to lose their money," he added. The result: foreign investors invest where they would not, or lower their risk premiums on existing investments. Countries send signals to the world not only by having treaties, but also by paying awards when they are challenged and lose. Noted one interviewee:

> It creates a perspective in investors, a sensation that this country is closer to Mexico than to [long pause] Zimbabwe. The best example of that is Mexico [. . .] They had a number of investment claims. They have defended them forcefully. Forcefully. When they lose, they pay. And they never put in doubt that they believe that investment treaties are good for Mexico. That is the attitude which gets the most out of investment treaties. It is like a sort of insurance. You pay a couple of investment treaty awards. That is like an insurance premium which you pay in order to convince the investment community that you're serious about the protection of investment [. . .] and the quality of the governance in your country. And that then has this beautiful effect that it gives you the advantage of reducing the rate of return requested by new investors.

Arbitration was useful not only for its direct effects, said most interviewees, but also for the indirect effects. One interviewee likened it to "preventative medicine; it is there on the shelf, but you do not take it." Others agreed, noting how little arbitration there is relative to the scale of foreign direct investment globally. Some arbitrators emphasized benefits from treaties to countries' domestic institutions. Treaties provide a guide for "how to behave" or, as another arbitrator quoted an influential arbitral colleague as saying, "This is a good government operation. Fucking little countries should be grateful! We are to teach them how to govern themselves." In short, treaties are part of the rule of law, and signing them creates an opportunity within countries to harmonize their constitutions to global best practice.

One advantage of having developed countries as parties to these treaties is that they also can be sued. Why would this be a good thing, above the diplomatic cover offered by formal reciprocity? One interviewee argued that hearing cases involving rich countries gives arbitrators an opportunity to shine a spotlight on what precisely rich countries do that makes them attractive to investment, a sort of model-pupil demonstration:

> [You can] begin to develop a set of developed country expectations which eventually you can hold developing countries to as well. And I think you begin to develop a more international body of law with respect to investment. If you really want investment to flow throughout the world in a relatively fair and equitable way, you develop this robust sense of law, and you are going to develop it in a more sophisticated way when you have a developed country as the potential defender rather than a developing country.

Another indirect effect of arbitration is the perceived spillover onto the quality of domestic institutions for domestic investors. As states treated foreign investors more favorably, nationals would demand the same treatment—leading to a virtuous cycle of improvements. Said one interviewee: "If you are scanning the world for likely capital, I would say, as a host country official, 'how about all those [domestic] investors that have big bank accounts in Miami and London and Switzerland? What can I do to get them to come back here?' Create a climate that says you will be treated fairly."

A final and significant benefit from treaties was civilizational, argued the interviewees. Said one: "the purpose of [arbitration] is to de-politicize investment disputes. Instead of diplomatic protection and that stuff, we are going to have arbitrators." Another arbitrator said that countries in the throes of decolonization hate their neighbors and colonizers, are not "open-minded," and are "lazy [. . .] the man of the future is somebody who can bypass their traditions and sort of handicaps what he inherited. If somebody had been subject in the past to [colonial] occupation, he has to understand that was a phase in history, and not to take it as an evil thing. On the contrary [. . .] colonizers made irrigation, roads, schools and everything better for the country." For this arbitrator, treaties help open up developing countries to a "universal culture" far better than their parochial beginnings. Eleven arbitrators suggested that without treaties gunboat diplomacy and war would proliferate. When I asked one if he thought investment treaties contribute to peace, he pointed to inherent features of states that need to be constrained: "Definitely. Yes. Yes, because I think it is a substitute to diplomatic protection. I think there is a great advantage. In fact, two states are not involved. The state of the investor has nothing to do with it. So you do not have an opposition between two states, which is *always dangerous*." (Emphasis added.)

Indeed, one interviewee suggested that investment treaties could have changed the course of twentieth-century history:

> We might have a very different world today if the Mossadegh government [of Iran] in 1951 had not violated the contract and its international legal obligation to arbitrate disputes under the Anglo American concession [. . .] If it had arbitrated, then we probably never would have had the intervention to overthrow the Mossadegh government, and if that had not happened, then you might well not have had the reaction which established clerical rule in Iran and so on and so on. So I think it is important stuff to have arbitration, rather than gunboat diplomacy, or simple plundering of investors by states, as you had with the Russian Revolution [. . .] I think it is a healthy thing. It is what is called, in the parlance of international law, the progressive development of international law. And I think it is a progressive development. And the oddity of the present situation is the people who say they are progressive are attacking it! I think they are all mixed up.

Figure 3.7 shows (unsurprisingly) that these lawyers, who have dedicated recent years of their life at least in part to investment arbitration, think the system worthwhile. It is an entirely intuitive point, and it underlines the important extent to which professionals of any stripe see their work as a calling that benefits more than themselves alone. More surprising were the two camps of dissenters.

The first group of contrarians was so skeptical of states' *bona fides* that they thought treaties would not help their economies, but would only help shield foreign investors from their dysfunction. For instance, all ten arbitrators who showed any familiarity with social-science research on the link between treaties and foreign direct investment flows knew that the research did not show a major positive impact. "The generally held view is that these treaties actually encourage foreign investment," noted one interviewee. "I mean, if that is true or not is debatable. There is no statistical evidence as far as I know that they actually increase foreign investment."

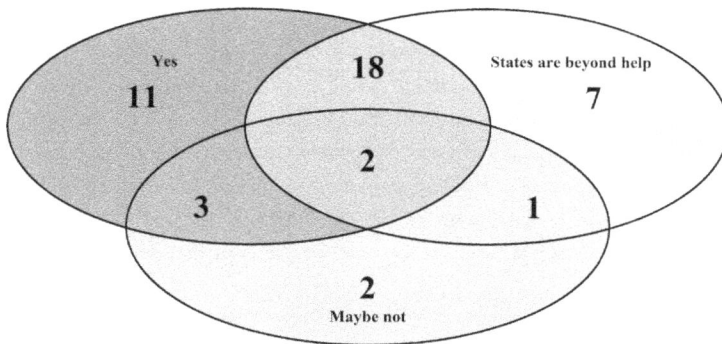

Figure 3.7 Do states actually need investment treaties?
Source: Author's grounded theory analysis of pertinent arbitrator responses (44).

Even without an economic benefit for host states, most arbitrators remained enthusiastic about treaties for what they meant for the investors. They doubted that states could ever really be trusted, no matter how many treaties they signed. An implication of this viewpoint is that the institutional change promised by treaties would not come. The ongoing pathology of states was blamed on localism, which impaired national judges from ever being able to render justice. As one interviewee said:

> When a tribunal that is going to assess or decide something is embedded in the culture of the local host country, they cannot be neutral. I feel myself very neutral when I try case against the Philippines, but I would not feel neutral in a case involving [my home nation]. Because I could not consider myself neutral if I am reading in the paper every day what is happening in that case. If an arbitration is against the Philippines, I know that there are plenty of headlines in the newspaper, but I do not care [. . . T]hat is the reason why, not only for judges, but even for arbitrators, it is very good to be far away from the psychological movement inside the country [. . .] I am not in a position to be neutral if I see what is happening at home. I am very neutral when I am deciding cases far away from my family, and from my professional and local activities that I am involved in. That is the reason why even domestic arbitration sometimes is not working very well, because in domestic arbitration you will see the man who is going to decide in the tennis club or at the swimming pool, it is not really very neutral kind of relationship.

For this arbitrator, local judges have denser social ties and more localized information, and this fuels bias. In contrast, what is difficult for national judges is easy for "three neutral [arbitrator] individuals sitting in a neutral place who are not responsive to an electorate," argued one interviewee. To the extent there was a drawback to cultural distance, it was easily remediable, said another: "The fact that you have people sitting that do not know much about the domestic aspect, I do not think that matters all that much. Very soon, you can talk to enough people and get some sort of clear idea what happened and why."

Localism was not just a Filipino problem, it was everywhere, the arbitrators agreed. As one interviewee said: "The local courts may side with the local party. It happens everywhere. I do not think that has much to do with developed or underdeveloped." And another said, "Even with what we somewhat loosely describe as the Western democracies, it is easy to understand that investors do not put 100 percent faith in the court system of what they perceive as their adversary." Norwegian courts, French courts, US courts, even New York courts for citizens from "contiguous states" such as Massachusetts: none inspired interviewees' confidence when it came to outside investment. National courts "around the world [...] are incompetent or corrupt or just nationalistic in their perceptions," said one interviewee. If private parties cannot reach a settlement, said another, then

> there is no other alternative but arbitration. I consider the British justice, the courts in England, as the best example in equity, in torts, in respect of due process, rule of law, and everything, but nevertheless they are not prepared to understand what is going on in the outside world. They are more legalistic in their approach than taking the economy, the environment, what is going in the world into account, because they follow rules and procedures. Very nice, that you have fair procedures, you have a rule of law that is established. But it is always evolving. You cannot keep it static and without change. So I am a believer in arbitration.

A second group of contrarians went further: investment treaties are not needed at all. This admission (from eight interviewees) is notable, since it goes against arbitrators' self-interest and is contrary to the academic views that if states sign treaties then they must be a rational response as either a complement or a substitute (to use the academic categories) for domestic institutions (Ginsburg 2005).

But for even these interviewees, the case against investment treaties was a very limited one, applying to only one nation: Brazil. The large South American nation has long attracted foreign direct investment despite having ratified no treaties. This should disturb advocates of arbitration as it would seem to undermine the justifications for the extraordinary system. But my interviewees had simple explanations that salvaged Brazil as the exception that proves the rule. Brazil, said one,

> has such a large market and such a bounty of natural resources that it can do that. There are other countries, like Singapore, that have no natural resources. And its main way of developing wealth is bringing investment in through adherence to the rule of law. Entering into these treaties gives the investor an added level of confidence to invest in Singapore rather than Malaysia. States are free to decide. Do they want investment?

While Brazil was the main example cited, it was not the only one cited by these interviewees. "Everyone believes" the Swiss and the Saudis "have so much money," and countries such as Bolivia and Norway have abundant natural resources, noted one arbitrator, adding that these factors may limit the need for treaties, although only for countries with such endowments. (For the record, these countries do have investment treaties, so the point was likely rhetorical.) In short, the exceptions to investment treaties' desirability prove the general rule. Indeed, several interviewees argued that Brazil would have gotten even more investment had it inked a number of treaties.

In sum, most arbitrators believe that their work has some positive social contribution. Three of four (34) say that treaties will help improve host states' economies and institutions. But 28 of them, including many of the same more-boosterish individuals, express doubts about whether treaties are necessary or sufficient for national progress. Alongside the notion that treaties embody the highest ideals of civilization and international peace, arbitrators were cynical about national institutions' ability to serve justice in a globalized economy. Even the world's best courts would favor local parties or simply be incompetent or corrupt. Arbitrators were the solution to such irresolvable government failure.

How Much Sensitivity Should Arbitrators Show States?

Despite the harsh disciplinary attitudes toward states expressed by interviewees in the previous sections, they also emphasized their own informal willingness to defer to states in some limited respects. At its most meaningful, this could involve adopting doctrines of deference to states, much like national courts did for sovereign immunity (as we learned earlier in the chapter). At its less ambitious, this regard could be as minimal as using kind tones when questioning states. States were deemed variously by them as "special entities," or "special animals" with "superior interests." They have democratic and representational concerns and "a lot of pride," explained one interviewee. Unlike corporations, "they never cease to exist," which affects their "time horizon" in and out of arbitration, said another.

Some arbitrators discussed how they could not help but be sensitive variously to states' "role, and their position, and their powers," the "taxpayer who is behind the defendants," or that "every one of these cases involves a public policy decision." States "were not coherent" or did not "operate according to some sociological model," said two interviewees. Some arbitrators also expressed awareness of negative perceptions of them in respondent countries. Said one: "Sometimes it is difficult for the population, for public opinion, to accept three men, three foreign people, who have decided about the regulation of electricity or things of that sort."

There was no uniform view among them about how far this discretionary sensitivity to states should go. Some criticized earlier arbitral decisions for being too tilted against the state, and they argued that arbitrators had since become more deferential to states after getting a "reality check." Others noted that cases were or should be decided with an eye to avoiding state backlash. The treaties themselves could be written with very state-restricting standards, but arbitrators could blunt the impact through issuing less harsh awards, and by ascertaining the intention of states rather than literally interpreting treaty texts. Observed one of the arbitrators:

> There has always been this general talk of investment arbitration being pro-business. It's not. You could say investment treaties are pro-business, or pro-private property, and they protect private property more than public interest. But once you have the treaty in place, which I mean, you can always change it, then investment arbitration is not pro-business.

Some arbitrators suggested they could probe the factual record more diligently to see if states could not be given the benefit of the doubt. But for others, such sensitivity was more modest:

> We know what environment we're working in, and we know the political currents. Now, it's not going to make you decide "a as opposed to b," or "yes as opposed to no." But particularly where you are dealing with sovereigns, you have to sort of have to know how to go about the things that, and have them feel they have had a complete hearing.

One arbitrator said that his colleagues should dismiss claims on jurisdictional grounds to spare states the expense of fighting misguided claims. In such a scenario, arbitrators would find that investors lacked standing to bring their case, or that investors made some other fatal technical flaw in their pleading. This would allow the state to get off the hook without much scrutiny into whether the investor was right or wrong on the merits. But others thought that this type of jurisdictional mercy was rare, citing cases where the chairmen of investment tribunals made parties argue the whole case only to dismiss it after the fact on jurisdictional grounds, wanting to keep cases going in order to be paid. One area where arbitrators showed willingness to be sensitive to states was in reducing the amount of quantum (arbitrator-speak for monetary damages) owed. (For more on this, see the discussion on horse-trading in the next chapter.)

These discussions did not illuminate any specific content that arbitrators attached to discretionary sensitivity. What areas or types of state behavior would be more likely to attract mercy? There was little clarity, suggesting that there would be little states could do ex ante to tailor their policy behavior to arbitrators' predilections. In the next section, I will show some of the (unpredictable) ways that sensitivity was shown in the case law.

Attractive Outputs: Ideology in Arbitral Decisions

As the first subsection showed, states are winning more than they are losing, and investors are recouping pennies on the dollar of their claims. But I have argued that these win–loss statistics obscure important developments. In particular, it obscures how ISDS tribunals have become a sort of norm laboratory. As I will now show, the input of ideologies identified in the second subsection above show up in the output of these cases: the awards themselves. Freed from the constraints of meaningful appellate review or a need to curry favor with states that are always and only on the receiving end of litigation, arbitrators are free to workshop ideas for appropriate state behavior in *dicta*—the reasoning portion of the awards. As I showed above, arbitrators have competing ideological loyalties, showing disdain for states at one moment and discretionary sensitivity to their plight in the next, which results in final arbitration decisions based on an overlapping mix of ideologies.

In the following sections, I provide a number of examples of the best- and worst-case scenarios for investors. Generally speaking, the best outcome for investors is to win a case, get compensation and have the reasoning in the case constitute a useful persuasive precedent for disciplining (or threatening to discipline) states in future interactions. But even in the worst-case scenario, investors as a class may still get something useful if arbitrators' reasoning presents a road map to how arguments could be tweaked in the future to win cases and effectively threaten states. To illustrate this point, I use a recent case or cases as a prism to examine how arbitrators have engaged with precedent and incrementally expanded the reach (or not) of the norms they were called upon to interpret. I make no call as to whether arbitrators reached the correct conclusion as a matter of law, an elusive task I will leave to others. Rather, my goal is to identify whether and how arbitrators' ideologies about politics and development show up in the awards.

"Best" Case: Damages for Political Change

Easily the most controversial standard in investment law is the obligation for states to provide fair and equitable treatment (FET). Unlike rules that have some objectively ascertainable content, such as do not expropriate, or do not impose capital controls, FET is elastic. University of New South Wales legal scholar Jonathan Bonnitcha finds that tribunals have interpreted the standard (variably) as: only requiring that foreigners be treated like nationals or that they receive better treatment; applying only to judicial acts or encompassing all branches of government; and as requiring good faith on the part of government or a guarantee of specific outcomes for investors (Bonnitcha 2014).

Early ISDS cases produced some very anti-state rulings. In *Metalclad v. Mexico* (2000), for instance, a unanimous trio of arbitrators determined that Mexico's federal government—having approved a federal construction permit for a hazardous-waste landfill—was required to block city governments from imposing environmental and social conditions on a municipal permit. The tribunal awarded nearly $17 million in damages, writing in highly categorical terms that

> *all* relevant legal requirements for the purpose of initiating, completing and successfully oper-ating investments made, or intended to be made, under [NAFTA] should be capable of being readily known to all affected investors of another Party. *There should be no room for doubt or uncer-tainty on such matters.* Once the authorities of the central government of any [country] become aware of *any scope* for misunderstanding or confusion in this connection, *it is their duty to ensure* that the correct position is promptly determined and clearly stated so that *investors can proceed* with all appropriate expedition in the confident belief that they are acting in accordance with *all* relevant laws [. . .] Metalclad was entitled to rely on the representations of federal officials and to believe that it was entitled to continue its construction of the landfill [. . .] Mexico failed to ensure a transparent and predictable framework for Metalclad's business planning and investment. (Lauterpacht et al. 2000, 23–27, emphasis added)

For years to come, tribunals favorably cited *Metalclad* for the proposition that national governments had to meet investors' expectations of a total uniformity in approach over time and territorial space. For instance, the investor in a hazardous-waste facility was awarded $5.5 million in the *Tecmed v. Mexico* case when the host state failed to meet the demanding requirement "to act in a consistent manner, free from ambiguity and totally transparently in its relations with the foreign investor" (Grigera Naon et al. 2003, 61). At the root of the state's sins: the elections in 1997 had elevated opponents of the landfill to local and provincial office, after which they (along with social movements) pressured the company to move the landfill's location.

In another case, *Vivendi v. Argentina (II)*, a water concessionaire bought a privatized utility from an incumbent provincial Argentine government in the heat of an electoral campaign where the nonincumbents opposed the deal. After a long legal battle, the company was awarded more than $100 million when the nonincumbents won and made good on their promise. As the arbitrators wrote in that case, "Under the fair and equitable standard, there is no doubt about a government's obligation not to disparage and undercut a concession (a "do no harm" standard) that has properly been granted, albeit by a predecessor government, based on falsities and motivated by a desire to rescind or force a renegotiation. And that is exactly what happened in Tucumán" (Rowley et al. 2007, 218). Notably, the same state-appointed arbitrator sat in both of these fundamentally anti-political and anti-state rulings. So much for the idea—influential in some literature on international courts (E. A. Posner and Yoo 2005)—that appointment authority necessarily gives states power.

"Worst" Case: Damages Only for Changes Unfavorable to Foreigners

By 2006, arbitrators began to articulate a more limited interpretation centered on domestic law—one more in keeping with the pitch made by the US Trade Representative and *The Economist* earlier in this chapter. In this new approach to fair and equitable treatment, the central issue was legitimate expectations. Namely, did a state make an enforceable promise under domestic law (or otherwise make very strong, direct and unambiguous representations) and was it legitimate to expect that the promise would be kept? Under this revised reading, it was deemed unreasonable for investors to expect no change. The arbitrators in one of the first cases to pivot to the new approach were careful to obscure the import of their move. Indeed, in writing that "investor's fair expectations [. . .] must exist and be enforceable by law," the tribunal favorably cited and made it appear that they were deriving the test from *Metalclad* and *Tecmed* themselves (de Maekelt et al. 2007, 39–40)!

What, then, is the obligation when the domestic legal regime itself is undergoing a process of change? Indeed, many significant cases now deal with the conduct of the national law interpreters themselves—national courts (Tucker 2013). The obligation of courts to investors was a key issue in the recently decided and highly controversial *Eli Lilly v. Canada* (2017) case. The underlying conflict in this case had roots that were decades old. In 2010–11, Canadian courts invalidated Eli Lilly's 1998 patent for Zyprexa (a schizophrenia drug) and its 2002 patent for Strattera (a treatment for attention deficit/hyperactivity disorder). In the years in between the patent approval and invalidation, Canadian courts began tightening criteria for patentability. In particular, they developed the so-called promise-utility doctrine, which requires the original patent application materials to spell out exactly how the product innovates and what novel benefit it will deliver. When Eli Lilly's generics competitors petitioned the courts for a second look at these materials, courts found that the 1998 and 2002 patents had not meaningfully innovated over patents granted in 1980 and 1979, respectively. In 2012, Eli Lilly filed an investor–state dispute settlement claim under NAFTA for $374.3 million, alleging that the patent invalidations were discriminatory, unfair, and inequitable. The arbitration tribunal ultimately sided with Canada, and against the investor.

Canada's win would seem to be a victory for regulatory prerogatives the world around, but a closer look reveals how qualified the right to regulate had become. Perhaps anticipating that arbitrators might be loath to rule against a highly developed country's courts' inherent powers to determine national law, Eli Lilly's lawyers framed their complaint as not against the promise-utility doctrine itself but against its application to the company's patents. The tribunal accepted this characterization for the purpose of assuming jurisdiction over the case, which overruled not just Canada but all three NAFTA governments that had made statements to the tribunal.[4] While Canada's power as a formal matter to determine its own law would be left intact, consider the implications of this line of reasoning: Had the arbitrators found that the patent invalidations consistent with Canadian law but inconsistent with the North American Free Trade Agreement, then Canada would have had to exempt Eli Lilly from the regime faced by other patent holders in order to comply.

Turning to the fair and equitable treatment question itself, the arbitrators argued that legitimate expectations would have indeed been violated had there been "a dramatic change in the Canadian law on utility" (van den Berg, Born, and Bethlehem 2017, 118). In the case at hand, the tribunal noted that this had not been the situation: the emergence of the promise-utility doctrine had roots in cases from the 1980s, and was crystallized in key decisions several years before Eli Lilly's patents were invalidated. The later decisions cited the earlier ones, as the tribunal noted. "While the promise standard may not have played a significant role in the Canadian jurisprudence before 2005, and courts looked to the disclosure for the promise in relatively few cases, the rule was clearly 'out there,' to be ignored at a patentee's peril," the tribunal ruled (ibid. at 99). Rather than an abrupt change, the tribunal saw a gradual change that other countries had not consistently complained about.

But this Canadian win had its own perverse implications. Say the facts had been slightly different. What if Eli Lilly's patent invalidations had come a few years earlier, before the doctrine crystallized? Or what if the George W. Bush administration or Obama administration had raised persistent objections to the promise doctrine, which (as the tribunal noted) stood at odds with US and international practice? The cost of pharmaceuticals is one of the most salient political issues today, with voices as varied as Senator Bernie Sanders to President Donald Trump calling for aggressive cost-saving measures that would be an abrupt change from the patent-holder-friendly current practice (Beavers 2017). The unavoidable conclusion from *Eli Lilly* is that investors facing an abrupt change in patent law could and would have a good ISDS case to claim damages based on legitimate expectations doctrine.

---

4. Indeed, had the tribunal found otherwise, it would have been fatal for Eli Lilly as a jurisdictional matter, because a complaint against the doctrine itself (articulated as early as 2002) would have surpassed NAFTA's three-year statute of limitations for launching a claim.

To be sure, an outright win is better than some norm workshopping (a la *Eli Lilly*) that a future investor might be able to use down the road. In *Windstream v. Canada*, a unanimous tribunal put the federal government on the hook for $20 million in damages after the provincial government of Ontario imposed a moratorium on offshore wind energy farms. In a nod to the government's concerns, they wrote that Canada's "evolving position was at least in part driven by a genuine policy concern that there was not sufficient scientific support for establishing an appropriate setback, or exclusion zone, for offshore wind projects" (Heiskanen et al. 2016, 106). But they then chastised the province, noting:

> At the same time, however, the evidence before the Tribunal suggests that the decision to impose the moratorium was not only driven by the lack of science. The impact of offshore wind on electricity costs in Ontario, as well as the upcoming provincial elections in November 2011, also appear to have influenced the decision, and the latter in particular in light of the public opposition to offshore wind that had emerged during the relevant period in many parts of rural Ontario [. . . T]he Government on the whole did relatively little to address the scientific uncertainty surrounding offshore wind that it had relied upon as the main publicly cited reason for the moratorium. Indeed, many of the research plans did not go forward at all, including some for lack of funding, and at the hearing counsel for the Respondent confirmed that Ontario did not plan to conduct any further studies. Nor have the studies that have been conducted led to any amendments to the regulatory framework. (ibid. 106–107)

This mixed finding produced mixed consequences. The moratorium itself was not a violation of the fair and equitable treatment standard. What was a violation was that the intervention of local politics derailed an idealized technocratic decision making process, and that the federal government did not intervene to force the provincial government to document (however flimsily) a scientific basis for their claim. This is a profound finding, sidelining the importance of public opinion in democracies, casting federalism as an obstacle to investment, and risking the demotion of science to a purely instrumental use.

The *Bilcon v. Canada* case a year earlier had even harsher implications for democracy. In that dispute, the US investor had received initially warm signals from the Nova Scotia provincial government for its offshore quarrying operation. Over time, however, public opposition to the project grew. A special review committee was set up, and instead of using cost-benefit analysis, the panel gave weight to the community's subjective sentiments. This offended the sensibilities of the tribunal majority, who urged the federal government to intervene not only in the province or the panel, but to alter the conclusions of the panel's recommendations themselves. They wrote, "Canada is one entity for the purposes of NAFTA responsibility" and "the mere fact that environmental regulation is involved does not make investor protection inapplicable" (Simma et al. 2015, 176–79). As the state appointee wrote in a sharply worded dissent,

> a chill will be imposed on environmental review panels which will be concerned not to give too much weight to socio-economic considerations or other considerations of the human environment in case the result is a claim for damages under NAFTA Chapter 11. In this respect, the decision of the majority will be seen as a remarkable step backwards in environmental protection. (McRae 2015, 19)

Canada was not the only developed country to be hit by the evolving notion of what fair and equitable treatment required. In 2007–8, in a bid to attract investment into the renewable energy sector, Spain pledged a variety of incentives to stay in place for 25 years. Less than a year later, the global financial crisis struck Spain's economy. While the country struggled to recover, European authorities insisted on spending austerity. Over the next several years, the nation's solar power subsidies were made less generous, leading dozens of investors to sue Spain in national courts and in investment tribunals.

In the handful of Spanish solar power cases decided thus far, arbitrators have come to more or less forgiving conclusions. In a first case, a 2-to-1 tribunal majority sided with Spain that an investor in shares of a solar company had no right to expect an unchanging regulatory environment. At the same time, they ruled that changes must not be sudden, must take into account the needs of investors, and must be "economically reasonable." The tribunal concluded by opining that other cases against Spain might have been more successful (Mourre et al. 2016, 117–23).

A second 2-to-1 decision with two of the same arbitrators reached a similar conclusion (in Spain's favor) under the 52-nation, Eurasia-wide Energy Charter Treaty, but arriving via a similarly anti-state reasoning. In particular, the tribunal found that the company—owned by nationals of Canada and Spain but registered in the Netherlands—could bring the claim against Spain despite some eye-catching irregularities. Namely, the first country (Canada) was not party to the treaty, the second country (Spain) was the home state itself (so the nationals were circumventing the domestic legal system), and European authorities argued before the tribunal against the application of the Energy Charter Treaty to two countries within the European Union (Derains et al. 2016). The sovereigns were ruled against on all these counts.

Spain dodged these bullets narrowly. The investor appointee was the same man in both cases,[5] and he argued that Spain's 2007 policies did create legitimate expectations that later governments needed to uphold (Tawil 2015; 2016). Mere months later, a whole tribunal in another Spain solar-power case agreed with this dissenter's line of reasoning, finding that states' obligations to ensure a reasonable rate of return trumps concerns over fiscal deficits—even when national supreme courts find the government blameless. The arbitrators awarded €128 million, placing particular importance on the fact that the investors had chosen to make highly leveraged upfront investments, amplifying the negative impacts of revised rates of return (Crook et al. 2017, 117–30).

In sum, arbitrators were able incrementally to move out the boundary of fair and equitable treatment. In the first phase of these decisions (roughly between 2000 and 2006) unanimous tribunals insisted on uniform and unchanging policy. In the second phase (around 2006), this investor right was curtailed by legitimate expectations doctrine linked to specific and legally enforceable state promises to investors. Finally, in the third phase of these decisions (from 2007 onwards), arbitrators often found a middle ground where the right to regulate was balanced against the right to earn a return.

---

5. As was the state appointee, although he did not dissent in either case.

*"Best" (and "Worst") Case: All (or Only Part) of Tribunals Agree That Regulations'
Impacts on Profits Are Compensable Takings*

In early ISDS cases, investors had success convincing tribunals that regulations that partially diminish the value of an investment (or wholly diminish part of the investment) should be compensated as full-scale expropriations. This stands in contrast to domestic US law, for instance, which typically requires that government actually assume possession of the asset (in the case of direct takings) or that all value be extinguished (in the case of regulatory takings) (Porterfield 2004). The tribunal in the aforementioned *Metalclad* case (despite featuring a former US attorney general, Benjamin Civiletti, who would have known the US practice) took a more capital-friendly tack, finding that, "expropriation under NAFTA includes [...] covert or incidental interference with the use of property which has the effect of depriving the owner, in whole or *in significant part*, of the use or reasonably to-be-expected economic benefit of property even if not necessarily to the obvious benefit of the host State" (Lauterpacht, Civiletti and Siqueiros 2000, 28). (Emphasis added.) While the tribunal did not offer a precise formula for "significant part," legal scholar Bonnitcha has found that *Metalclad*'s reasoning was taken up in numerous cases in the decade to come (Bonnitcha 2014, 250).

Nonetheless, findings of expropriation, especially of the regulatory variety, have been rare. The balance articulated by a trio of influential arbitrators in *Electrabel v. Hungary* turned back to the US approach, requiring a loss of *"all* significant economic value,"* which would make an investment "financially *worthless*" (Veeder, Kaufmann-Kohler and Stern 2015, para 6.53; emphasis added). The tribunal majority in the recent *Blusun v. Italy* case praised *Electrabel* as a more "careful formulation" than *Metalclad's* "sweeping definition," finding against the investor's claim that a requirement to restrict the maximum amount of agricultural land usable for solar panels constituted an indirect expropriation (Crawford et al. 2016, 142).

Even in this "worst case," however, the claimant (and, by extension, other investors) got recognition of the potential merit of their claims. The *Blusun* tribunal favorably cited *Metalclad* for the notion that land-use restrictions that make "it impossible to use the property for its intended purpose [...] can amount to indirect expropriation" (*Blusun*, 145). This goes beyond US law, which looks to whether a property owner retains title and some value after a regulation takes place, and deemphasizes private hopes and aspirations. *Blusun*'s partial rehabilitation of the investor-friendly *Metalclad* precedent comes with pedigree: the chair in the case was none other than James Crawford, a sitting judge on the prestigious International Court of Justice. And the investor appointee, Stanimir Alexandrov, actually agreed with the investors' claim, finding that the "land use restriction would have amounted to half, or more, of the value of the Project. Because the land use restriction amounted to an indirect expropriation, damages should follow notwithstanding this uncertainty—at a minimum, in the amount of the lost incremental value of the land" (ibid. 148). A calculation that a 50 percent reduction in value amounts to an expropriation goes even further than the *Metalclad* "significant" threshold. This suggests the arbitral pool remains open to investors' more adventurous claims.

"Best" (and "Worst") Case: Foreigners Can Override Treaty Commitments of Their Home Country (or Are Bound to Only Those)

Perhaps the most contentious issue in investment case law is, at first blush, mind-numbingly procedural: most-favored-nation (MFN) rules. As we will explore in more detail in chapter 5, MFN offers a way for investors from a given home state to get treatment above and beyond what the home state negotiated. Some investment treaties, for example, require states to first litigate their dispute in domestic courts for a period of time before invoking treaty proceedings. Other treaties place no such precondition, and sometimes the same state has signed both types of treaties. Thus, the legal issue is whether investors can circumvent the rules from the more stringent treaties in favor of the laxer ones. Out of dozens of cases to examine the question, about half have said yes, and about half no. One string of cases followed the *Maffezini v. Spain* approach. In that 2000 case, an Argentine investor was able to sue Spain, despite not complying with local litigation requirements in the Argentina–Spain investment treaty, by invoking more-favorable rules in an Argentina–Chile pact (Orrego Vicuna et al. 2000). In contrast, in the *Plama v. Bulgaria* case (2005), a tribunal ruled that a Cypriot investor could not rely on more-favorable treatment enjoyed by investors under a Bulgaria–Finland treaty—though they did find jurisdiction on other grounds (Salans et al. 2005).[6]

The issue is ideological, but not in the way it might first appear. According to analysis by University of Amsterdam legal scholar Stephan Schill, when arbitrators with a background in business arbitration have looked at the most-favored-nation question, they have tended to side with the state, finding that foreign investors just as much as states must comply with the letter of the treaty responsibilities in order to get the treaty rights. In contrast, arbitrators with a background in public law have argued that it is better to be consistent across treaties and not allow jurisdictional questions such as MFN to get in the way of spreading international law (Schill 2017). In other words, the arbitrators we might expect to align with states are (on this issue) the ones perhaps most tempted to give investors more options for asserting private rights. The deeper implication of the still-unresolved split is that, in a given year, a given state might experience two arbitrations that arrive at opposing conclusions. In sum, while the *Plama* followers found that host states were bound (only) to follow the (substantial) obligations of treaties they did sign with home states, the *Maffezini* followers found an even broader sphere of obligation because of the MFN clause.

Truly Worst Case: Unusable Protections

There are two treaty protections that have never lived up to their hype for investors: rules on nondiscrimination and capital controls. They have in common a high degree of precision, which limits tribunals' ability to stretch norms in pro-investor directions.

---

6. As the cases moved to the merits, Maffezini prevailed (winning a few hundred thousand dollars), while Plama lost.

First, let's examine nondiscrimination. As noted earlier in this chapter, the idea that investor–state dispute settlement might help rein in protectionism has a strong appeal among many observers. Indeed, even determined critics of the system argue that it would be more legitimate if it limited itself to guaranteeing that foreign investors will be treated no worse (and no better) than nationals (Lester 2013).

Yet arbitrators have interpreted treaties as making it virtually impossible to bring claims against governments on this basis, even in cases of some egregious governmental double standards. In the nearly 350 cases to date, investors have only convinced arbitrators to hear national treatment claims in 53 cases, and have been sided-with in only 10.[7]

Some, but not all, of the difficulty in using national treatment rules can be linked to the treaty clause that evenhandedness is only required for investors in "like circumstances." In *Rusoro v. Venezuela,* for instance, arbitrators noted that small-scale gold producers (who were mostly national) were forced to hand over only 15 percent of their production to the government, while the figure for the larger scale companies (including the prominent foreign-owned claimant in the case) was 50 percent. In the tribunal's view, the treaty

> only requires that Venezuela grant treatment no less favourable to Rusoro than that which, "in like circumstances," grants to its own investors. The Bolivarian Republic [i.e., Venezuela's formal name since a 1999 constitutional change] has adopted an official policy, differentiating between small scale, traditional miners and large mining companies and offering additional support and less stringent requirements to small miners. Thus Rusoro (and other large miners) and small scale miners are not "in like circumstances," and the difference in treatment is justified by valid policy reasons. (Fernandez-Armesto et al. 2016, 124)

This hurdle also affected claims involving developed countries. In the aforementioned *Eli Lilly v. Canada* case (2017), the company argued (and was not contradicted) that "only patents held by foreign firms have been invalidated pursuant to this doctrine, despite its facially neutral character [. . .] the main beneficiary is the prominent Canadian generic drug industry." The tribunal refused to give these asymmetric benefits any weight, saying they only prove that "the largest pharmaceutical companies in the world are not Canadian" (*Eli Lilly*, paras. 401, 441), eliding the issue of whether national champions that do not respect patents would be better positioned relative to patent holders as a result.

In *Windstream v. Canada* (2016), the investor had compelling evidence that the renewable energy investments of both Canadian national and South Korean investors were allowed to prosper, while the US-owned Windstream was subjected to a clumsily handled moratorium that killed the latter's business plans. While the dispute-settlement tribunal sided with the investor on other counts, they found no discrimination, as the Canadian and South Korean investments were subject to slightly different legal

---

7. Author's calculations. The numbers would be slightly higher if examinations of fair and equitable treatment claims where discrimination was a factor in the analysis were concluded. But such parsing is not straightforward as a methodological matter, because tribunals tend to mix and combine the factors in their FET analysis.

oversight (Heiskanen et al. 2016, 118). In other words, investors have not only to sell similar products (the threshold for likeness in the World Trade Organization), but also be given equal regulatory treatment. Since it is the regulatory treatment itself that serves as the basis of the complaint, national treatment rules are a circular, difficult right for investors to access.

If nondiscrimination rules are seemingly unusable, then treaty bans on capital controls are not far behind. These standards have been subjected to withering criticism by development scholars in the wake of the 2008 financial crisis, who saw active capital-account management as a way for countries to avoid capital floods and flights (Gallagher 2010). Nonetheless, treaties have become progressively more forgiving of government's right to institute temporary capital controls, with a patchwork of balance-of-payments and prudential exceptions being grafted onto more recent iterations. Perhaps as a result of these exceptions (and the relative rarity of countries using highly restrictive capital controls in the first place in recent history), dispute-settlement tribunals have only entertained a dozen investor claims on this front, and only found three violations.

In the first case, the Slovak Republic's mandatory reinvestment/ban on profits in the healthcare sector (which the country's Supreme Court eventually overruled) had the consequence of also blocking repatriation of profits, thus violating treaty rules. The tribunal, however, engaged in no real parsing of the issue in their paragraph of treatment, focusing instead on fair and equal treatment (Lowe et al. 2012, 97). The second award was similarly brief in its paragraph of analysis, faulting Zimbabwe's failure to provide foreign exchange to tobacco investors (Fortier et al. 2015, 199). In the third case, an investor claimed success using the rules against Venezuela, but the award is not yet public (*GRUMA* 2017). In short, for a policy area that has generated substantial concern from champions of active public policies, the treaty rules are sufficiently precise and limited that investors have gotten little practical benefit from them.

Summing Up

This chapter explored why there is a demand for investment law. First, it can make companies better off financially. Investors as a whole make back the money they spend on lawyers many times over, and occasionally have restored some of what they claim to have lost. Second, ISDS standards are flexible enough that they create the possibility of arbitrators creating new investor rights. Even when investors lose cases, they might rack up useful tribunal opinions (dicta) or dissents that can be used by latter claimants to win cases (or pressure governments to settle). The inputs arbitrators bring to the cases—their ideologies—are largely favorable to investors and antagonistic to the messy realities of states. The outputs they produce—their decisions—reflect these inputs, but are layered incrementally over the decisions that came before. The interaction between standards' imprecision, ideology and past case law can produce pro-business awards even in cases that side with the state. Even in these best-case scenarios for governments, arbitrators are likely to encourage states to behave less like states (with attributes such as democracy, federalism and political bargaining) and more like a contractual counterparty. For companies, this is welcome news.

Table 3.2 Compatibility of arbitral ideology with development scholarship

Ideology *(legalist or anti-state in tenor)*	New Institutional Economics Compatible?	Institutionalist Political Economy Compatible?
Anti-predation (legalist)	Yes. State bureaucrats are inherently predatory and must be restrained.	No. What seems like predation could be necessary rent redistribution—an activity which only the state has capacity to undertake.
Anti-protectionism (legalist)	Yes. Favoring local firms gets the prices wrong and leads to static inefficiency.	No. Countries may be underdeveloped without protecting national champions.
Pro-foreign capital (anti-state)	No. There is never a justification to provide preference to any party on the basis of nationality (foreign or domestic).	No. If preference is to be provided to any class of firms, it should be nationals with a social stake in the country's development.
Pro-proceduralist (legalist)	Maybe. Predictable procedures help private parties plan their activities. But procedures may be solely about optics rather than getting the correct policies.	Maybe. Generally the same concerns as the mainstream. But there are also situations where elements of surprise are necessary to avoid private predation on the public.
Anti-political (anti-state)	Yes. States' monopoly of force gives them a privileged position which encourages predation.	No. The division between politics and market is socially constructed. There can be no de-politicizing: policy comes from political settlements.
Policy should stay static (anti-state)	No. States have a special role to play, reacting quickly to events for which private actors would be unable to resolve collective action problems. Moreover, veto players play an important role in checking executive power (which entails a certain inconsistency across government branches).	No. Shares the mainstream's concerns with states acting quickly when policy requires. In certain political situations, strong executive power may need to override veto players. In other political situations, policy experimentation at different levels of government means beneficial variance.
Treaties provide a valuable judicial forum outside of countries, even if they do not bring in foreign direct investment (anti-state)	Objectionable. Treaties are only valuable if they incentivize domestic institutional upgrading, or bring in more foreign direct investment than their combined negotiating and sovereignty costs.	Objectionable. Generally the same concerns as the mainstream, but also a skepticism about outside actors with no social stake in a country's success.

Source: Author's grounded theory analysis of arbitrator interviews and development literature.

Of course, my conclusions in this chapter only take us so far. I have not delved into specific investors' motivations for bringing cases, which could vary widely. Only an ethnography of general counsels and chief executive officers involved in multinational business could shed light on how individual capitalists perceive their interests. That would be a separate book, focusing as much on pre-case bargaining in the shadow of investment law as it would on the law itself, which is my concern here. Nonetheless, even without peering inside particular companies, arbitrators' inputs and outputs are infused with a pro-business, legalist ideology that values vested rights above democratic change.

Arbitrators' ideologies sit uneasily with development theory. Some of the ideologies could be described as legalist in orientation, and thus broadly acceptable to new institutional economists (but not to institutionalist political economists). Other ideologies, however, could be described as anti-state—a perspective that goes beyond what most development scholars of any stripe would be willing to advocate. The poor fit between arbitral ideology and development scholarship should trigger *prima facie* concerns about investment treaties in both schools. Arbitrators may not have set out to be development policy makers, but the preponderance of developing countries in the arbitrations (see Table 3.1) has thrust them into that role anyway. Table 3.2 plots arbitral ideologies from Figures 3.5, 3.6 and 3.7 against development schools of thought.

At the same time, none of what I have discussed here tells us whether arbitrators are any better or worse than other types of adjudicators. What if Justice Ruth Bader Ginsburg, a progressive idol, were asked to judge whether Venezuela's capital controls are excessive, or whether Argentine bureaucrats are so brusque that it amounts to unfair and inequitable treatment? We cannot know.[8] Yet I will argue in the final chapter that arbitrators may be simply reflecting the biases of lawyers as a profession. If that is true, we need to better understand the peculiarities of what sets arbitrators apart from tenured judges, in order to decide which flavor of lawyer we like better. To that we now turn.

References

Acemoglu, Daron, and James A. Robinson. 2012. "Industrial Policy Déjà Vu." *Why Nations Fail Blog* (blog). April 12.

Acemoglu, Daron, and Simon Johnson. 2005. "Unbundling Institutions." *Journal of Political Economy* 113 (5): 949–95.

Acemoglu, Daron, Simon Johnson, and James A. Robinson. 2001. "The Colonial Origins of Comparative Development: An Empirical Investigation." *American Economic Review* 91 (5): 1369–1401.

Amsden, Alice H. 1989. *Asia's Next Giant: South Korea and Late Industrialization.* Oxford: Oxford University Press.

---

8. Actually, we have some sense. In *BG Group PLC v. Republic of Argentina,* Ginsburg signed onto an opinion written by fellow liberal justice Stephen Breyer that rejected the country's request for review of an adverse ISDS award. The majority (over a sharp dissent from Chief Justice John Roberts), wrote that "international arbitrators are likely more familiar than are judges with the expectations of foreign investors".

AP. 2007. "Venezuela to Sell off US Refineries." *Taipei Times*, May 1.

Arndt, Christiane, and Charles Oman. 2006. *Uses and Abuses of Governance Indicators*. Development Centre Studies. Paris: OECD.

Bates, Robert H. 1981. *Markets and States in Tropical Africa: The Political Basis of Agricultural Policies*. Berkeley, CA: University of California Press.

Beavers, Olivia. 2017. "Sanders Will 'Absolutely' Work with Trump to Lower Prescription Drug Costs." *The Hill*, March 26.

Bekker, Pieter, and Akiko Ogawa. 2013. "The Impact of Bilateral Investment Treaty (BIT) Proliferation on Demand for Investment Insurance: Reassessing Political Risk Insurance After the 'BIT Bang.'" *ICSID Review* 28 (2): 314–50.

Berg, Albert Jan van den, Gary Born and Daniel Bethlehem. 2017. Eli Lilly and Company v. Government of Canada (Final Award). ICSID.

Bergsten, C. Fred. 1996. "Globalizing Free Trade." *Foreign Affairs* 75 (3): 105–20.

Bonnitcha, Jonathan. 2014. *Substantive Protection under Investment Treaties: A Legal and Economic Analysis*. Cambridge: Cambridge University Press.

Chang, Ha-Joon. 2002a. "Breaking the Mould: An Institutionalist Political Economy Alternative to the Neo-Liberal Theory of the Market and the State." *Cambridge Journal of Economics* 26 (5): 539–59.

———. 2002b. *Kicking Away the Ladder: Development Strategy in Historical Perspective*. London: Anthem Press.

———. 2010. "Hamlet without the Prince of Denmark: How Development Has Disappeared from Today's 'Development' Discourse." In *Towards New Developmentalism: Market as Means Rather than Master*, edited by Shahrukh Rafi Khan and Jens Christiansen, 47–56. London: Routledge.

Clarke, Simon. 1991. *The State Debate*. New York: Macmillan.

Crawford, James R., Stanimir Alexandrov and Pierre-Marie Dupuy. 2016. Blusun S.A. v. Italian Republic (Award). ICSID.

Crook, John R., Stanimir Alexandrov and Campbell McLachlan. 2017. Eiser Infrastructure Ltd and Energia Solar Luxembourg SARL v. Kingdom of Spain (Award). ICSID.

Dam, Kenneth W. 2007. *The Law-Growth Nexus: The Rule of Law and Economic Development*. Washington, DC: Brookings Institution Press.

Derains, Yves, Guido Santiago Tawil and Claus von Wobeser. 2016. Isolux Infrastructure Netherlands, B.V. v. Kingdom of Spain (Award). SCC.

Eberhardt, Pia, and Cecilia Olivet. 2012. "Profiting from Injustice: How Law Firms, Arbitrators and Financiers Are Fueling an Investment Arbitration Boom." Amsterdam: Transnational Institute.

Economist. 2014. "A Better Way to Arbitrate." October 11.

Evans, Peter B. 1995. *Embedded Autonomy: States and Industrial Transformation*. Princeton, NJ: Princeton University Press.

Fernandez-Armesto, Juan, Francisco Orrego Vicun, and Bruno Simma. 2016. Rusoro Mining Limited v. The Bolivarian Republic of Venezuela (Award). ICSID.

Fortier, L. Yves, David A. R. Williams and Michael Hwang. 2015. Bernhard von Pezold and others v. Zimbabwe (Award). ICSID.

Franck, Susan D. 2009. "Development and Outcomes of Investment Treaty Arbitration." *Harvard International Law Journal* 50 (2): 435–89.

Fukuyama, Francis. 2013. "What Is Governance?" *Governance* 26 (3): 347–68.

Gallagher, Kevin P. 2010. "Policy Space to Prevent and Mitigate Financial Crises in Trade and Investment Agreements." G-24 Discussion Paper 58. United Nations Conference on Trade and Development.

———. 2016. *The China Triangle: Latin America's China Boom and the Fate of the Washington Consensus*. Oxford: Oxford University Press.

Gerschenkron, Alexander. 1962. *Economic Backwardness in Historical Perspective: A Book of Essays.* Cambridge, MA: Belknap Press of Harvard University Press.

Ginsburg, Tom. 2005. "International Substitutes for Domestic Institutions: Bilateral Investment Treaties and Governance." *International Review of Law and Economics* 25 (1): 107–23.

Grewal, David, and Jedediah Purdy. 2015. "Law and Neoliberalism." *Law and Contemporary Problems* 77 (4): 1–23.

Grigera Naon, Horacio, Jose Carlos Fernandez Rozas and Carlos Bernal Verea. 2003. Tecnicas Medioambientales Tecmed, S.A. v. The United Mexican States (Award). ICSID.

GRUMA. 2017. "Gruma Provides Information About the Decision in the Arbitration of Its Spanish Subsidiaries Against Venezuela."

Heiskanen, Veijo Aulis, Doak Bishop and Bernardo M. Cremades. 2016. Windstream Energy LLC v. Government of Canada (Award). Permanent Court of Arbitration.

Hirschman, Albert O. 1958. *The Strategy of Economic Development.* New Haven: Yale University Press.

Hodgson, Matthew. 2014. "Costs in Investment Treaty Arbitration: The Case for Reform." *Transnational Dispute Management (TDM)* 11 (1).

Howell, Llewellyn. 2013. "ICRG Methodology." The PRS Group. 2013.

Hudson, Manley O. 1932. "The Central American Court of Justice." *American Journal of International Law* 26 (4): 759–86.

Jackson, John H. 2006. *Sovereignty, the WTO, and Changing Fundamentals of International Law.* Cambridge: Cambridge University Press.

Johnson, Chalmers A. 1982. *MITI and the Japanese Miracle: The Growth of Industrial Policy, 1925–1975.* Redwood City, CA: Stanford University Press.

Kagan, Robert A. 2003. *Adversarial Legalism: The American Way of Law.* Cambridge, MA: Harvard University Press.

Katzenstein, Suzanne. 2014. "In the Shadow of Crisis: The Creation of International Courts in the Twentieth Century." *Harvard International Law Journal* 55 (1): 151–209.

Keohane, Robert O., Andrew Moravcsik and Anne-Marie Slaughter. 2000. "Legalized Dispute Resolution: Interstate and Transnational." *International Organization* 54 (3): 457–88.

Khan, Mushtaq H., and Kwame Sundaram Jomo. 2000. *Rents, Rent-Seeking and Economic Development: Theory and Evidence in Asia.* Cambridge: Cambridge University Press.

Koskenniemi, Martti. 2005. *From Apology to Utopia: The Structure of International Legal Argument.* Cambridge: Cambridge University Press.

Krasner, Stephen D. 1982. "Regimes and the Limits of Realism: Regimes as Autonomous Variables." *International Organization* 36 (02): 497–510.

Krueger, Anne O. 1990. "Government Failures in Development." *Journal of Economic Perspectives* 4 (3): 9–23.

La Porta, Rafael, Florencio Lopez-de-Silanes, Cristian Pop-Eleches, and Andrei Shleifer. 2004. "Judicial Checks and Balances." *Journal of Political Economy* 112 (2): 445–70.

Lal, Deepak. 1997. *The Poverty of "Development Economics."* London: Institute of Economic Affairs.

Landes, William M., and Richard A. Posner. 1979. "Adjudication as a Private Good." *Journal of Legal Studies* 8 (2): 235–84.

Larsson, Olof, and Daniel Naurin. 2015. "Split Vision. Multi-Dimensionality in the International Legal Policy Space." Working Paper.

Lauterpacht, Elihu, Benjamin Civiletti, and Jose Luis Siqueiros. 2000. Metalclad Corporation v. The United Mexican States (Award). ICSID.

Lester, Simon. 2013. "Liberalization or Litigation? Time to Rethink the International Investment Regime." 730. Policy Analysis. Washington, DC: Cato Institute.

Lowe, Vaughan, Albert van den Berg and V. V. Veeder. 2012. Achmea BV (the Netherlands) v. Slovak Republic (I) (Award). PCA.

MacLean, Nancy. 2017. *Democracy in Chains: The Deep History of the Radical Right's Stealth Plan for America.* New York: Viking.

Maekelt, Tatiana de, Albert Jan van den Berg and Francisco Rezek. 2007. LG&E Energy Corp., LG&E Capital Corp., and LG&E International, Inc. v. Argentine Republic (Award). ICSID.

Maine, Henry Sumner. 1861. *Ancient Law: Its Connection with the Early History of Society, and Its Relation to Modern Ideas*. London: John Murray.

Marshall, Monty G., Ted Robert Gurr and Keith Jaggers. 2013. "Political Regime Characteristics and Transitions, 1800–2012 Dataset Users' Manual." POLITY IV Project.

McRae, Donald. 2015. William Ralph Clayton, William Richard Clayton, Douglas Clayton, Daniel Clayton and Bilcon of Delaware Inc. v. Government of Canada (McRae Dissent). PCA (UNCITRAL).

Mieville, China. 2006. *Between Equal Rights: A Marxist Theory of International Law*. Chicago: Haymarket Books.

Monbiot, George. 2013. "This Transatlantic Trade Deal Is a Full-Frontal Assault on Democracy | George Monbiot." *The Guardian*, November 4.

Mourre, Alexis, Guido Santiago Tawil and Claus von Wobeser. 2016. Charanne and Construction Investments v. Spain (Award). SCC.

North, Douglass C. 1990. *Institutions, Institutional Change and Economic Performance*. Cambridge: Cambridge University Press.

Olson, Mancur. 1993. "Dictatorship, Democracy, and Development." *American Political Science Review* 87 (3): 567–76.

Orrego Vicuna, Francisco, Thomas Buergenthal and Maurice Wolf. 2000. Emilio Agustín Maffezini v. The Kingdom of Spain (Award). ICSID.

Pelc, Krzysztof J. 2016. "Does the International Investment Regime Induce Frivolous Litigation?" Working Paper.

Polanyi, Karl. 1944. *The Great Transformation*, edited by Robert M MacIver. New York: Farrar & Rinehart.

Porterfield, Matthew C. 2004. "International Expropriation Rules and Federalism." *Stanford Environmental Law Journal* 23: 3–90.

Posner, Eric A., and John C. Yoo. 2005. "Judicial Independence in International Tribunals." *California Law Review* 93 (1): 1–74.

Posner, Richard A. 1998. *Economic Analysis of Law*. Fifth edition. New York: Aspen Publishers.

———. 2010. *Economic Analysis of Law*. Eighth edition. New York: Aspen Publishers.

Rogers, Brishen. 2016. "Three Concepts of Workplace Freedom of Association." *Berkeley J. Emp. & Lab. L.* 37: 177.

Rowley, J. William, Gabrielle Kaufmann-Kohler and Carlos Bernal Verea. 2007. Compania de Aguas del Aconquija S.A. and Vivendi Universal S.A. v. Argentine Republic (Vivendi II) (Award). ICSID.

Rueschemeyer, Dietrich, and Peter B. Evans. 1985. "The State and Economic Transformation." In *Bringing the State Back In*, edited by Peter B. Evans, Dietrich Rueschemeyer and Theda Skocpol. Cambridge: Cambridge University Press.

Salans, Carl, Albert Jan van den Berg and V. V. Veeder. 2005. Plama Consortium Limited v. Republic of Bulgaria (Decision on Jurisdiction). ICSID.

Schill, Stephan W. 2017. "Maffezini v. Plama: Reflections on the Jurisprudential Schism in the Application of Most-Favored-Nation Clauses to Matters of Dispute Settlement." Research Paper 2017–11. Amsterdam Center for International Law. Amsterdam: University of Amsterdam.

Schwebel, Stephen M. 2014. "In Defense of Bilateral Investment Treaties." *Columbia FDI Perspectives* 135: (November).

Simma, Bruno, Bryan Schwartz, and Donald McRae. 2015. William Ralph Clayton, William Richard Clayton, Douglas Clayton, Daniel Clayton and Bilcon of Delaware Inc. v. Government of Canada (Award on Jurisdiction and Liability). PCA (UNCITRAL).

Smith, Mick. 2012. "Mechanics of Third-Party Funding Agreements: A Funder's Perspective." In *Third-Party Funding in International Arbitration*, edited by Victoria Shannon and Lisa B. Nieuwveld, 19–38. Alphen aan den Rijn, Netherlands: Kluwer Law International.

Songer, Donald R., Susan J. Johnson, C. L. Ostberg and Matthew E. Wetstein. 2012. *Law, Ideology, and Collegiality: Judicial Behaviour in the Supreme Court of Canada*. Montreal and Ithaca, NY: McGill Queens University Press.

Tawil, Guido Santiago. 2015. Charanne and Construction Investments v. Spain (Dissent). SCC.

———. 2016. Isolux Infrastructure Netherlands, B.V. v. Kingdom of Spain (Dissent). SCC.

Tucker, Todd. 2013. "Investment Agreements versus the Rule of Law?" Discussion Paper 9. IPFSD-Forum. Geneva: UN Conference on Trade and Development.

USTR (US Trade Representative). 2014. "The Facts on Investor–State Dispute Settlement: Safeguarding the Public Interest and Protecting Investors." USTR.Gov. March.

Veeder, V. V., Gabrielle Kaufmann-Kohler and Brigitte Stern. 2015. Electrabel S.A. v. Hungary. Washington, DC: ICSID.

Wade, Robert. 1990. *Governing the Market: Economic Theory and the Role of Government in East Asian Industrialization*. Princeton, NJ: Princeton University Press.

———. 2010. "The Market as Means Rather than Master: The Crisis of Development and the Future Role of the State." In *Towards New Developmentalism: Market as Means Rather than Master*, edited by Shahrukh Rafi Khan and Jens Christiansen, 21–46. London: Routledge.

Weber, Max. 1978. *Economy and Society: An Outline of Interpretive Sociology*. Berkeley, CA: University of California Press.

Williamson, Oliver E. 1975. *Markets and Hierarchies: Analysis and Antitrust Implications, A Study in the Economics of Internal Organization*. New York: Free Press.

Woo-Cumings, Meredith. 2006. "The Rule of Law, Legal Traditions, and Economic Growth in East Asia." 2006/53. Research Paper, UNU-WIDER, United Nations University (UNU)..

Zywicki, Todd J., and Anthony B. Sanders. 2008. "Posner, Hayek & the Economic Analysis of Law." *Iowa Law Review* 93 (2): 559–603.

Chapter Four

WHY ARBITRATORS SUPPLY
INVESTMENT LAW

Imagine a purely private market in judicial services. People would offer their services as judges, and disputants would select the judge whom they mutually found most acceptable. The most popular judges would charge the highest fees, and competition among judges would yield the optimum amount and quality of judicial services at minimum social cost [. . . O]ne could even] give judges property rights in precedents—e.g., a royalty every time one of their decisions was cited.

— William Landes and Richard Posner (Adjudication as a Private Good, 1979)

Serving as an arbitrator is a relatively poor way to get rich. Working as counsel to an investor can net a private lawyer more than $1,000 per hour. In contrast, arbitrators (at least at the World Bank) earn $3,000 per day. What an arbitrator gets in a day of hearings, counsel earns by lunch. Moreover, serving as counsel can fill up significant chunks of one's professional calendar for years, while an arbitrator who charges for more than a few weeks of work would seem overly costly, raise eyebrows, and risk future appointments.

What motivates arbitrators to supply investment law? I argue that a big part of the answer lies in inter-arbitrator relationships and collegial norms, even if money explains part of the motivation. This chapter represents the first scholarly attempt to formally model arbitration tribunals. It is derived from the first-hand stories of the only people who have seen inside the black box of deliberation and interpretation: the arbitrators themselves. Applying grounded theory methods (see Appendix), I show how arbitrators' personal strategies, interests and affinities make for a perpetual fount of uneven law creation. The result is an investment arbitration system that relies heavily on the ingenuity, self-regulation and self-policing of a sprawling cohort of untenured adjudicators. The portrait in the following pages shows that arbitrators are human, like the rest of us and like other lawyers. They drink, they bicker and they gang up on one another. But they also resolve tricky issues of international political economy without armies of government or corporate bureaucrats helping them. Can we learn from their model?

How Arbitrators Are Appointed

Most investment tribunals are composed of three arbitrators.[1] Conventionally, the complainant investor will first appoint an arbitrator, a move the respondent state will then follow with an appointment of its own. Depending on the case, a chairman arbitrator will

---

1. Although it is a rarely used option, some treaties also allow sole arbitrators to decide cases. In the universe of finalized cases, there were only a handful that were decided by sole arbitrators.

be appointed either by the two parties, the two other arbitrators (referred to as "wingmen" in ISDS parlance), or an arbitral center such as the World Bank's International Centre for Settlement of Investment Disputes (ICSID). The male-gendered monikers, chairman and wingmen, are emblematic of the profession, as nearly 95 percent of arbitrators that have served finalized arbitrations are men.

Arbitrators face few constraints on their behavior. There are no stringent requirements for who can serve on a tribunal, nor for how to deliberate or interpret the law. While ICSID maintains a panel of arbitrators, parties can nominate to tribunals individuals who are not on that panel. The center rules only instruct tribunals to decide questions by (at least) majority vote, write and sign their awards and deal with all the questions submitted to them. Dissenting and separate opinions are allowed (ICSID Convention Article 48). The chairman is instructed to conduct hearings and preside over deliberations, which are secret and not open to non-tribunal members—unless all tribunal members agree (ICSID Rules 14–16). Under non-ICSID rules, each tribunal is allowed to conduct "the arbitration in such manner as it considers appropriate," subject to general requirements such as the obligation to avoid "unnecessary" delays (New York Convention Article 17). Awards and decisions are by majority vote, except the chairman "may decide alone" on purely procedural matters when there is no majority (Article 33). Other than these minimal rules, interpretation of the law applying to the merits (and arbitral deliberation more generally) is not regulated in any constraining fashion.

Several features of arbitration distinguish it from national judging. The first is place. A national judge will typically do his work close to home. In investment arbitration, it is more likely that arbitrators will be working far away from home. This means flying and staying in hotels. Instead of going home to his family for a home-cooked meal, an arbitrator needs to forage for meals in the streets and suites of wherever the hearings are taking place. This creates at least the possibility of sharing meals with fellow arbitrators, who are often staying at the same hotel. In Washington, DC, for example, the World Bank's ICSID reserves rooms for arbitrators at the Fairmont Hotel in the "Foggy Bottom" neighborhood of the city. On the ninth floor, arbitrators can make use of the Fairmont Gold executive entertainment suite, where there is an open bar in the evening, complete with lamb kabobs and elegant hors d'oeuvres. (This location was the site of much of my fieldwork.)

Seeing colleagues at breakfast in the morning through nightcaps in the hotel at night increases the intensity of the collegial interaction, at least relative to national judging. And because the parties, counsel and arbitrators are flying in from all across the world, the hearings are compressed into a few days or weeks. In order to stay on schedule, arbitrators may be asked to work through the weekend, or start hearings early in the morning and keep them going until late at night. These timelines make it difficult to schedule other appointments or make social plans. This also increases the intensity of the collegial interaction, as well as the potential for exhaustion.

Arbitrator Types

Arbitrators serve in teams of three. Not consistent trios: the precise line-up is always changing depending on who appoints them for each case at hand. But even with shifting personnel, there are distinct types of colleagues and collegial relations that shape the arbitrators' experience in a case. Both chairmen and wingmen vary by their relationship to the litigating parties, which I call "tilt," and to each other, which I refer to as "affinity." I explore these variations in the sections to come.

Chairman Types

The chairman in each case influences the deliberations from the beginning. The three appointees often already know one another, by reputation if not by prior shared tribunal and other experience. When there is mutual admiration and similar beliefs among the three, it is easier to exchange views informally before, during and after the hearings. The exchanges resemble discussions among friends, with everything from substantive to gossipy comments about counsel being suitable topics of conversation. In contrast, if one or more arbitrators are an unknown quantity, a group norm for deliberation quickly develops. But in either case, the tone is often set by the chairman, who displays one of several different affinity, or leadership, types.

A first type is social.[2] These chairmen work to create camaraderie through shared meals, coffee and drinks at the beginning and end of hearings. At meals, the chairman can choose whether to discuss scheduling matters, the substance of the case or simply personal interests. One interviewee emphasized the role of socializing in getting to agreement:

> I always look for opportunities early in the evolution of the case for a nice dinner with a few glasses of wine between members of the tribunal. As I said earlier, after all these years, you know one another. But some you know better than others. So, I create social occasions, and make sure that after the conclusion of the hearing, and again all too often this does not happen, that you set some time aside. If the hearing finishes at five, you should not make plans to be to be in a 6:30 flight going back home [. . .] [In one case] My colleagues came to the dinner table, with some views. And at the end of the dinner, two hours later, I could see that we had a consensus.

Others described tools as varied as inviting fellow arbitrators out for cocktails—"after the third tequila [. . .] everyone agreed"—said one frequent chairman interviewee—or out to their country homes where "the mobile phones do not work" to share Burgundy wine in order to get to consensus, said another.

Socialites are highly dissent-averse. "I try to find ways where we can agree, because I think if you have a unanimous decision, it gives greater legitimacy in the eyes of the parties than if it is divided," said one arbitrator who has served as a chairman. "I work to try to bring about a meeting of the minds." The legitimacy comes through the cultivation

---

2. These labels are of my own making, although they are derived from words and descriptions used by my interviewees. In developing these labels, I do not mean to tarnish or even describe any particular individual. Rather, as noted above, the labels correspond to sociological ideal types.

of the impression that "these decisions couldn't go any other way," he explained. Not going any other way is impossible if dissents surface, showing the world that a number of different decisions would have been possible. As another interviewee said:

> As chair [...] you search for a consensus. That is one of the, if not the, central objective of your remit, to have unanimity [...] I will go the extra mile. Not to the point of being intellectually dishonest. But I will go the extra mile, or the extra kilometre, in order to try and convince the person, or convince myself. [laughter] I am not happy when there is a dissent. I feel that at the end of the day, you know, I flagellate myself, because I think as chairman, I must've done something wrong.

There are a few approaches at the disposal of the dissent-averse socialite. He can lobby the wingmen one by one and give them space to say to him what they may not wish to say in each other's presence. Or he can reduce the strength of an award until both wingmen sign on, with the risk that the end product will be unclear or "anodyne."

A second chairman type is managerial. A managerial chairman does not socialize or discuss his views of the case until the very end. He might take his meals alone, ordering room service while he works on his writing for other cases. He runs hearings and deliberations as if they were board meetings, following a strict agenda. He avoids playing favorites between the wingmen: if he looks left to ask a state appointee their point of view, then he immediately turns right to ask the investor appointee the same question. This equanimity extends even to email correspondence. If he begins one email "Hello Tim and Joe," he alternates the name order on the next email to "Hello Joe and Tim." He makes detailed chronologies of all litigation-triggering events and distributes them to the wingmen in advance of the first hearings. He makes sure to read all the submissions ahead of time, or at least a summary from his assistant. And he often calls meetings to review what is known and unknown after each day's hearings.

The managerial-type chairman's goal is to establish the facts necessary to decide the case and move cases along, not to be universally beloved. Yet he needs at least one arbitrator to go along with him, and unlike the social chair, he values clarity—even at the expense of completeness.

Deft case management requires skillful colleague management, through tactics such as smoking out, co-optation, judicial economy and sequencing. A smoke-out is when the chairman asks the wingmen to declare their points of view and stage a debate in front of him or in writing. This can help him make up his own mind on the merits, or simply see which of the two wingmen correspond most to his already-formed views. But as frequent arbitrator Albert Jan van den Berg notes, this is a risky strategy because a chairman who asks wingmen to articulate their views in writing before the chairman announces his point of view encourages dissent, as "the arbitrator whose note is not chosen feels left out" (van den Berg 2010, 830).

Co-optation occurs at the end of the case when a chairman includes footnotes in the award, noting where there were minor disagreements with the tribunal majority, so as to salvage the formal unanimity of the award. In contrast, judicial economy is the tactical refusal to decide all points before the tribunal. If, for example, a tribunal agrees that a state violated rules on fair and equitable treatment but not expropriation, then the chairman can steer the award to focus on the lowest common denominator. As one interviewee mused: "Why get into [things] you do not have to?"

Then there is sequencing, which is a tactic that frontloads points of agreement. Say a chairman suspects that a state appointee will balk at a large award of damages but might agree on the merits of the case. Then the chairman can circulate the merits section (the legal assessment of state behavior) before the quantum section (the monetary damages portion), or simply leave a blank space where the dollar damages will go. After obtaining his colleagues' agreement, he can introduce the number at the very end. This limits the room for the state appointee to walk back his support of the award without some loss of face.

The socialite-type and the manager-type chairmen may differ on how they use law to reach consensus, but both benefit from a tool unavailable to other types of adjudicators— damages. In the US legal system, judges decide the law, but juries award damages. At the World Trade Organization, there is likewise a separation between legal interpretation and allocation of states' retaliation rights. But in investor–state dispute settlement, tribunals get to decide both the law and the damages, often in the same award. This empowers a chairman to horse-trade in the service of consensus, getting a state appointee to agree on the merits that a state violated a treaty, in exchange for a reduction in the amount owed. As one arbitrator explained it:

> With respect to these key issues, I mean, "is this an investment, is this expropriation or not?" There is in my view and experience very little room for let's say horse-trading. I mean, when it comes to amounts, if you decide "this is indeed an expropriation, we now need to fix the compensation," of course there is a lot more leeway to give and take as far as the amounts are concerned.

For all chairmen, a major benefit of all of the above inter-arbitrator interactions is to feel out the wingmen. Which way are they leaning? Are they partial to the party that appointed them?

This consensus-building process helps maximize reappointments. As one interviewee said, reputation is "all you have" as an arbitrator in a system without tenure. Although my interviewees came into treaty arbitration by diverse means, those who stay in arbitration do so because law firms, arbitral centers and (crucially) their peers recommend them. One interviewee captured how these informal recommendation networks build on themselves:

> I get asked two or three times a week now about people who might serve as arbitrators. Either in cases that I'm involved with, or more often, someone will call me up and say, "We are looking for an arbitrator to chair this tribunal. Do you know Lord Mucketeymuck?" Or whatever his name is. Or Professor So-and-So. And if I think that Lord Mucketeymuck or Professor So-and-So is a good guy, I will say: "Excellent. Thoughtful, hard-working." If I do not, I will say something like, "You could do better, or, just between us, he does not listen."

According to another arbitrator:

> If the chair perceives that a wingman who he highly respects and might orchestrate his appointment in other cases, is getting pissed off, is getting upset or irritated or isolated [. . .] that is a leverage point. You do not want to have someone who is very, very key in this field to walk away disenchanted, because you may depend on them professionally later [. . .] You do not want them to badmouth you. You do not want to be un-appointable in the future, especially if you rely upon it as your only job.

Those who can worry the least about reappointment are those who get outside remuneration, typically what is referred to as wearing a "double hat" as counsel to parties in other arbitrations, or working as a commercial arbitrator, where appointees are paid three and four times the going rates for treaty-based arbitration. Otherwise, explains one interviewee, for arbitration to become your "bread and butter" and to make a "nice living" on it, you need the support of others in the arbitration community. Even those arbitrators who do not need the money may value the fame and prestige that come with repeat appointments.

This takes us to a third style of chairman: dictatorial. Once he has made up his mind on the merits of a case, the dictator will announce his position or circulate a finalized draft award without having engaged in any meaningful deliberation. This type of chairman will make the assumption that, whichever party he favors, there will be at least one wingman vote to go along with his own. As one interviewee said about a dictator-led arbitration:

> Some arbitrators feel they have been dissed, disrespected by the majority. It started I think with [one particular case that the interviewee requested remain confidential]. The [state appointee], who was new to arbitration, it was his first case, was incensed about the majority [. . .] I think he felt that [the chairman] had sort of undervalued him, compared to [the investor appointee . . .] Apparently, [the chairman] would always, on any issue, turn to [the investor appointee] first, and then second to the [state appointee]. Something small like that, the body language, develops, and of course the [state appointee] thought that was not only a disrespect to him, but also an insult to his country. Obviously, his countrymen were seeing what was happening to him, and he took it personally [. . .] yet there is an awful lot of shortcuts now, because of time pressure, on producing awards. Some chairmen say, "This is it, take it or leave it."

Dictator-type chairmen can also be more subtle. As one interviewee said, the wingmen "know that you [the chairman] will decide. If they don't agree, you will be the one deciding [. . .] you need only two, so you don't need to [explicitly] push your weight around. They know that." Another said: "I also have no problem with just doing my own opinion and see who is joining me [. . .] You write your award and you know that whatever the outcome is, one of the arbitrators will go along." By limiting the amount of compromise, dictators can be more coherent, laying out a consistent worldview on appropriate state behavior.

The social, managerial and dictatorial styles are all potentially effective in moving tribunal cases across the finish line. Other styles, which are characteristic of chairmen whom I collectively deem to be "weak," are not effective. Chairmen who are seen to be ineffectual by other arbitrators move slowly and let the parties or wingmen guide the proceedings. Some arbitrators also see weakness when a chairman delegates award-writing to wingmen. In contrast, chairmen who are seen as effective make procedural decisions themselves and relatively quickly. As one interviewee said, they are attentive to the fact that states (as perennial respondents) will try to drag out the procedure, and they counter this practice.

Chairmen from academic backgrounds also are prone to weakness, according to some interviewees. Said one: "You get some professorial types who are kind of new to the game and they do not know how to run a hearing. They are useless. They let things go on and on and on, they waste time, they drive me batty, I try not to let it show, but I'm sure it does." Another arbitrator, when I asked this question—"how can a chairmanship go wrong?"—responded:

> If it is weak [. . .] I always refer to the Scandinavian disease or the Nordic disease, which is, [in a mocking tone] "well perhaps the parties can get together." It drives me crazy. I do not think that's the way Alfred Nobel thought either. Someone who does not have a firm grip, or who is uncertain, or seems to be kind of wishy washy, who lets counsel run over him. That is awful. That is the only way one can really go wrong.

The aforementioned affinity types—socialite, manager, dictator and weak—are separate from a chairman's tilt toward states and investors. This tilt is rarely obvious: most savvy chairmen moderate their rhetoric or risk disqualification or annulment. (As I discuss in the next chapter, disqualifications are decided by majority vote of the two co-arbitrators, or by an outside authority.) Nonetheless, it is useful for the logic of the ideal types to conceive of chairs as pro- or anti-state, as we will see below.

Wingman Types

There were three types of wingmen identified by my interviewees: followers, neutrals, and partisans. I also extrapolate a fourth: the turncoat.

A follower wingman is "somebody who does not read the material, is unintelligent, lazy," explains one interviewee. He adds that the consequence is that "if you are a completely passive arbitrator, then you can disregard them [because] they do not help." Neutral wingmen, for their part, do not systematically favor states or investors. As one self-described neutral arbitrator said, "When I am a party-appointed arbitrator, I am simply neutral. But I am not always sure that the parties like that! [Laughter] If they interview me before, I say, 'I will make sure your arguments are heard, but I will not defend them unless I think they are good arguments of course.' But then that has nothing to do with who puts them forward or who appointed me."

A neutral-inclined wingman often hides his predilection in pre-interviews. A number of arbitrators describe pre-interviews (like the one mentioned above) as a common tactic used by parties, who ply potential appointees with facts from the case in the hope of seeing what their gut reaction would be. A neutral wingman may shut down these pre-interviews out of hand, or instead commit only to ensuring that the party's perspectives get a full and fair hearing. Consequently, a neutral wingman can play a pseudo managerial role in the proceedings, leveraging accounting skills, native English speaking or fast writing to get the chairman to delegate work to him. At the extreme of this type of delegation, a wingman can become the *faux* chairman.

The turncoat is another logical possibility of a type. This type, whether a state's or an investor's appointee, can be not only open to voting for the investor or the state, but also determined to do so. Why would a turncoat ever get an appointment? One possibility is that states, especially those with little prior experience as a respondent, pick a famous arbitrator, thinking such a man will have more influence with the other members of the tribunal. Unfortunately for the state, famous arbitrators (for reasons discussed in the rest of this chapter) are likely to be biased against states. By the time the state realizes its mistake, it is too late.

The final type of arbitrator (partisan wingmen) requires more explanation, as it's a type of adjudicator only made possible by the unique attributes of arbitration relative to traditional judging. While judges can be Democratic or Republican, more or less pro-property, more or less against civil liberties, arbitrators have the added distinction that they owe their appointment to one of the parties litigating before them. In this, they can be categorized along the spatial axis models often used by political scientists that we discussed in chapter 3: Are they closer to the point of view of the investor or state appointer?

The simplest form of partisanship is relentlessly to take the side of your perceived patron on everything from procedural matters to merits to the final damages awards (quantum). As a number of interviewees explained, a partisan will do this inside the hearings in front of the parties, and in deliberations in private. The partisan advocates in emails, in edits to draft opinions and in dissenting opinions, where they might even copy word for word from their appointer's written submissions. For this type of partisan, the only thing that matters is that your appointer knew that you took his side. If the ceaseless advocacy leaves the man without allies or influence on the tribunal, so be it.

But this type of partisanship is not particularly helpful to your appointer's bottom line, according to interviewees. Chairmen, they say, discount everything they say, and may tilt to the other side. One partisan arbitrator was described by another as "catastrophically hopeless" and "universally thought to be a complete idiot as he just goes to absolute extremes." The most the appointer will get in this case is a dissent, said another, and "dissents are not good. It does not get you anything for the party that appointed you." Ceaseless partisans lose influence early. One interviewee told of a party that

appointed a guy who was really, really partisan [. . .] Apparently, the party that appointed the partisan arbitrator had a weak case on jurisdiction [whether the investor had standing and cause to bring the case], a weak case on breach of contract [also known as merits or liability phase], but a very good case on quantum [the amount of damages owed]. What I'm told by one of the persons who was on this tribunal, the other side's arbitrator, is that that guy made himself so obnoxious at the beginning of the arbitration in connection with the arguments on jurisdiction and liability, that when they got to the end on quantum, where he might have said something to help the party that appointed him, no one was listening to him anymore. So, I do not think that partisanship is in [a party's] best interests.

But there are several models for a more effective partisan arbitrator. The first is the cunning partisan, who withholds his point of view until the last possible moment. One arbitrator, when asked this question—"At what stage in the process do you normally figure out that there is going to be a dissent?"—responded:

> That depends on how intelligent the arbitrator is. Very intelligent party-appointed arbitrators, they never disagree with any of your intermediary decisions because they know that that is not the beef. And very intelligent people will only, very good party-appointed arbitrators, will only dissent, if at all, at the very end.

When asked, What are the consequences to showing one's cards earlier? the arbitrator replied: "That you lose any credibility. If I know that you will dissent, what interest do I have to get closer to your arguments?"

In order to throw their colleagues off the scent, effective partisans counter-signal, sending intentionally disorienting messages. As one arbitrator put it:

> You get this very interesting dynamic where people are very keen, wingmen are very keen, to show their neutrality cards early. That is, you play a card early against the party who has appointed you in order to gain credibility with the chair that you are not going to be predisposed to that party. So early on [. . .] you get an arbitrator who was appointed by one party, who will violently disagree with an unimportant point being made by their appointing party [. . .] you go into the deliberation room, you say 'I am outraged that the investor has suggested a two-day extension. Outraged!' [. . .] on the basis that you are signaling that 'I am not for the investor.' When it comes to something important, they are for the investor!

A second type of effective partisan is the leveraged one. This type of arbitrator accepts a large number of tribunal appointments by investors—more than he could prepare for on his own. This type of wingman, says one arbitrator, has "a back-office full of people working for him full time, incredibly impressive, but unnamed people, and they do all the work for him and research. And what happens is that [such a wingman] will arrive at a deliberation with memos that have been done by his back-office." Importantly, the leveraged wingman saves the chairman from having to do this work and is able to out-maneuver the other wingman by being more prepared than they are. Even if a chairman is not predisposed to follow the leveraged wingman's line, the constant stream of memos subtly shapes the course of the arbitration.

A final type is the jawboning partisan. As one interviewee told me, some state arbitrators are "bleeding hearts for states," and will take their position on every matter. Arbitrators say one arbitrator in particular "has driven people absolutely berserk" and will "talk talk talk."[3] As one interviewee told me about another: "[A certain state appointee], if you

---

3. Out of deference to privacy, when interviewees discussed specific arbitrators, I redacted the names of the latter unless the fact formed part of the public record.

are an investor? Wuuuh. This is not good." Asked whether this particular jawboning wingman had much of an influence over the award, the interviewee replied:

> Do you think? He is so tiresome that I think some people just to stop the pain will give in. He is [long pause] extremely [long pause] tiring. And some people are just that way. He will never ever listen, and he just kicks and screams, and is dogmatic. It is not fun at all [. . .] he thinks it is wrong to change your mind. "You are appointed, and you have your convictions, and you stick to your convictions." So why are we deliberating? That is not good.

While partisanship goes against the supposed need for neutrality in arbitration, my interviewees admitted that it is a rational approach to take because the partisan wingman is guaranteed a steady stream of appointments (so long as you are at least somewhat effective at influencing your peers).

One of the most important choices a neutral or a partisan wingman must make is whether to issue a dissenting opinion. There are highly dissent-averse wingmen, who for collegial reasons have a firm rule against dissenting, even when they disagree with the award. As one interviewee said,

> If you sign one award where Argentina is said to be [exempt from needing to comply with a treaty because of] *force majeure* for two months, and then you sign another one that says *force majeure* for two days, people are going to say, you know, "This guy has made a deal, because he cannot be inconsistent." For Argentina, it is really clear, because it is exactly the same facts. And you get [a certain arbitrator] signing for instance different opinions because he believes in unanimity. But if you do not do the dissent, people will assume you bargained for your agreement. For your consent to the award, you got something in exchange.

By creating a long paper trail of dissents, a neutral or partisan wingman documents what he in particular (rather than the tribunal as a whole) believes. On the one hand, this advertises that the wingman has not been bought off in a given case because his views have a documented and ethically unimpeachable consistency. On the other, dissents enable wingmen to advertise to law firms and potential appointers that if selected to the tribunal they will be useful to the appointer.

There are still other benefits to dissent. Dissenters can influence the development of case law. Some dissents become required reading at law schools and can clarify issues and contribute to the proper development of the law, according to interviewees. Moreover, dissents can lead to changes in the awards themselves, assuming that a chairman is not dictatorial or overly eager to wrap up the deliberations. As one chairman explained: There is this tension between the dissenter who says, 'Are you two interested in what I am going to write?' We say, 'Sure we are interested. But there is a limit. We want to get out'

I asked a few dissenters if there was any particular stigma to the practice. While some arbitrators expressed concern about writing dissents in a courteous tone, most did not hesitate to issue them. One said, "Nobody said anything to me, and I still have more work than I can do." But a potential drawback to being seen as a frequent dissenter or partisan is that chairmen know (or think they know) exactly how you will vote before you walk in the door. If they agree with your position, then such situational awareness is no problem for the partisan wingman (and in fact, this may reduce the influence of the other wingman, who is no longer needed for a majority). But if the chairman does not agree with the wing's presumptive position, then he discounts what the partisan wingman says and may tilt toward the other side. When serving on a tribunal with colleagues such as these, one interviewee said "the deliberation then is not a normal deliberation, because it is not three people with open minds who are just dealing with the instant case. It is a battle of competing portfolios."

Types in Interaction

Arbitrators vary by their position on the tribunal (whether they are chairmen or wingmen), their affinity to colleagues, and their tilt toward the litigating parties. Figure 4.1 displays how these variations interact. (If you do not recall my disclaimer, I will repeat it: These graphics are knotty and gnarly on purpose.) The vertical axis shows wingman tilt, from a pro-investor bottom to a pro-state top. Partisan arbitrators who lean toward the interests of multinational companies would fit in the bottom, as would state-appointed turncoats who covertly harbor the same views.

The horizontal axis models different affinities and chairman leadership styles within tribunals. Weak chairs who are dominated by their colleagues register all the way to the left, while dictatorial chairs who try to lord over their tribunals clock all the way to the right. At intermediate levels, the social-type chairman shares content development with the wingmen to get to unanimity, while the managerial chairman makes only the smallest compromises necessary for a majority award. The rectangles show the region of greatest influence for the wingmen. The possibility of outright partisanship is something that stronger chairmen guard against—unless they share in the partisanship, in which case one or the other (and perhaps both) of the wingmen simply duplicates the chairman's preferences rather than drives the result. Partisan wingmen are most able to influence the outcome if there is a weak chairman, or a consensus-driven social chairman. Neutral wingmen are less agenda-driven, but they will scrutinize the facts of the case and attempt to convey these to the chairman if he has not appreciated them. Their influence is thus greatest on the line between social and managerial chairmen. Follower-type wingmen lack influence, so are outside the shaded zone.

The long arrow running from the far right to the far left in Figure 4.1 indicates one possibility not yet discussed: that the wingmen will gang up against the chair. The dictatorial chairs' assumption that there will be an automatic majority of two seems to presume the existence of partisanship. But wingmen do not always vote for their appointers. As an example, my interviewees referred to the *Tokios Tokelēs v. Ukraine* case under the Ukraine–Lithuania treaty, where the distinguished French law professor Prosper Weil made the argument that Ukrainian citizens should not be able to use a Lithuanian investment vehicle to obtain standing as "foreign investors" against Ukraine, their home state. Surprisingly, both wingmen disagreed, including Piero Bernardini, who had been appointed by Ukraine. As one interviewee put it, this led to a "famous chairman's dissent [against the two wings in the majority], and as a result of which [Weil] has never been re-appointed in a case again. And you can look at that and say, 'Okay Prosper, you weren't

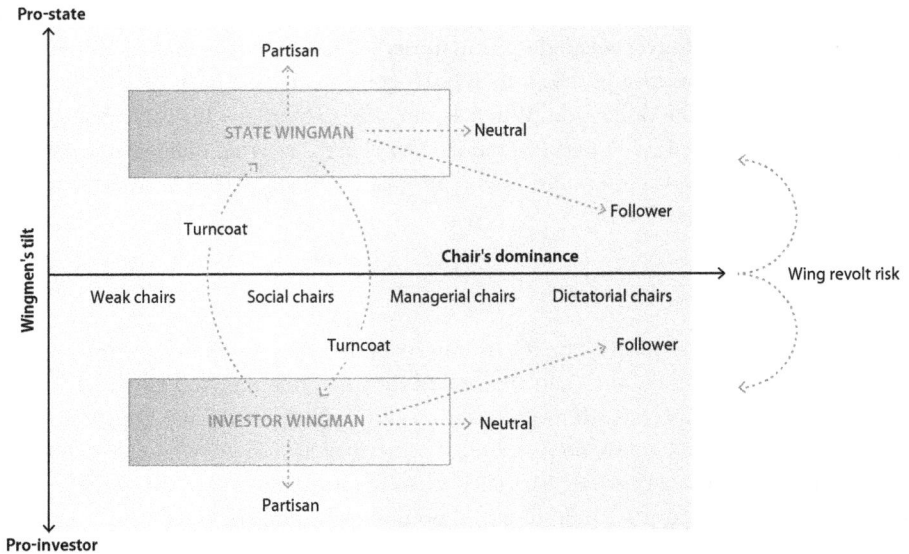

Figure 4.1 How do arbitrator types interact with one another?
Source: Author's grounded theory analysis of interviews and documentary materials.

thinking.' Apart from the fact that I think he was wrong!" In more recent cases, the fact that Weil was in the minority was cited as a reason to ignore his opinion (Derains et al. 2016, 181).

Tribunal Types and Implications for States

What types of chairman and wingmen are best for states? To explore this question in my ideal type framework, I assume that a state's interest once sued is to win (not lose), and to have an arbitral award that qualitatively leaves them more (rather than less) policy space.

Let us first consider the type of chairman a state would prefer. Obviously, a state would prefer a state-tilting chairman to an investor-tilting one. But recall that dictator-type chairmen are marked by low affinity, meaning they make no compromises—even at the risk of being left in the minority. Manager-type chairman, in contrast, will compromise the least necessary to remain in a majority of two. Socialite chairmen go farther and will compromise to the point necessary to secure a unanimous award. Weak chairmen are unable or unwilling to influence the tribunal. Among state-tilting chairmen, then, states would prefer a dictator to a manager who will make compromises on the facts, a manager to a socialite who will make compromises on the law, and a socialite to a weak chair who is of no consequence. Among investor-tilting chairmen, the state would generally prefer the reverse order.

Turning to the wingmen, a state would prefer to have its wingman as a guaranteed vote. If it cannot secure a partisan one, then the state would like to be able to know with certainty that the investor's appointee is a turncoat. If the state cannot benefit from a partisan or turncoat, then it would like to have at least a gettable appointee—a neutral wingman. Next, a state would settle for a follower appointee who will just follow the chairman's lead (whose decision-making is exogenous at this point in our story). The worst of all state appointments is a state-side turncoat. Thus, a state's preference for the investor's appointee goes in the order turncoat, neutral, follower then partisan.

With four chairmen and four wingman types, there are 64 possible tribunal combinations. If we further assume that chairmen can have a tilt toward states or investors, then the number of tribunal combinations doubles, to 128. Table 4.1 graphically displays the 64 tribunal combinations with a state-tilting chair, while Table 4.2 does the same for investor-favoring ones.

A few comments are in order to better understand the tables from both a quantitative and qualitative point of view. First, as a quantitative matter, each combination of wingmen presents a range of possible "votes" that a state could pick up from the tribunal members, with lower and upper bounds ranging from 0 to 3. For instance, row 1 on Table 4.1 represents a tribunal with a state-tilting chairman, a partisan state appointee, and a turncoat investor appointee. This combination would be predicted to deliver a solid three votes for the state at both the lower and upper bounds. Thus, when it came time for this particular trio to decide whether the state was "thumbs down, guilty" or "thumbs up, not guilty," all digits in the room would point toward the floor. For these men who value the prerogatives of governing, they would not wish to saddle the government with the embarrassment of a merits loss or the expense of a damages order.

In contrast, a state-tilting chairman paired with a follower state appointee and a neutral investor appointee (shown seven rows down in Table 4.1) would deliver a lower bound of two votes, and an upper bound of three. Why is this? Recall that a follower will simply follow the lead of the chair. Here, because the chair favors the state, so too will this particular state-appointed wingman. So, without even thinking about the investor's man, the state is guaranteed at least a majority award. Of course, the ultimate prize is that the neutral investor appointee also happens to see matters the same as the chair and is willing to sign on to a unanimous award. A three-out-of-three vote, while not strictly necessary, will certainly better inoculate a state from investors determined to relitigate the case after losing (whether formally or in the public sphere).

But as we learned in earlier chapters, quantitative votes are not the only thing that matter, with risks even when states win. For instance, pair a state-favoring dictator with at least one wing willing to go with the state or chair, and the state will win every time, garnering two (if not three) votes. Yet with every such tribunal combination (types 1–12 in Table 4.1), states can have better or worse qualitative outcome. Such a chairman, if he is dense or myopic, may fail to appreciate what specific award content would most serve the state's interest. He puts a great of faith in at least one other arbitrator coming his way, and they often will.[4] But because a dictator does not consult with his wingman colleagues, he does not benefit from their constructive criticism and expertise. Thus, in his haste, he might include his own idiosyncratic rhetorical asides that diminish the award in the

---

4. But note the wing revolt scenarios in types 13 thru 16 under the dictatorial chair.

Table 4.1 Tribunal types and hypothesized outcomes for states with state-tilting chair

Wing Types		Quantitative Range of Voters States Can Expect			Qualitative Variation by Chair Types *Tribunal type numbers*—*Outcome, risk*			
State Wing	Investor Wing	Low Bound	Top Bound	Maximum Loss	Dictator	Manager	Socialite	Weak
P	T	3	3	0	1 – Win, reckless content	17- Win, reckless content	33- Win, unnecessary bargaining	49- Win, inter-wing bargaining over terms
P	F	3	3	0	2 – Win, reckless content	18- Win, reckless content	34- Win, unnecessary bargaining	50- Win, faux president for state
F	T	3	3	0	3 – Win, reckless content	19- Win, reckless content	35- Win, unnecessary bargaining	51- Win, faux president for state
F	F	3	3	0	4 – Win, reckless content	20- Win, reckless content	36- Win, unnecessary bargaining	52- Muddle
P	N	2	3	−1	5 – Win, reckless content	21- Win, reckless content	37- Win, some concessions to neutral	53- Potential loss, concessions to neutral
N	T	2	3	−1	6- Win, reckless content	22- Win, reckless content	38- Win, some concessions to neutral	54- Potential loss, concessions to neutral
F	N	2	3	−1	7- Win, reckless content	23- Win, reckless content	39- Win, major concessions to neutral	55- Potential loss, neutral as sole arbitrator
N	F	2	3	−1	8- Win, reckless content	24- Win, reckless content	40- Win, major concessions to neutral	56- Potential loss, neutral as sole arbitrator

P	P	2	2	−1	9- Win, reckless content	25- Win, reckless content	41- Loss on merits, with horse-trading to reduce quantum	57- Loss on merits with inter-wing horse-trading to reduce quantum
T	T	2	2	−1	10- Win, reckless content	26- Win, reckless content	42- Loss on merits, with horse-trading to reduce quantum	58- Loss on merits with inter-wing horse-trading to reduce quantum
F	P	2	2	−1	11- Win, reckless content	27- Win, reckless content	43- Loss, center of gravity is partisan investor wing	59- Loss with low judicial economy
T	F	2	2	−1	12- Win, reckless content	28- Win, reckless content	44- Loss, center of gravity is partisan investor wing	60- Loss with low judicial economy
N	N	3	1	−2	13- Potential loss if wing revolt	29- Win, potential concessions to neutral	45- Potential loss, unpredictable horse-trading	61- Potential loss, wing bargaining
N	P	2	1	−2	14- Potential loss if wing revolt	30- Win, potential concessions to neutral	46- Loss, possible horse-trading	62- Loss, neutral determines extent
T	N	2	1	−2	15- Potential loss if wing revolt	31- Win, potential concessions to neutral	47- Loss, possible horse-trading	63- Loss, neutral determines extent
T	P	1	1	−2	16- Loss with expansive ruling by wing revolt	32- Loss with high judicial economy	48- Loss with low judicial economy	64- Loss with expansive ruling

Source: Author's grounded theory analysis of interviews with arbitrators. F = follower; N = neutral; P = partisan; T = turncoat.

Table 4.2 Tribunal types and hypothesized outcomes for states with investor-tilting chair

Wing Types		Quantitative Range of Voters States Can Expect			Qualitative Variation by Chair Types *Tribunal type numbers—Outcome, risk or opportunity*			
State Wing	Investor Wing	Low Bound, Predicted	Top Bound, Predicted	Maximum Loss, Predicted	Dictator	Manager	Socialite	Weak
P	T	2	2	-1	65- Win, expansive ruling by wing revolt	81- Win on narrow factual basis	97- Win, convoluted reasoning	113- Win with expansive ruling by wing revolt
P	N	1	2	-2	66- Potential win if wing revolt	82- Possible win on narrow factual basis	98- Possible win, convoluted reasoning	114- Possible win, subject to bargaining with neutral
N	T	1	2	-2	67- Potential win if wing revolt	83- Possible win on narrow factual basis	99- Possible win, convoluted reasoning	115- Possible win, subject to bargaining with neutral
N	N	0	2	-3	68- Potential win if wing revolt	84- Possible win on narrow factual basis	100- Possible win, intense neutral bargaining	116- Possible win, subject to bargaining between neutrals
P	F	1	1	-2	69- Loss, state-side dissent	85- Loss, state-side dissent	101- Loss, major concessions to state	117- Possible win, if state wing leads coup
F	T	1	1	-2	70- Loss, state-side dissent	86- Loss, state-side dissent	102- Loss, major concessions to state	118- Possible win, if state wing leads coup

P	P	1					
T	T	1	-2	71- Loss, state-side dissent	87- Loss, state-side dissent	103- Loss on merits, horse-trading to reduce quantum	119- Loss with investor-tilting faux president, state wing dissent
F	N	1	-2	72- Loss, state-side dissent	88- Loss, state-side dissent	104- Loss on merits, horse-trading to reduce quantum	120- Loss with investor-tilting faux president, state wing dissent
N	F	1	-2	73- Loss, potential dissent by neutral	89- Loss, potential dissent by neutral	105- Loss, potential concessions to state	121- Possible win, with neutral as faux president
P	P	1	-2	74- Loss, potential dissent by neutral	90- Loss, potential dissent by neutral	106- Loss, potential concessions to state	122- Possible win, with neutral as faux president
N	N	0	-3	75- Loss, potential dissent by neutral	91- Loss, potential dissent by neutral	107- Loss, potential small concessions to state	123- Loss with investor-tilting faux president, possible neutral dissent
T	T	0	-3	76- Loss, potential dissent by neutral	92- Loss, potential dissent by neutral	108- Loss, potential small concessions to state	124- Loss with investor-tilting faux president, possible neutral dissent
F	P	0	-3	77- Loss	93- Loss	109- Loss, accidental concessions	125- Loss by investor-tilting faux president
T	F	0	-3	78- Loss	94- Loss	110- Loss, accidental concessions	126- Loss by investor-tilting faux president

(continued)

Table 4.2 (*continued*)

Wing Types		Quantitative Range of Voters States Can Expect			Qualitative Variation by Chair Types *Tribunal type numbers—Outcome, risk or opportunity*			
State Wing	Investor Wing	Low Bound, Predicted	Top Bound, Predicted	Maximum Loss, Predicted	Dictator	Manager	Socialite	Weak
F	F	0	0	−3	79- Loss	95- Loss	111- Loss, accidental concessions	127- Muddle
T	P	0	0	−3	80- Loss	96- Loss	112- Loss, accidental concessions	128- Loss, wing bargaining over terms

Source: Author's grounded theory analysis of interviews with arbitrators.

eyes of the broader arbitration community, who may be averse to citing its arguments in future cases. Similar risks abound with the managerial chair, who is not above compromise, but only does so when necessary to secure a tribunal majority. In types 17–31, the state-favoring manager is guaranteed at least one state-favoring wing and so need not water down his award, nor be swayed away from counterproductive brash conclusions. In such instances, a solid victory for states becomes an isolated event in the broader war for a sovereignty respecting international law.

Or consider the qualitative outcomes under the socialite chair (types 33 through 48). While, on paper, a state-favoring socialite will increase the odds of a favorable outcome for states, such chairs will water down the strength of the award, often unnecessarily, in order to be well-liked and reach unanimity. In such settings, a hard-charging partisan investor can pull the center of gravity of the tribunal further towards him than (by quantitative considerations alone) he would have any right to do. Thus, the best case for states with a socialite at the helm is a watered-down win, and the worst case is an outright loss.

Then there is the other side of the equation from Table 4.1, where the chairman tilts toward the investor. In Table 4.2, we see that there are some instances in which states can do quite well even when the chairman is against them. For instance, state-tilting partisan or neutral wingmen combinations can revolt against investor-tilting dictators or weaklings (Types 65, 68, 113 and 116), and proceed to write their own majority award. These wingmen combos can also bargain with managers or socialites to produce narrow wins for the state, or water down the extent of the loss (Types 81, 84, 97 and 100). With dictators and managers, there is also the possibility of having a state-favoring dissenting opinion (Types 69–76 and 85–92). While dissents do not change the immediate outcome, they may add grist to later state efforts to set aside an unfavorable award.[5] Finally, a state partisan wingman could lead a coup against a weak investor-favoring chairman and follower co-wingman (Types 117–18).

All else being equal, states would prefer west columns to east, and north rows to south, as presented in Tables 4.1 and 4.2. But there are cases where this pattern is disrupted. States, for example, generally prefer state-tilting dictators to managers. But this preference is reversed when paired with two neutral wingmen. In that case, a state is better off with a manager chairman that will assure that both wingmen do not revolt. So, type 29 is preferred to type 13, in contravention of the general geographic preference ranking.

To take another example, even though a state would generally prefer the secured vote of a partisan wingman, this is diminished when a socialite is chairing the tribunal. Two neutral wings are a better bet for the state than two partisan ones when a social chairman is involved, who in his quest for unanimity will encourage horse-trading that leads to partial state losses. In contrast, there is a chance that neutral wingmen could take the state's side, so they are thus a better bet (Type 46 > 41 in the tables).

---

5. This was Argentina's tactic in a recent bid to set aside the arbitral award in the *AWG* case under the UK–Argentine investment treaty, where it drew attention to the split in the tribunal (Slater 2015).

A state would generally prefer a socialite chairman to a weak one. But in the case where the investor appointee is a follower and the state appointee a strong partisan, then a weak chairman is better. In such a case, the state appointee becomes the faux chairman and determines the case unilaterally. Meanwhile, a social chairman in similar circumstances could unnecessarily pander to a follower investor wingman, who would have voted with the chair regardless (Type 50 > 34). But under a weak chairman, a state would prefer to take its chances with two neutral wingmen rather than two partisan ones. In the latter case, the arbitrators will have to horse-trade merits (for the investor) for quantum reduction (for the state) in order to even produce an award. With two neutral wingmen, there is at least the possibility that they could agree with the state's case (Type 61 > 57). Finally, a partisan state appointee could lead a coup against a weak investor-favoring chairman and follower co-wingman (Types 117–18).

Summing Up

Investment arbitration is a remarkable legal system. For more than 25 years, arbitrators have shown themselves to be ingenious and capable of creative management solutions, performing a difficult task under unusual conditions. Through their ingenuity, they have transformed investment law into one of the most active fields of international legal practice. In each case, arbitrators must structure their collegial interactions *de novo*. It resembles a market where buyers and sellers determine for each case whether to finalize a transaction. Sellers of legal decisions with good reputations who are well known in the market place will get work. Those who do not, will not, or will have to get lucky with a first appointment and then build their reputation from there. Through the use of strategic dissenting, agreeing and socializing, arbitrators help to make the market work. There is surely much that other fields of international law and justice seeking could learn.

Yet, like any market, investment arbitration suffers from market imperfections. There are transaction costs in searching for arbitrators and ascertaining their likely disposition. And many tribunal combinations leave states at a disadvantage from the jump. In investment treaty arbitration, investors have asymmetric control over the caseload, and thus indirect control over reappointments. Investors are well served to pick vigorous partisans who have been known to vote or dissent in favor of investors. Chairs who want reappointments must be seen as giving something to the investors who drive the demand for dispute settlement. State-friendly dictators are unlikely to survive in such a system, as they would be blocked by investor-side law firms and appointees. The more likely scenarios for states is that they will deal with investor-friendly dictators (in which case states get nothing), social chairmen (who through the logic of horse-trading will assess states lower damages but proliferate investor-friendly merits decisions), or managerial chairmen (who will generate fact-intensive decisions and concede as little to the state as possible, and only then if the state appointee is needed for a majority vote). Thus, the center of "tilt gravity" on the typical tribunal is closer to the investor interest from the outset.

Even for the one appointment that states control, uncertainty abounds. A state could appoint a supposed partisan, only to guess wrong, or appoint a partisan who alienates the other tribunal members. Indeed, wingmen who survive for long in the system will be dependent on their reputation in the arbitration community. If states are conscious of these incentives, then they should appoint arbitrators who are closer in ideological-spatial terms to the median (pro-investor) arbitrator than to the outlier zealous protectors of sovereign interests. This is especially true when the amount of damages on the line has the potential to make a major dent in state budgets. In those instances, a state would be foolish to not eat a merits loss as the price of reduced damages.

All of this seems less than ideal for states. Why do they not take back these tremendous powers?

References

Berg, Albert Jan van den. 2010. "Dissenting Opinions by Party-Appointed Arbitrators in Investment Arbitration." In *Looking to the Future: Essays on International Law in Honor of W. Michael Reisman*, edited by Mahnosh H. Arsanjani, Jacob Katz Cogan, Robert D. Sloane and Siegfried Wiessner, 821–44. Alphen aan den Rijn, the Netherlands: Martinus Nijhoff Publishers.

Derains, Yves, Guido Santiago Tawil, and Claus von Wobeser. 2016. Isolux Infrastructure Netherlands, B.V. v. Kingdom of Spain (Award). SCC.

Slater, Matthew D. 2015. Republic of Argentina v. AWG Group Ltd (Petition to Vacate Arbitration Award). Washington, DC: US District Court for the District of Columbia.

Chapter Five

WHY INVESTMENT LAW LASTS

Judicial empowerment through constitutionalization is best understood as the product of a strategic interplay between three key groups: threatened political elites, who seek to preserve or enhance their political hegemony by insulating policy making in general, and their policy preferences in particular, from the vicissitudes of democratic politics while they profess support for democracy; economic elites, who view the constitutionalization of rights, especially property, mobility, and occupational rights, as a means for placing boundaries on government action and promoting a free market, business-friendly agenda; and judicial elites and national high courts, which seek to enhance their political influence and international reputation.
—Ran Hirschl, *Towards Juristocracy* (Hirschl 2004, 12)

In the last two chapters, we have focused on the world inside arbitration. In the next two, we zoom our lens outward to put it in a political context.

How has the world responded to investment-treaty arbitration and arbitration to the world? More than twenty years ago, sociology-and-law scholars Yves Dezalay and Bryant Garth (1996) had a prediction. Their book was the first major study of international arbitrators. At that time, arbitration was mostly an inter-corporate affair. A typical case might involve a London insurance company that insured a Massachusetts shipper but failed to pay out on the policy. Instead of going to a court in the United Kingdom or the United States (where one party might have a home-country advantage), the two companies could opt for private arbitration in a chamber of commerce. To the extent the story involved the public sector, it was limited to the strategies the arbitration community used to get national courts to agree to help enforce the awards. Nonetheless, with the 1995 publication of the University of Miami's Jan Paulsson's famous article celebrating the first investment-treaty case (*AAPL v. Sri Lanka*, discussed in chapter 2), there were hints that states might soon be more directly embroiled in arbitrations. Dezalay and Garth wondered whether this meeting of private and public actors might push arbitration in a more social democratic and green direction (Dezalay and Garth 1996, 312).[1]

By any interpretation, the hope of a greening of investment law has not been realized, even if critics' worst fears have also not come to pass. So why does investment law survive? It is not for lack of challenges to its legitimacy—of which many have been launched but few landed. After losing a string of cases after their 2001 financial crisis, for example, Argentina refused for many years to pay any damages. The Obama administration even

---

1. There have been subsequent studies of commercial arbitrators, many of whom also serve in investment-treaty disputes. See, for instance, Karton (2013) and Mattli and Dietz (2014). These disputes primarily involve contractual issues.

agreed with the populist Nestor and Cristina Kirchner governments in US court filings that certain investment-treaty tribunals had overstepped their bounds (Breyer 2014). Despite this, Argentina eventually buckled, paying out in the cases it lost (Peterson 2013b). Some of President Kirchner's left-leaning counterparts in Latin America renounced the very notion of investor–state dispute settlements, but they ended up leaving most of their treaties intact (Polanco 2014). Only Ecuador successfully renounced all of its treaties, but in a process that took ten years to complete.

The critique has spread beyond Latin America. Australia strenuously objected to investor–state dispute settlement (ISDS) in its trade agreements with other developed nations, until buckling under pressure during the Trans-Pacific Partnership (TPP) negotiations. In 2016, European citizens and governments made similar objections, proposing major overhauls that would judicialize the system even more. Finally, in 2017, the Donald Trump administration proposed changing the North American Free Trade Agreement (NAFTA) to allow states to opt-in or opt-out of the ISDS mechanism. While the ultimate fate of this proposal was still under negotiation between the United States, Canada and Mexico when this book went to press, the strong opposition by the corporate sector in all three countries suggests a total gutting of the dispute-settlement mechanism is unlikely (Simson 2017).

This misfiring of reform is puzzling from a conventional political-science perspective. Chapter 2 explored the primary mechanisms states have of controlling adjudicators to whom they have delegated power. In the principal-agent framework, states write the rules and monitor their enforcement. They screen who gets to be an adjudicator and fire the ones they do not like. They manipulate courts' budgets (Hawkins et al. 2006). In settings where a higher degree of adjudicator–trustee independence is needed, states still retain some control, but they must use more legalistic tools such as rewriting treaties, influencing the development of case law, invoking provisions for terminating the treaty or citing legal defenses as excuses for noncompliance (Helfer and Slaughter 2005). In these accounts, sovereign states that want reform have ways of getting it.

This chapter argues that investment law's resilience is due to historical institutionalist factors, including path dependence, the logic of unintended consequences and the complexities of institutional layering. In the sections that follow, I show how, first, the imprecision of key treaty obligations provides arbitrators with substantial interpretive discretion. Second, the delegation of authority they enjoy comes from multiple principals, making it harder to rein them in. Finally, investment-treaty rules are dispersed in numerous institutions and treaties around the globe. As such, reform in one pocket of the system does not neatly diffuse—if it diffuses at all. (See Table 5.1 for a preview of these main arguments.) Through this prism, we see that states end up with only partial control over the system they created. The end result looks a lot more like strong forms of judicial review in domestic legal systems than voluntary, flexible, quick arbitration.

Exploiting Imprecision

One of the primary tools that states have over international adjudicators is to specify very clearly what the latter's delegated power entails. States can choose to make treaties very

Table 5.1 Investment law: Beyond control?

How States Could Control Adjudicators (in Political Science Theory)	But May Not Function If...
Rule writing	Rules are imprecise, and interpretation is back-loaded
Monitor them through reporting requirements	Behind-the-scenes interpretations and deliberations are not public (though final decisions often are)
Screen them or fire them	States do not have a monopoly on appointments and do not control firing
Cut their budget	States do not control tribunal budgets
Make it harder to sue states	Litigants can treaty-shop around the hurdles
Leave treaties	To be effective, state must leave a whole suite of treaties at once, incurring economic and reputational costs
Do not comply	Enforcement can happen without their cooperation

Source: Author's analysis, adapting work by Hawkins, Helfer, Slaughter and others.

precise so that it would be clear ex ante what a violation would entail (Abbott et al. 2000). In this way, arbitrators would have little to no discretion.

But there are good reasons to leave the law vague. Treaty negotiators do not have a crystal ball and cannot look into the future to identify every scenario they might want to discipline. Clever policy makers can always find ways to obey the letter of the law while violating its spirit. By empowering adjudicators to determine what the spirit requires, negotiators save themselves time at the negotiating table and may even enhance the efficacy of their creation (Pauwelyn and Elsig 2013). Moreover, more precision in a treaty system can trigger greater political opposition within countries (as the costs of signing the treaty are more apparent). Precise agreements may thus be less likely to be signed in the first place (Goldstein and Martin 2000).

States such as the United States, with ample outbound investment, may also push for arbitrators to retain maximum discretion. For instance, Ecuador recently attempted to get the United States to agree to a reinterpretation of the US–Ecuador investment treaty. This would have aided the administration of President Rafael Correa in its dispute with Chevron Corporation and provided a useful example for other states that wished to reduce arbitral autonomy. One interviewee told me:

Within the State Department, there was a tremendous fight about how to deal with that case. Some of the defense people in the State Department said, [agitated] "We got to defend it on the merits." I said, "That's a no-brainer. You can't defend it on the merits. You just repeat, 'There's no dispute. There's no dispute. There's no jurisdiction. We don't have a view on what the right interpretation is [. . .] We don't have a United States view. We have said nothing.'" But people wanted to fight it on the merits. It would have dug a very deep hole. Fortunately, better heads prevailed.

In short, even if precision would benefit the United States as a defendant, it might not help US investors as complainants.

That is not to say that there are no bounds placed on interpretations of investment law's standards. The Vienna Convention on the Law of Treaties, drafted at the United Nations' International Law Commission from 1949 to 1969, codifies how international law is to be interpreted and how conflict between treaties resolved. As we learned in chapter 2, there had been an explosion of treaty activity in the nineteenth and early twentieth centuries. To international lawyers, the purpose of treaties is to see that states keep their promises (*pacta sunt servanda*). However, to keep these commitments from becoming straitjackets, a parallel norm existed alongside: when objective circumstances change, relations between states must also change (*rebus sic stantibus*). The ILC's mission was to keep *rebus sic stantibus* from becoming a too-easy escape clause by limiting its invocation to situations where the change in circumstances radically changes states' burden of obligations. In other words, not feeling like complying is not a good enough reason to break promises (Rosenne 1970).

Other provisions of the Vienna Convention direct themselves to adjudicators. According to Article 31, a treaty's terms are to be assigned their ordinary meaning (derivable from dictionaries and their legal context) and in light of a treaty's object and purpose. As legal scholar Andrea Saldarriaga of the London School of Economics has written, the convention privileges an "objective method, placing emphasis on the meaning of the text, over the subjective approach which seeks to uncover the parties' intentions. In doing so, the VCLT sought to eliminate (or at least alleviate) the uncertainty that preceded its adoption as to which interpretative method to apply" (Saldarriaga 2013, 201).

Saldarriaga's analysis shows that, while two-thirds of investment tribunals cite the convention, many do so incorrectly or apply it inconsistently. In light of investment law's particularly capacious standards, this is unsurprising. As we saw in chapter 3, the obligation of host states to treat investors fairly and equitably is vague and as a result has been interpreted in wildly different ways. Moreover, many investment treaties allow arbitrators to determine what system of law to interpret, whether the provisions of the treaty itself, outside contracts, outside treaties, domestic laws or international custom (Gaillard and Banifatemi 2003). Finally, under the Washington Convention (which governs arbitrations at the World Bank's International Centre for the Settlement of Investment Disputes), arbitrators are forbidden from not coming to a legal conclusion on the basis that the applicable law is unclear (a legal doctrine called *non liquet*) (Commission 2007). Such openness demands creativity.

Given such imprecision, can arbitrators simply invent law?

The Law Appliers

First, a minority of arbitrators say no. For these individuals, the law itself left little space for discretion. One interviewee, summed up this view by claiming that arbitrators just "apply the law; that is it." Unlike national judges, arbitrators "cannot make the law change," said another interviewee. There will be a right and a wrong answer, he said, which means "ambulance chasers, [. . .] who will throw to arbitration anything, absolutely anything, without limit and without consideration to any standard of logic [. . .] will most certainly be defeated."

As another interviewee explained: "To me, it's not an art, it's a science. Once you get the rules right, the sequence of the rules right, and you apply them, and you get the result [. . . t]he law is supposed to make things predictable." When asked about the great many complicating factors—political changes, regime changes, macroeconomic changes—and their relationship with predictability for the parties involved in dispute-settlement cases, this arbitrator replied: "That's a difficult question. But it should hold true that law has rules, and you should be able to figure what is the outcome, including in a change of policy or change of regime from liberal to socialist or whatever, because there are rules about that [. . .] Investment arbitration is one of these specialized areas where you should have fewer and fewer problems basically because the law is very repetitive."

Far from being runaway agents improvising new legal rules, one interviewee said, "It can get a little boring. I am kind of tired of it now. [Laughter] Always the same stuff!" Still, another said, "All things being considered, I prefer the diversity of commercial arbitration [. . .] There is a little monotony to investor–state arbitration." When I asked how another arbitrator "put meat on the bones" of the fair equitable treatment standard, he said, "I am not sure I even thought about that too much. I was just applying the treaty as I thought *it had to be understood*." (*Emphasis added.*)

Who benefits from the supposed precision in the law? Some said the existence of a right answer ensures equal justice for countries at different levels of development. Another interviewee said ISDS arbitration does not have "different standards as between the rich and the poor, the rich and the rich, and the poor and the poor." For others, the existence of a right answer might mean that the law was correctly applied, but that justice in a moral sense might not be served. One said, "Our job is to simply interpret the treaty. And take account of the facts. It is not to do the right or decent thing. It is simply to apply the law." Another claimed:

> The likelihood is that most of [the awards] are correct. Correct in the sense that they are rendered in accordance with the law. Whether they are correct in a more philosophical sense of justice being done and all that, is obviously to some extent a different story. Particularly when it comes to a state winning on the basis of there being no jurisdiction under the treaty. The investor may well have reason to be aggrieved by whatever has taken place, but for some reason or another, not being able to invoke treaty protection. And that is something you just have to live with. The treaties say what they say.

For these law appliers, arbitration is boring and clerical, consisting of a careful assembling of factual chronologies and consulting dictionaries to get at the plain meaning of words.

Fact-finding is a middle ground between applying and creating the law. As one arbitrator said, fact-finding could help states:

> I have found that there is a normal tendency [among arbitrators] to say, for instance in Russia, "Putin controls everything." Does he? We have to look. Does he really? I do not know. I have to look at every single case and see whether it is really Putin who is controlling Gazprom. I do

not know, if I do not see the real facts of the case. And then once you ask these questions, you have perhaps a different approach to interpretation.

In other cases, the search for facts benefited the investor. Said one interviewee,

> I have had cases where the investor says he was in the shower and then some men came into the shower and took him out and gave him a beating. Is it true, is it not true? Was it the state, was it the Secret Service, or was it just that he had a girlfriend who had another boyfriend and it was the other boyfriend who was [. . .] You know? The problem for this is, once you have established the facts, and you have established, say, harassment by the state, or that the state was bugging this person, or that there was an order by the president of the government to do something nasty to this investor. Once you have established the facts, it is rather simple.

Nonetheless, fact-finding involves limited discretion. Arbitrators cannot travel back in time to ascertain whether Russian President Vladimir Putin put the pressure on the country's largest energy company, Gazprom, or whether a state official of a certain country invited an investor's lover into the shower. They are constrained by a preexisting menu of facts, much like law appliers are bound by a preexisting treaty text.

The Law Creators

It is unsurprising that there would be self-described "law appliers" among the arbitral pool. After all, fealty to law is part of any good lawyer's training. But over the course of my interviews, a more complicated picture emerged. While some arbitrators claimed a modest role, they gave countless examples where they or their colleagues improvised solutions to legal problems. As one said: "There is too much judicial creativity in investor–state arbitration. That is not the function of international arbitration, to create common law jurisprudence as if they were common-law lawyers [. . .] It is not our function."

But creativity still happens, which is what makes it worth complaining about. When I categorize all of my interviewees by what they saw as their primary function—law applying, law creating, fact-finding, or some combination thereof—the clear weight is toward the creative middle, with over 95 percent of respondents conceding substantial arbitral discretion. (See Figure 5.1.)

For many interviewees, creativity is why they keep accepting appointments. "You are really creating the law as you go along," said one. "There are many open issues, many open questions," said another. These innovations were celebrated in triumphant terms: "I feel very proud to have been involved in that kind of revolution in the legal system"; and, "I felt like a pioneer." In their view, because investment law is developing, arbitrators get to teach the world. One arbitrator said that professors unaccustomed to practicing law tell him that investor–state arbitration is as intellectually challenging as any theory they teach in the classroom. And a longtime arbitrator added: "Because it is [intellectually challenging] you are on the front edge. It's being developed. The law is being made. You can have an influence on it."

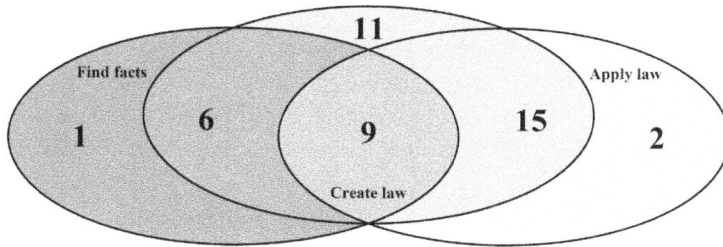

Figure 5.1 What is an arbitrator's role?
Source: Author's grounded theory analysis of pertinent arbitrator responses (44).

This creative spirit takes advantage of gaps in the law, and of parties who are not able or do not want to fill them. As one interviewee said, "Because we have a flat legal system with no appellate review and each arbitral tribunal is sovereign, we are free to disagree with each other." Another said:

> This investment-protection treaty had a pretty terrible arbitration clause because it did not say [. . .] under which rules it would be conducted. So there was first an exercise I did, namely write a sort of innocent-sounding letter saying, "Gee. I am now sitting in this arbitration. I'm looking forward to doing this with you people. So are my colleagues. We were wondering whether we should perhaps use [a certain set of] rules [. . .] If you have any objections to this, please let us know." Or something like that, you know? And fortunately, they had no reaction to this.

The creative spirit came from deep within arbitrators' bodies and minds. "I think most people get a gut feeling as to whether the conduct was correct or right or whether the claimant really got done in," said one, with a chuckle. It was arbitrators' moral assessment of the facts of the case that guided this gut. On the merits, said another, the rulings

> usually go by the facts of the case, and how offensive they are to you, you know, what has happened. So that then from that, you bridge it to fair and equitable. Most people have a sense of their belief [in] what it should be. On damages, we are totally free to do whatever we think is reasonable.

Another confirmed this view:

> Ultimately, if the arbitrators have the conviction that somebody has really been shafted, they are unlikely to adopt a body of legal reasoning that will say, "Yes, this guy has been shafted, but he is out of luck" [. . .] If you get to the merits, and you have the sense that somebody really has been the victim of inappropriate behavior, that is going to be the driver. Not some verbal refinement of "what do we mean by fair and equitable treatment, what are reasonable, did this guy have a reasonable expectation of it?" No.

The consequences of this adjudicating from the gut is less predictability for states and investors. "Everybody has a different conception of fair and equitable treatment," said one. "It is almost impossible to give advice now, because ultimately all advice comes to the same thing: it depends who the arbitrators are," said another. A third opined: "Different tribunals, formed by different lawyers [means] the results could be very different, because simply they think differently." Variance in interpretations stems from variance in talent. As one interviewee said: "Always look at the names. 'Gabrielle Kaufmann Kohler, 10 out of 10. Mr. X, do not bother to read it.' The name is very important. I think it reflects the quality of the reasoning."

In more predictable legal systems, states can try to influence the development of case law by seeking good precedents. This is a normal strategy in other, more hierarchical legal contexts, like US courts, the European Commission for Human Rights and the World Trade Organization (Galanter 1974; Lupu and Voeten 2012; Pelc 2014). Indeed, one of my respondents argued that he follows prior case law "when the precedents are so numerous, so constant, that a change in the case law would be a complete revolution." As another said, present decisions "whether we like it or not, rightly or wrongly, will affect future arbitrations." Another said, for "human beings, it is natural for us to look around, and say, 'How was this done before? Who has decided it?'" Or as another put it: "If a really respected group of arbitrators decides a particular set of principles, you think a lot about that. You think long and hard before you say that that does not make any sense."

Nonetheless, strategic litigating has unpredictable payoffs in such a flat legal environment. As one said, "my function is not to decide for the world; it is deciding this case for these parties." Or as another said, "If I had to decide a question which had been already decided in the past, why should I necessarily be influenced by my former opinion?" Indeed, as one state appointee wrote in a 2012 dissenting opinion, where he reversed course on a 2004 award he had joined:

> with regard to the practical possibility for an arbitrator on an ICSID tribunal to change, clarify or alter in any way his opinion or his position, he clearly has in principle complete freedom to do so, particularly after considering developments in the case and subsequent decisions [. . .] My change of heart between the decision in the arbitral award concerning the claim by Siemens against Argentina and the current case [also against Argentina] can be [. . .] fully justified by the obvious fact that each arbitration is different. (Bello Janeiro 2012)

In this unpredictable landscape, arbitrators' citation of case law is more akin to that of litigants—citing the favorable and being unbound by the rest. As one arbitrator explained, "You can all point to something [from the case law] to buttress the position that you are trying to bring across to your colleagues." Another said, "Arbitrators will refer to the trend of awards they like, not to the other ones." Another said citation was an afterthought.:

> You have too many prima donnas, who want to justify themselves. And probably in half of the arbitrations they are citing, they are quoting arbitrations they have been involved in before [. . .] In my personal experience, I decide what I consider and then I ask some people to help me to look at what the citations could be [after the fact].

Even arbitrators who felt themselves bound by case law have to struggle to make this case to colleagues. As one said:

> States need to know what is right and what is wrong, and investors as well. Whether it is a good solution or not, it is actually less important [. . .] I very much insist on people trying to follow clear lines of cases, and to be relatively disciplined.

In sum, past decisions are a resource for litigating states to draw on in their filings, but the utility of doing so is not knowable in advance.

What types of arbitrators were more prone to create law? No clear pattern emerges. Interviewees pointed fingers at commercial lawyers and public international lawyers, practitioners and academics, younger and senior arbitrators, continental civil lawyers and Anglo-Saxon common law lawyers. One arbitrator said he "was persuaded that most of these negotiators did not know what they were doing," but added that "no one knew what these treaties meant." He recalled one of the negotiators telling him "'the common lawyers will work out what the terms mean,' [so] lawyers went to work on them—hammered them!"

But another interviewee took the opposite view:

> Deep in the common lawyer's heart, they still believe in natural law. There can be only one correct and just decision. A continental lawyer would say, "No. There is paradise for later, but here on earth, it is politics and you have the evolution of society and you have the evolution of international relations, you have globalization. So problems change and the solutions have to change." And that is why a continental lawyer has perhaps less problems with an evolving case law.

Another interviewee scorned arbitrators from legal traditions that emphasized legal citation for "prefer[ing] to wash their hands by quoting six precedents." He said these kinds of arbitrators "do not want to move things [. . .] they do not want to be the one to break the precedents."

Academics came in for particular ridicule from other arbitrators, either for being too improvisational or too timid. But one academic interviewee explained why this might be the case. "One of the reasons that law firms do not like to appoint academics as arbitrators is that they are afraid that academics will be thoughtful and creative and come up with something new and unexpected. That is not what they want." An investment arbitrator who also has heard purely commercial arbitration cases responded that academics do not know "what makes people tick" in the real world. He went on:

> I find them to be much too theoretical, not practical enough. Because they have not had much experience if any in the real world. I think it helps to have had some experience in the business world, to have been an advocate in courtrooms, in different places, rather than having been a theoretician of the law for decades and decades [. . .] I say, "This is the way it happens out there you know in the boardroom, on the executive floor, in the actual confines of the government. This is real life!" And if you are going to be an arbitrator, you cannot

simply say, "Well that is not the way [laughter] my textbook has taught me.' So you need to have gone to the school of hard knocks [laughter].

This common view among most arbitrators probably explains why academics may want arbitration work—by some estimates, they can double their annual income by serving in a case (Waibel and Wu 2017), but they may not be in high demand.

This criticism of academics, though, begs the question: Are the law creators among arbitrators abusing imprecision? It is impossible to know with any certainty states' true ex ante preferences or expectations. The evidence is that many states knew precious little about what they were signing when they inked the treaties (Poulsen 2015), so many of them probably had no firm prior beliefs on the content of such provisions as fair and equitable treatment. Nonetheless, my interviewees did suggest that states and other observers were taken aback by the pushing outward of investment law. As one interviewee said of a 1998 case (*Lanco v. Argentina*), "Argentina thought they had not signed any contracts, any arbitration clause, and that Argentina itself as a state was not involved, it was just [a contract by] the municipality of Buenos Aires." When the tribunal found otherwise, "that was really a surprise for everybody."

Another arbitrator observed of the 2000 award in *Maffezini v. Spain*: "Everyone was scandalized in Spain. I mean how is it that this Argentine who has a business in Galicia is able to file a claim against Spain?" As one interviewee said of NAFTA, "The United States, Mexico and Canada did not know what they were signing, and they knew as much as anybody!" According to recently disclosed documents under the US Freedom of Information Act (Nolan et al. 2000), the case of *The Loewen Group Inc. and Raymond L. Loewen v. the United States* surprised the United States by showing jury awards could be the basis of claims under NAFTA, which had been negotiated just years before. This anecdotal evidence, and the fact that more precise obligations are less successfully invoked, are consistent with imprecision mattering.

Benefiting from Complex Delegation

It is one thing for arbitrators to make use of imprecision to expand their power, but why do states not rein them in? In conventional social-science theory, such mission drift should not occur. In the 1970s, economists theorized about when the mechanisms of control within a firm might break down, allowing management to do more or less than what owners might prefer. Liberal merger-and-acquisition rules were said to be one way of keeping management on their toes (Alchian and Demsetz 1972). Social scientists later extended this framework to government, to try to account for how legislatures could use oversight, whistleblowers and court review to check the power of executives (McCubbins, Noll, and Weingast 1987).

Yet international relations are substantially more complex than individual firms, and a single agent can respond to multiple principals. This relationship can take the form of parallel delegations or revocations of authority, or of a single delegation and revocation that requires the collective consensus of multiple actors. The governance of multilateral development banks, for example, is overseen by numerous governments, meaning a change in preferences by a single government will not likely be sufficient to change the behavior of the banks' management (Lyne et al. 2006). The United Nations' cumbersome collective decision-making rules have incentivized individual countries to contract separately with UN agencies for their own nationally branded initiatives (Graham 2015). Finally, the World Trade Organization could be described as a complex agent, where a chain of delegated authority connects home-country governments (sovereign principals) to their Geneva-based staff (proximate principals) and to Secretariat staff (agents). Principal-agent problems can arise at any point in the chain (Elsig 2011). Indeed, by one count, most new international organizations are created not by states but by other international organizations (Johnson 2014).

Investment arbitration is even more tangled, characterized by what I call a principal complex. This concept combines several elements:

- **Collective principals**. Bilateral investment pacts are underpinned by two multilateral treaties, each with more than 150 member states: the 1959 New York Convention and 1965 Washington Convention. Under these pacts, signatories agree to have their national courts defer to, and help enforce, arbitral awards rendered in other member nations. The Washington Convention also set up an international organization, the International Centre for the Settlement of Investment Disputes (ICSID), while the New York Convention and its associated UN Commission on International Trade Law (UNCITRAL) allow disputes to be held at a variety of private and inter-state bodies. Changes to either convention require unanimous agreement of state members.
- **Complex delegations**. In investment-treaty cases, there are multiple parallel and chained delegations of authority, with states empowering private investors and arbitral centers to play principal-like roles of their own, screening and appointing arbitrators.
- **Weak principals**. Strong principals must be able to delegate authority to agents and revoke it if the agent slips or shirks, yet investment-arbitration appointees only weakly meet these criteria. Arbitration wingmen are not formally instructed to side with their appointers. Arbitrators can be removed from a case, but only by their fellow arbitrators or the arbitral center. Finally, most arbitrators' decisions are not reviewable in national courts or the World Bank. (As I argue in more detail below (and also in chapter 2), national laws and treaty obligations forbid courts from overturning arbitration decisions for all but narrow reasons.) Figure 5.2 models these relationships; recall my warning in previous chapters about the knottiness of these graphics.

The following subsections take stock of four ways state control breaks down because of this principal complex: screening, monitoring, sanctions and institutional checks and balances.

Screening

In the right circumstances, the power to hire is a highly efficient way for principals to control their agents. If government officials only allow the ideologically like-minded to rise

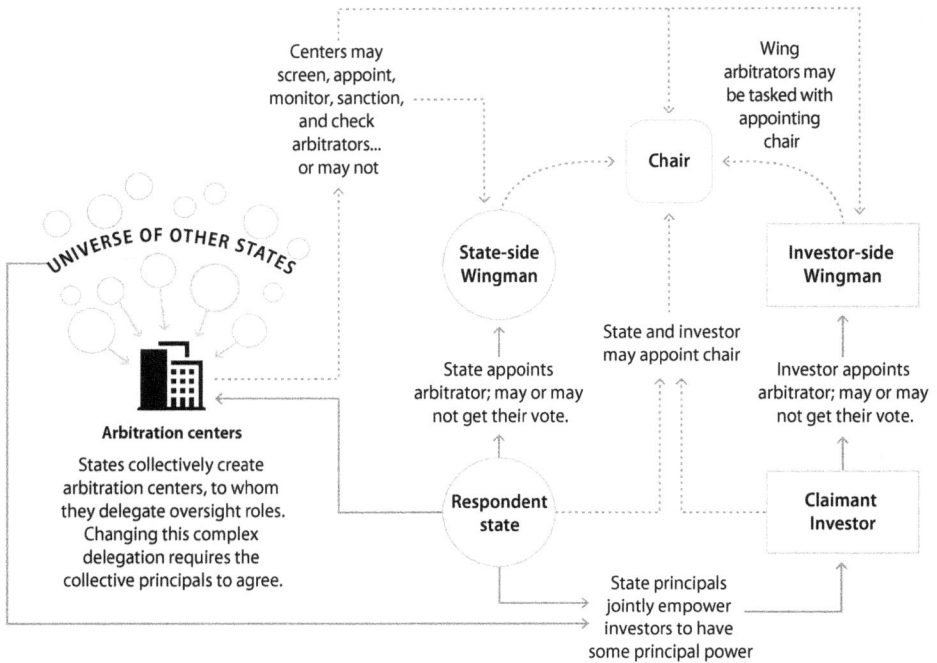

Figure 5.2 Division of labor and power complicates investment regime reform
Source: Author's grounded theory analysis of interviews and documentary materials.

to the top ranks of a given agency, then this ensures the double benefit of faithful policy implementation while saving time. US Republican politicians, for example, only appoint judges who have come up through the ranks of partisan-oriented law associations such as the Federalist Society (Teles 2010).

Unfortunately for states, they are not the only ones with screening powers in investment arbitration. As discussed in chapter 4, some arbitral center rules give states the option of appointing one of the three arbitrators and of attempting to come to an agreement with the investor about a mutually acceptable chairman. But it is also possible that the two nominated wingmen will be allowed to select the chairman. And if nominations are not forthcoming (or if arbitral center rules so dictate), then the arbitral center can fill any of the three vacancies.

The formal weakness of screening power might not matter if states had informal control over who becomes an arbitrator. But even informal powers are highly attenuated. Each contracting state gets to designate four individuals to the standing Panel of Arbitrators maintained by the International Centre for Settlement of Investment Disputes and are free to appoint arbitrators of their choice, even if they are not on that panel. But if the parties do not appoint their wingmen or do not agree on the appointment of a chairman after a certain amount of time, then the World Bank president must fill the vacancies with individuals from the standing Panel of Arbitrators.

There are various asymmetries involved. The World Bank president gets to name ten individuals: more than any one state. And the United States by tradition picks the World Bank president. (Outside of cases overseen by ICSID, tie-breaking powers are wielded by chambers of commerce or by heads of international courts.)

My interviewees confirmed that states cannot screen to any great effect, but their coprincipals in the arbitral centers might. On the front end, many arbitrators discussed being recruited informally by lower-level contacts at the World Bank who would recommend appointment to the ICSID's Panel of Arbitrators or to a specific investment tribunal. These contacts were creative in how they would see the people appointed, finding a member state that was low on its panel numbers and recommending that arbitrators work their political connections to find someone in that government who could support his designation.

The arbitrators themselves game this system, running highly political self-promotional efforts in both their home countries and in Washington. One arbitrator told a friend in his home-country government that it "looked silly" to have unfilled vacancies, and successfully encouraged them to designate him to the ICSID's Panel of Arbitrators. Then, he made a side trip to Washington when he was arbitrating a commercial case in New York. "I said, 'Let's just say hello to the people at ICSID where I have never been.' I just said hello, and these chances in life, suddenly there were all these cases with [developing countries]. And they were desperately looking for arbitrators. They appointed me to two cases on the same day!"

Ultimately, arbitrators and law firms are the most effective screeners. There is a paradox here: if there is an unlimited pool of talent, and anyone can be an arbitrator, then agents would be in excess supply. This would (all else being equal) enhance the relative bargaining position of principals, including states (Hawkins and Jacoby 2006). This excess supply, however, is only on paper. In practice, as discussed in chapter 4 and consistent with other research,[2] there are only a few dozen arbitrators that risk-averse law firms will appoint, or that arbitrators will decide are worthy to join their club's ranks. Thus, even for the one wingman appointment that states control, the governments are better off if they pick from those prescreened as appointable by elite insiders.

The power of multiple principalship is evident in its absence. A limited form of investor–state dispute settlement is overseen by the Organization for Islamic Cooperation (OIC). Under that 57-country pact, a disputing investor and state are instructed to pick arbitrators. If they do not, or if the two appointees cannot agree on a third arbitrator to chair the case, then the OIC secretary general is instructed to fill in the missing appointments. Yet, as reported by Hepburn and Peterson (2017), the Organization for Islamic Cooperation has failed to step into its designated role in a handful of cases that have been lodged there. As a consequence, states that do not appoint an arbitrator can effectively kill a case (or force it to other venues). In short, agents will have more autonomy if they can be summoned without reliance on the states that they are judging.

---

2. See, among many others, Dezalay and Garth (1996), Puig (2014), and Langford et al. (2017).

Monitoring

States' monitoring capacity is weaker still. The most consequential actions arbitrators take is their conduct in inter-arbitrator deliberations, which are held behind closed doors. This vacuum creates more room for the types of collegiality-driven pressures explored in chapter 4.[3] Because arbitrators rely on colleagues for reappointment recommendations, they will have little incentive to "rat" on their colleagues, explained one arbitrator. In any case, no whistleblowing mechanism exists.[4]

As with pre-hearing screening, arbitrators were generally underwhelmed by states' conduct during tribunals, when monitoring could take place. My interviewees said that states' attempts to object to jurisdiction or disqualify arbitrators (which take place after a tribunal has been convened) were likely to be dismissed, as arbitrators just see these as delaying tactics. Arbitrators generally agreed that states were more "theatrical" and "sanctimonious" in hearings than investors, and prone to making false accusations. States have difficulties making themselves "understood by the chairman," explained one interviewee.

Indeed, the interviewees agreed that states were best off when they did less. Arbitrators gave states kudos for hiring counsel from outside their countries. Explained one interviewee: The "sophisticated" states use the "best law firms" from the United States while the "undeveloped countries [. . .] that did not have much experience in this area [hired] domestic law firms" or "one of their retired diplomats" who will use "language [. . .] from the diplomatic world" and "deliver speeches" instead of making strong legal arguments. "They were outgunned badly," he concluded. And as another arbitrator noted:

> When it started, states were [. . .] not arrogant, but they thought they could do it alone. But these are complicated things [. . .] A Georgian lawyer, or a Russian lawyer, as intelligent as he might be, cannot compete with Freshfields [a leading law firm in investment arbitration]. It is impossible. They do not have the practice, they do not have the international network, they do not have the possibility to do what big firms can do.

---

3. Venezuela suggested as much in a recent application for annulment, arguing that a strange award was a result of horse-trading within a tribunal. The ad hoc committee noted the state had no evidence for this and deferred to the tribunal's own self-representation of its process (Yusuf et al. 2016, para. 88, 146).
4. In a long-running case—the first ever "mass claim" in ISDS history—a respondent appointee repeatedly tried to "rat" on his colleagues, only to be ineffectually batted back. As Kabra (2017) reports: "Mr. Torres Bernárdez [Argentina's appointee] opined that [. . .] the tribunal had failed to issue a merits award within a reasonable time. On his view, this was contrary to the principles of good administration of international arbitral justice, and the corollary that justice delayed is justice denied. In response, the other tribunal members issued an additional declaration, alleging that the information disclosed by Mr. Torres Bernárdez was irrelevant, partially inaccurate, and in breach of the principle of secrecy of tribunal deliberations. Mr. Torres Bernárdez issued a further declaration, clarifying yet again that he did not share the view of his co-arbitrators." In the end, his opposition mattered little, as Argentina settled with the investors out of court.

Relative to states, arbitral center staffers were seen as better able to meaningfully monitor tribunals' work. They helped with the writing process, either formally through the editorial process or informally in chats. Arbitral center staff members help "a lot in providing precedents, insights, not only the administrative aspect," said one interviewee, and even recommend changes in how awards are written. Some types of arbitrators, such as academics without a large legal staff, would not even take a case unless an arbitral center could guarantee staff support. Staff members are careful to make sure that their role is not formally acknowledged in the awards, as they know it is not appropriate. As such, the precise influence of staff is difficult for outside researchers to identify. As one interviewee summed up:

> The [ICSID] secretariat is really excellent. They help enormously. Those are the arbitrators of the arbitrators! [. . .] They worked until three in the morning. That experience. They had ideas [. . .] they helped a lot [. . .] They very gently said, "Oh, I remember a single case where a Dutch arbitrator said this or that, or a French arbitrator was annoyed with this and that." They did it lightly, at lunchtime. Or sometimes [. . .] we would have a cigarette outside the World Bank. And then we had a chance to have a five-minute conversation.

Recent cases confirm states' individual and collective inability to steer arbitrators in preferred directions. As the European Union has pushed toward deeper economic integration that involves region-wide competence over investment issues, it has sought to roll back investment treaties concluded in decades past by member states. Tribunals have not been sympathetic, with a recent tribunal hearing a lawsuit by Belgian investors against Italy opining:

> Despite the fact that the European Commission has intervened in many other intra-EU arbitrations, as far as has been publicly reported, no tribunal yet has upheld this objection to jurisdiction. Overall the effect of these decisions is a unanimous rejection of the intra-EU objection to jurisdiction. (Crawford et al. 2016, 104)

Similarly, while the three NAFTA governments have sought to steer interpretation in cases through so-called "non-disputing party" submissions, investment arbitrators have shown themselves able and willing to disregard these filings (Hepburn 2016). Finally, states that try to aggressively defend themselves by raising many jurisdictional objections may try the patience of a tribunal, which could decide to saddle a country with costs even when that country wins (Derains et al. 2016, 226).

Sanctions

A third form of principal-agent control for states—sanctions—is only a little stronger than monitoring and screening. Control of budgets as a sanction tool would be a powerful way to discipline wayward agents, but investment arbitration is not reliant on state contributions. The International Centre for Settlement of Investment Disputes is financed primarily out of revenue paid by the arbitrating parties (ICSID 2014). In non-ICSID cases, investment tribunals are entirely financed by the litigating parties. Thus, it is true that states may share in the arbitration costs. Covering these costs, however, is not at their discretion but rather by order of a tribunal. In short, states lack formal financial leverage.

Absent having control of arbitrators' salaries, the main way states can sanction individual investment arbitrators is through removal from a case. After being appointed, an arbitrator in an ICSID dispute can be subject to a disqualification challenge by one of the parties if he has a "manifest lack" of "high moral character and recognized competence in the fields of law, commerce, industry or finance" or if he cannot "be relied upon to exercise independent judgment" (ICSID 2006).

But, like screening and monitoring, states do not control this second sanctioning mechanism, either. They can at most trigger it. The disqualification challenge is decided by the other two arbitrators on the tribunal. If two or more arbitrators are challenged or if the two unchallenged arbitrators are unable to come to agreement with one another about the disqualification of their peer, then the World Bank president decides on the challenge. If an arbitrator is disqualified, the chairman must select the replacement from the ICSID's Panel of Arbitrators where, as noted above, the World Bank president has both formal and informal influence.

Under the New York Convention and its associated UN Commission on International Trade Law, disqualification procedures are broadly similar to those at the International Centre for Settlement of Investor Disputes, but the absence of a similarly institutionalized secretariat requires that treaties and related instruments designate alternative disqualification mechanisms. For instance, India's investment treaties give the president of the International Court of Justice the authority to rule on disqualification challenges to tribunal majorities.

States cannot even be certain as to how and when other entities will disqualify arbitrators. Standards for disqualification at the International Centre for Settlement of Investment Disputes are highly malleable: the terms "manifest lack," "recognized competence," and "independent judgment" are not defined. In practice, standards have ranged from a high threshold through World Bank President Robert Zoellick's 2007–12 tenure (requiring "highly probable" evidence of dependence or bias) to a lower threshold under his successor, Jim Yong Kim (who only requires easily perceptible evidence of "an appearance" of dependence or bias). Neither test is particularly demanding; only four out of more than 40 disqualification attempts (10 percent) have been successful (Daele 2014).[5]

Indeed, the case history shows that disqualification is a clumsy and unreliable sanction tool to better align arbitrators with state policy goals. In 2013, World Bank president Kim rejected Argentina's effort to disqualify Francisco Orrego Vicuna on the basis that the Chilean arbitrator was irreparably biased against Argentine interests (Kim 2013c). The government cited as evidence his past work for Chile's Pinochet dictatorship (which collaborated in the torture of Argentine nationals) and his public writings against Argentina's use of an "essential security" exception defenses. Moreover, in a book

---

5. This number does not account for instances in which arbitrators resigned voluntarily.

chapter, the arbitrator colorfully argued that the defense (which governments have long incorporated into treaties) could unravel the "rationale of all the major legal systems of the world, international law included" (Orrego Vicuna 2010: 750–51). Kim saw no conflict and refused Argentina's request.[6]

In a separate case, India was more successful in its challenge to the same arbitrator. The country focused its argument also on Orrego Vicuna's hostility to the security defense. In a disqualification ruling under UNCITRAL rules, the president of the International Court of Justice, Peter Tomka, took issue with the Chilean arbitrator publishing his anti-state views after his arguments has been subject to a rare annulment at the International Centre for Settlement of Investor Disputes. But, in the same case, India was unsuccessful in disqualifying the chairman, Canada's Marc Lalonde, who had also served as a wingman on some of the same tribunals in question as Orrego Vicuna (Tomka 2013).

In other words, Orrego Vicuna's particular offense was not to have endorsed troubling views, but was refusing to publicly bow to the legal hierarchy, minimal as it is. As if to show their autonomy, the reassembled Lalonde-led tribunal eventually found that India could not wholly rely on the essential security defense; Orrego Vicuna's replacement, David Haigh, found they could not use it at all (Peterson 2016c). And when the Kyrgyz Republic cited the *Tomka* decision as a basis to challenge the fixity of Jan Paulsson's views on denial of justice (a legal question about which Paulsson wrote the leading reference book and on which he has clearly defined views), the deciding authority rejected the claim with little explanation (Sibelesz 2014).

In sum, disqualification is a very rare event—and for ideological conflicts, practically nonexistent. Nonetheless, some of my interviewees claimed to worry about disqualification, making them watch what they say to the press, in conference proceedings and to researchers. Some resigned from tribunals voluntarily rather than be dragged through a disqualification process. This prospect left some arbitrators wistful for national courts. Said one: "We wouldn't think about challenging a judge because he has already three or four years ago pronounced on a particular point of law."

But interviewees confirmed that this worry is not tied to what states in particular think of them. Instead, arbitrators saw non-state entities as having more sanctioning power. As one said:

> I have not found that [disqualification proceedings] created particular difficulties in the arbitral process itself. After all, the arbitrators are not the ones putting the complaint or the challenge. I suppose one could say in the ICSID case, it is rather embarrassing to be put in the position of having to pronounce on one of your colleagues with whom you have been sitting for six months, or whatever. But, there are precedents, and you still have to decide these matters on the basis of fairness, and what the grounds for challenges are. There is no particular advantage in kicking him out, or her, or keeping him in, or her in. It is not a major issue.

---

6. Also that year, Kim twice disqualified arbitrators over perceived conflicts of interest, rejecting states' arguments about ideological bias (Kim 2013a, 2013b). A similar conflict was also at issue in the one case where two co-arbitrators voted to disqualify their colleague (Levy and Aynes 2014).

Another interviewee cast doubt on the meaningfulness of disqualification more generally, saying that the standards for disqualification were so high that "you would have
to get an email by mistake or something of the sort, be copied by mistake" on out-of-
court communications between a party and an arbitrator arranging how to vote. "It
does not happen," he concluded. Indeed, in late 2017, an investor appointee (Stanimir
Alexandrov of Bulgaria) resigned from the *SolEs Badajoz v. Spain* case after losing the confidence of at least one of his colleagues in a disqualification challenge. In other words,
the challenge by the state itself was not enough to shame the arbitrator, but the existence
of discord within the tribunal apparently did.

If states lack control over formal sanctions, what about informal ones? The arbitration community is rife with lore of the handful of times when states attempted to
bully arbitrators. In the *Loewen v. United States,* the United States famously pressuring their
appointee to vote against the investor (Veeder 2013). In the end, the US did win the
case, helped along by the Canadian investor, which reincorporated as a US company,
destroying the basis for jurisdiction. The incident was a source of embarrassment for
many interviewees. As one interviewee noted:

> There was one case in which the United States was clearly wrong, and that was the *Loewen*
> award. I don't know if it has many supporters or defenders. It was just wrong. There was a
> case of arbitrators really keeling over for the United States. It creates a sort of lopsided sense
> that certain countries are less likely to lose. That is problematic.

Another interviewee added that this is occasionally a problem for state appointees of all
nations:

> I have had instances where one of the arbitrators was all along coming along with the con-
> clusion and everything. Two cases in particular. In the end, the third arbitrator was a party-
> appointed arbitrator, with the state-appointed arbitrator, saying, 'Well I agree, but I live here
> and I cannot come out, so I have to be the dissident on this particular point or something.'
> I had another case involving another country [. . .] [and the arbitrator said] said, 'Listen, I am
> a lawyer, living in that country, and if I want to survive even physically, I better not. I fully
> agree with you, but I have to say that I am a dissident.' [. . .] What can you do? But thank
> God that is not frequent.

Recourse to informal leverage is possible, but at a reputational risk for the bullying
state—and may be effective for only one of the three arbitrators.

Institutional Checks and Balances

With limited ability to screen, monitor, or sanction, states are left to the mercy of the
checks and balances that have accumulated over the past several decades among the
institutions that now handle investment arbitrations. As with the other controls explored
above, these mechanisms are weak.

Under the Washington Convention, any party dissatisfied with an ICSID award
can request annulment on narrow procedural grounds. Once the request is registered,

the World Bank president appoints three new arbitrators from the standing Panel of Arbitrators to an ad hoc annulment committee. If a committee annuls an award, then either party can request an entirely new tribunal to rehear the case. Annulled awards are not enforceable in domestic courts. This mechanism has done little to align arbitrators with state interests. Annulment committees cannot correct legal errors or rewrite awards to make them more consonant with state interests (Schreuer 2011). What is more, only twelve out of hundreds of ICSID investment-treaty awards have ever been annulled (see Table 5.2).

Investors ended up retaining or adding to their victories in the majority of those twelve annulment decisions. In 2002, the French water company Vivendi SA successfully argued for annulment of a 2000 award that had gone in favor of Argentina. The original tribunal had found that the investor in a privatized water facility was contractually obligated to litigate any dispute in local courts rather than under the France–Argentina Bilateral Investment Treaty (Rezek et al. 2000). The annulment committee disagreed, finding that national contractual obligations do not control investment treaties: "It is not open to an ICSID tribunal [. . .] to dismiss a claim on the ground that it could or should have been dealt with by a national court" (Fortier et al. 2002: para. 102). This paved the way for re-litigation of the entire case, where Argentina was ordered to pay Vivendi $105 million (Rowley et al. 2007).

The annulment committee in *Malaysian Historical Salvors v. Malaysia* made a similarly revolutionary finding—from the perspective of limiting the applicability of state policies in investment disputes. In 1991, a British investor had signed a contract with Malaysia to salvage the contents of a boat shipwrecked in 1817, in return for a share of any proceeds. The original tribunal found that the salvage company had a contract to perform services, but that the mere existence of this legal relationship did not qualify as an "investment" since it made no "significant" contribution to Malaysia's economic development. This finding was consistent with a line of ICSID cases that utilized the so-called *Salini* criteria that required investors to make measurable contributions to economic development—such as creating jobs, building roads, or investing capital—in order to obtain standing under investment treaties (Hwang 2007). The 2009 *Salvors* annulment committee disagreed, writing that there are little to no "outer limits" on how peripheral an investment can be to permit investor standing (Schwebel and Tomka 2009: paras. 69, 78). This decision attracted a dissent from the third member of the committee, who argued that there would be no sense housing the International Centre for Settlement of Investor Disputes at the development-oriented World Bank if promotion of development were not a prerequisite for launching arbitral claims (Shahabuddeen 2009). This break with consensus was notable because annulment committees rarely see dissents.

Nonetheless, the dissenting member's views did not carry the day in the 2-to-1 decision. The practical import of the annulment for the British investor in the case at hand was minimal, since the firm did not have the funds to re-arbitrate the case with a new tribunal (Peterson 2009). The decision of the annulment committee, however, appears to have cast a chill on further efforts by arbitrators to require that investors support economic development in host countries before launching arbitral claims (Sattorova 2012, 290).

Table 5.2 Outcomes for states in annulment cases before the International Centre for Settlement of Investment Disputes

Case name	Date	Outcome	Who prevailed originally	In whose favor was annulment?	State ultimately "loser"?	Ruling
Vivendi Universal S.A. v. Argentina	July 2002	Annulled in Part	State	Investor	Yes	Investor not obligated to litigate in local courts; paved way for re-litigation and success by investor
200B Patrick Mitchell v. Democratic Republic of the Congo	November 2006	Annulled in full	Investor	State	No	Tribunal did not define "investment," but state incorrect that this would include development benefit
CMS Gas Transmission Company v. Argentina	September 2007	Annulled in part	Investor	State	Yes	State entitled to use essential security defenses, but still owes same amount, $133m
Malaysian Historical Salvors, SDN, BHD v. Malaysia	April 2009	Annulled in full	State	Investor	Yes	No investment too marginal to benefit from protection
Sempra Energy International v. Argentina	June 2010	Annulled in full	Investor	State	No	Sequence of tribunal's legal argument wrong, so state off hook for $128m
Helnan International Hotels A/S v. Egypt	June 10	Annulled in part	State	Investor	No	Contra tribunal dicta, investor would not have had to litigate in local courts. Overall ruling (for Egypt) left unchanged
Enron Creditors Recovery Corporation v. Argentina	July 2010	Annulled in part	Investor	State	No	Sequence of tribunal's legal argument wrong, so state off hook for $106m
Fraport AG Frankfurt Airport Services Worldwide v. Philippines	December 2010	Annulled in full	State	State	No	Tribunal was correct to dismiss, but should have heard more evidence first

Victor Pey Casado and President Allende Foundation v. Chile	December 2012	Annulled in part	Investor	State	Yes	Part of damage calculation wrong, needs a new tribunal to recalculate
Occidental Petroleum Corporation v. Ecuador	November 2015	Annulled in part	Investor	State	Yes	States owes less in damages (as per a dissenting opinion in tribunal), but still owes and merits claims rejected
TECO Guatemala Holdings, LLC v. Guatemala	April 2016	Annulled in part	Investor	Investor	Yes	State may owe investor more than original tribunal said
Tidewater Investment v. Venezuela	December 2016	Annulled in part	Investor	State	Yes	State may owe less in damages, but must cover 70% of annulment proceeding
Total investor wins			8	4	7	

Source: Author's analysis.

More recently, Guatemala and a US investor both applied to annul a 2013 award. The original decision had found that Guatemala's alleged failure to follow its own laws in handling an electricity concession constituted a treaty violation, even though the country's Supreme Court had found no wrongdoing. The state argued that the original decision amounted to an improper appeal of a decision by a nation's highest court. Not only did this argument not sway the annulment committee, but the latter sided with the investor's claim for even further damages as well, paving the way for re-litigation of the case (Hanotiau et al. 2016).

Even when states won annulment victories, none made as much headway in favor of state interests as those won by investors did for investor interests. In its *CMS Gas* annulment request, Argentina alleged that the tribunal (chaired by the aforementioned Francisco Orrego Vicuna) had radically expanded the content of the fair and equitable treatment that states must provide investors, while sharply limiting states' abilities to use essential security defenses. A 2007 decision by an ICSID annulment committee sided with Argentina on some of this critique but determined these were not annullable errors. In the end, the annulment committee arbitrators found on other grounds that Argentina was still liable for the same amount (Guillaume et al. 2007). Two later annulment decisions against awards rewarded by Orrego Vicuna succeeded in erasing Argentina's monetary liability but did not go even as far as *CMS Gas* on siding with Argentina on the merits. Instead, their decision faulted the original tribunal's sequence of legal arguments (Soderlund et al. 2010; Griffith et al. 2010).

Outside of the International Centre for Settlement of Investment Disputes, matters are little better for states. The New York Convention allows an award to be set aside by a national court if the arbitration had procedural irregularities or if "recognition [. . .] of the award would be contrary to the public policy of that country" (Article V). On paper, this suggests that awards by the UN Commission on International Trade Law carry particular enforceability risks relative to those awarded by the ICSID, where the grounds for annulment are more precise. Yet national laws implementing obligations under the New York Convention in the United States and the United Kingdom and continental Europe (Speidel 2006: 196) (Horn 2008: 592) instruct national courts to be highly deferential to arbitration awards rendered under UNCITRAL rules. Investors know this, which means they often pursue enforcement in these countries. In addition, national courts make very limited use of the so-called public policy exception.

Of the more than a hundred finalized, non-ICSID investment-treaty awards, only a few have been modified by courts in the seat of arbitration. As noted in chapter 1, a Canadian court modified *Metalclad v. Mexico* after finding that the arbitral tribunal erred in finding that the North American Free Trade Agreement required governments to be transparent in their policy making. The court then made a modest reduction of the amount awarded to the investor (Levesque 2014). But far from being bound by this court interpretation, later tribunals doubled down on the *Metalclad* transparency finding, claiming the Canadian courts got it wrong (Orrego Vicuna et al. 2010: para. 231). In a second case, *RosInvestCo UK Ltd v. The Russian Federation*, Swedish courts in 2013 dismissed an award against Russia after the British investor refused to expend any resources to collect on it (Peterson 2013a).

Thus, for the first 25 years of investment-treaty law, hardly any awards were set aside. In 2016, the pace picked up notably. In 2016, Dutch courts set aside the largest investment award ever in *Yukos v. Russia*, after faulting arbitrators for taking jurisdiction even though Russia had not ratified the relevant treaty (Peterson 2016b). The same year, French courts set aside two awards for legal errors in *Energoalians v. Moldova* and *Sutter v. Madagascar*, including overly lax definitions of what should constitute sufficient investment in order to have standing to bring a claim (Peterson 2016a). A year later, the French judiciary went on to vacate a third case, *Belokon v. Kyrgyz Republic*, finding that the investor may have used their investment as a vehicle to launder money—an offense to French "public policy" (Charlotin 2017).

Will French and Dutch courts continue this more activist stance? If they do, investors may begin insisting that the "seat of arbitration" (i.e., the country registered as the jurisdiction with review powers in UNCITRAL awards) be countries with more deferential courts, like the United States, not France. US courts, for instance, have upheld recent pro-investor decisions against states' environmental policies in *Crystallex v. Venezuela* on the grounds that an investment "award does not interfere with Venezuela's environmental rules or regulations, but only requires Venezuela to compensate Crystallex for the results of its inequitable actions and expropriation. Venezuela fails to meet the demanding threshold by demonstrating that holding it to the terms of its own treaty would violate our basic notions of morality or justice" (Contreras 2017, 28).[7] The United States could make a bid that it is a more hospitable country for sovereign wealth than France and the Netherlands after their recent pro-state decisions.

Did the arbitrators themselves feel constrained by these institutional checks and balances, such as they are? Annulment committees were viewed with suspicion by some interviewees, who said they were sometimes not at the same level, qualification-wise, as the original tribunal members, or can make strange decisions or opine on matters that were not at issue. Another interviewee said that annulment harmed collegiality and increased cleavages in the arbitral community:

> I have a bad impression of a number of annulment proceedings. Which is related to a view which I find frankly discriminatory, which is that, if there is an award coming out of a tribunal which is, for example, composed of, or presided over by someone from a country not regarded as forming part of the club—the selected club, Europe, the United States, a couple of others, Canada and so forth. If you are from elsewhere, or a developing country, then the annulment committee feels that it has to exercise its power by annulling [. . .] But they would never do this when the tribunal or the arbitrator is part of the club, or part of a major law firm, part of an institution where all these appointments are made, he is in a level of respectability different from that applied to the rest of the world. I think that is really pitiful, but I have sensed that it happens.

---

7. As further evidence of the stickiness of international legal standards, the US judge ruled that arbitration panel was within its rights to apply the 1926 *Chorzow* standard, neglecting to mention that this standard is alien to US claims against the state (ibid. 25).

So-called set-aside proceedings (the term for domestic court review of non-ICSID cases), also came in for scorn. One interviewee noted that most courts "followed the rules and stay the hell out of the merits," yet the Canadian judge who reviewed *Metalclad* "waded way more into the merits than it had any right to do." Another arbitrator reviled the same judge for being too literal-minded: "His opinion was a joke! He did not even consider any arguments. He just said, 'this is what [fair and equitable treatment] says. And what it says is what it says.'"

Far from reining in arbitrators, institutional review often tilted the balance of power away from states. One arbitrator confirmed that "the ICSID did not lay down itself a criteria for [defining an] investment," so arbitrators had to come up with one. According to another, staff at the International Centre for Settlement of Investment Disputes pressured arbitrators not to annul awards because it was bad for the system. As with earlier principal-agent controls, my interviewees saw non-state entities having more power in checking and balancing. In an initial tribunal, an appointed wingman arbitrator "may be more cautious when he asks questions to the party that has appointed him," noted one interviewee, [but] when you are in an annulment situation, where you have to be all three appointed by the institution, you do not have this inhibition" and worry more about what the arbitral center thinks.

How Viable Is Voice or Exit?

If arbitrators exceed their remit and cannot be disciplined using traditional principal-agent controls, then states are left with two choices: voice (amend your treaties) or exit (get out of them). Yet these tools do not seem to be much in use.

By one count, only about 6 percent of treaties (196) have been renegotiated (Haftel and Thompson 2017). States have only unilaterally terminated a few dozen (Pohl 2013). Only three states—Bolivia, Ecuador and Venezuela—have officially denounced the Washington Convention (Parra 2013), and none have denounced the New York Convention (Port et al. 2010). Neither of these conventions has ever been amended (Schreuer et al. 2009).

Ecuador's relative activism may be the exception that proves the rule. The Andean nation has the distinction of being the only country to have successfully eliminated its entire portfolio of investment treaties. Because Ecuadoran president Rafael Correa was able to remain in power for more than ten years—thanks to a collapse of the country's previous political party system, his own charisma, redistributive policies, and a rewriting of the constitution while in office—he had enough of a time horizon to see a difficult project of eliminating all investment treaties through to the end. President Correa's political longevity far exceeds the global average presidential tenure of four years in office and even tops the average maximum permitted tenure of eight years (Ginsburg et al. 2011). Yet even in such beneficial circumstances, his investment reforms were piecemeal. A first batch of terminations in 2008 only targeted smaller trading partners. To eliminate the treaties with powerful countries took a full ten years and a willingness to deal with sustained diplomatic tensions.

This lack of a meaningful exit strategy from investment treaties is explained in part by design within treaties. Most investment treaties include a so-called overhang provision such that the state continues to be bound by the rules for an average of 12.5 years (and as long as 25 years) after withdrawal (Pohl 2013). As most governments will not be in office for such a long period of time, they will not be able to enjoy whatever sovereignty benefits come from cancelling treaties, and instead incur only the immediate costs—spending money on renegotiation and risking capital flight.

In Ecuador's case, national judges have found the survival clauses to be binding for decades to come.[8] One batch of treaties, including the one with the United States, will last until 2027. Its longest-lasting pact (with the United Kingdom) will last until 2037 (CAITISA 2017). Ecuador will have five elections between now and then. At any point, a right-leaning government could win (as almost happened in 2017) and cancel the termination.[9] With European governments immediately greeting the terminations with a threat of capital flight, the story is far from over (Ecuavisa 2017).

The threat is real, or at least seen to be. As one interviewee put it:

There is a long-term price I believe to be paid for [exit] in terms of general reputation in the world. That is perhaps a big way of putting it, but I think there is some truth to it. It has got a political price, and [...] it may be, although it is not certain, that there's also a price in terms of having less inflow of investments. And I think that perhaps the effect may be more of an issue if you demonstrate that you want to get out of the treaties that you once concluded. I mean that really signals the intention that you want to be free to treat your investors as you please. If you are the investor, that is probably a little bit more of a red flag than having never signed a treaty at all.

Another explanation for investment treaties surviving intact without amendments is the relationship across treaties. Most investment treaties have most-favored-nation rules permitting investors to claim the most favorable level of protection in any of a country's portfolio of treaties. The inclusion of these clauses in bilateral investment treaties allowed more favorable Chilean treaty standards to be imported into an Argentina–Spain treaty, more favorable Kuwaiti standards into an Australia–India treaty, and Danish standards into a Russia–Mongolia treaty (Paparinskis 2011). So even if a country modified one pact's rules to be more state-friendly, an investor might be able to use the unreformed rules under another.

Moreover, so long as a state remains party to the multilateral Washington and New York Conventions, that state may still be dogged by claims. A sovereignty-minded government would have to modify its entire network of treaties, or at least its most investor-friendly one. The first option is extremely costly. The second option is also of

---

8. This is only for investments made before the termination of the treaty.
9. Indeed, it might not take even that long. As of early 2018, it appears that Correa's handpicked successor (Lenin Moreno) stood ready to reverse Correa's policies and reinstate all of the canceled treaties, citing a need to reassure foreign investors in the midst of an economic downturn.

scarce practical use because a cosignatory country that pushed an especially pro-investor treaty in the first place (say the Netherlands) is unlikely to agree to pro-state changes.[10]

Political scientists have developed a term for this dense layering: a regime complex. As University of California, Los Angeles's Kal Raustiala and University of California, San Diego's David Victor write:

> Regime complexes are marked by the existence of several legal agreements that are cre-
> ated and maintained in distinct fora with participation of different sets of actors. The rules
> in these elemental regimes functionally overlap, yet there is no agreed upon hierarchy for
> resolving conflicts between rules. Disaggregated decision-making in the international legal
> system means that agreements reached in one forum do not automatically extend to, or
> clearly trump, agreements developed in other forums. (Raustiala and Victor 2004, 279)

A burgeoning scholarship focuses on the consequences of regime complexity. When there are multiple overlapping rules, for example, states may be able to choose which to join, leave or comply with—empowering some regimes over others and inviting inter-regime turf wars. Complexity also creates an opening for small groups of experts to help states navigate their options. This creates the risk that the small group will be overly insular and not focused on the big picture (Alter and Meunier 2009). By creating focal points and lowering transaction costs, arbitration institutions helped states pursue goals that would be impossible in a world governed solely by short-term power calculations. When regime complexity frustrates these institutional tasks, some predict a reassertion of state power (Drezner 2009). This can be for the good of society, such as when the European Union leverages its place in the spaghetti bowl of bilateral trade agreements to push its human rights values on countries that could use more of them (Hafner-Burton 2009). It could also be for evil, as when states sidestep onerous anti-torture treaty requirements by simply never declaring war or peace (Fazal 2013).

But regime complexes need not always re-empower states. In investment arbitra-tion, states share governance responsibilities with arbitrators, arbitral centers and even national courts. This mix of institutions means that different principals and constituen-cies can block change in any of these forums. Consider the regime complex from the per-spective of the investor (modeled in Figure 5.3). Say an Argentine financial regulation put a crimp on the profits of a US company's local affiliate. The firm could pursue its case in a straightforward way by accessing the protection afforded the parent company under the US-Argentina investment treaty, have its case heard in the perennially operating facil-ities at the World Bank's International Centre for Settlement of Investment Disputes, and later seek enforcement in US courts.

But suppose this direct line of attack did not get the investor all they hoped for. Maybe the US–Argentina treaty was riddled with loopholes that protected states' rights to regu-late. Perhaps the new World Bank president is a little too quick to pounce on arbitrators

---

10. More recently, India began the process of replacing its investment-treaty network. An initial
     draft contained obligations not only for states but for investors. Yet for reasons that are not
     clear, these investor rules were walked back in the final versions (Hepburn 2017).

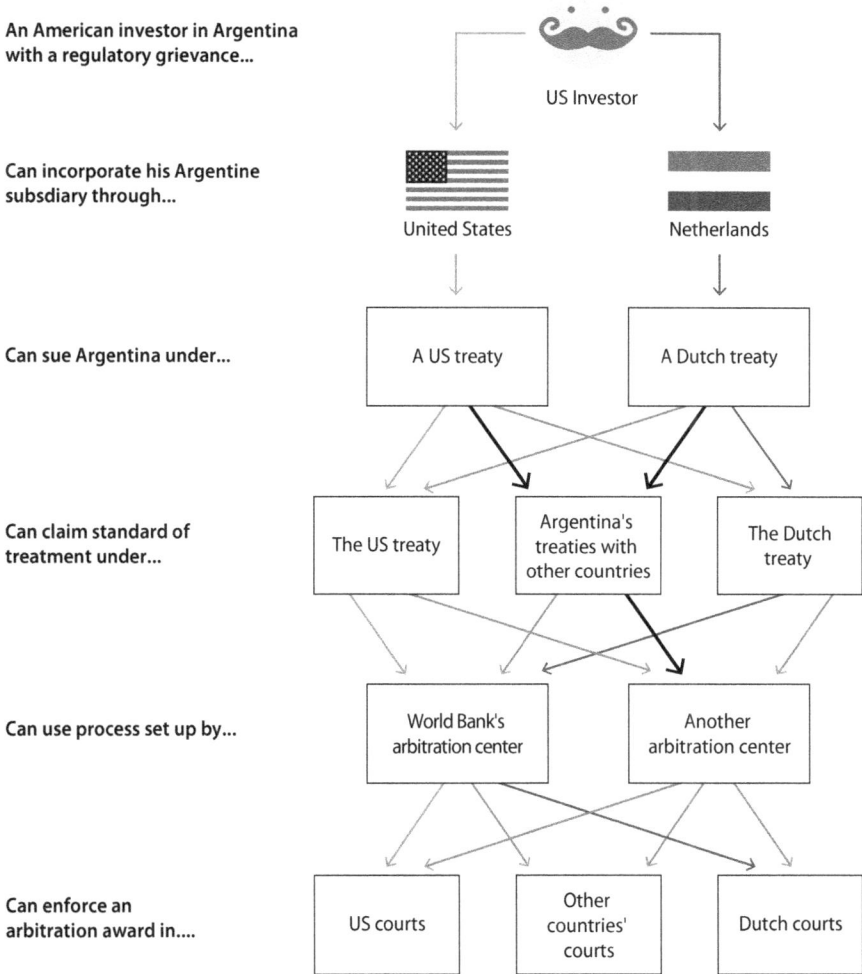

Figure 5.3 How investors can game the investment regime complex
Source: Author's grounded theory analysis of interviews and documentary materials.

who have been too solicitous of investor interests. The US Supreme Court could have taken a left turn under justices nominated by President Bernie Sanders, putting in doubt their deference to the arbitration process. Or it is possible that Argentina has moved all its assets out of the United States, so enforcement in US courts would too much of a hassle for no chance of gain.

Investment law's regime complex gives the ambitious investor plenty of options. The US investor could manipulate its multinational holdings structure so that a Dutch subsidiary would be the legal owner of its Argentine operations. In so doing, the company could then bring the case under the Dutch–Argentina treaty, get that treaty's protections, arbitrate the case at the International Chamber of Commerce's headquarters, and seek enforcement in Dutch courts. At any step of the way, still other permutations are possible. The US-cum-Dutch company could invoke the most-favored-nation standard to access favorable treatment under Argentina's treaties with countries beyond America and the Low Countries, could pick still another arbitration center, or could pursue enforcement in London, Paris or any other venue that had favorable attitudes towards arbitration and lots of Argentine cash. In short, instead of going through the front door, there's always a side-door option.

The flip side of plenty of investor offensive options is the need for lots of state defensive ones. It would not be enough, say, for Argentina to renegotiate its pact with the United States, if the Dutch or Chilean ones survived. It would not suffice to pull out of the Washington Convention that set up ICSID if there is the possibility of arbitrations at centers not housed at the World Bank. Amending that convention (or the New York Convention governing non-ICSID arbitration) would require the buy-in of all the states that created them, a collective action nightmare. Finally, it would not cut it to make Argentine courts less deferential to arbitral awards if the national laws of the United States, Netherlands, Chile, Canada, Germany and so on had more accommodating doctrines.

Perhaps unsurprisingly, then, my interviewees were skeptical that states would be able to make reform a reality. Arbitrators variously viewed attempts at reform as "jokes" that "clever" arbitrators can "get around" with "a bit of fiddling" by simply acknowledging the reform language and then advancing their own preferred interpretations. Multiple interviewees criticized North American countries for attempting to rein in interpretations via a declaration of their understanding of the fair and equitable treatment standard. As one said, "A lot of the arbitrators won't pay any attention to what the governments are saying, because it is insane." Another said:

> [States] are pushing back, [requiring a] greater margin of appreciation [in recent treaties]. You know there is more "regulatory takings will nominally not be attacked." I wonder about how long that is going to hold up, and whether arbitrators will live with that. I doubt it. They are going to find us an extraordinary case where there is discrimination of some sort. [. . .] Because most of the arbitrators, although they will definitely hold for governments, their instinct is, certainly the Anglo Saxon ones, American ones in particular: They are capitalist. And they say, "these guys want our investment, they've got to" [. . .] It is very easy, because governments do behave terribly.

I attempted to gauge arbitrators' openness to reform by asking for their take on a perennial reform idea: should the annulment system at the International Centre for Settlement of Investor Disputes be replaced by a full-fledged appellate mechanism that can reexamine the merits of cases? Their responses were telling: more than 70 percent (32 arbitrators) said no. They gave various reasons. As one said, "Could you set up an appellate body and then engraft it onto the other [treaties]? Highly unlikely. And is it wise? Because at a certain point, I mean, it is already too much of a lawyer sandbox."

Other interviewees hewed to a states-are-the-problem narrative. These arbitrators worried that an appellate body would be only appointed by states that, one said, would "name people who have been in their service" or in service of diversity (what he referred to as the "around-the-world spread"). The impartiality and quality of rulings would diminish, these interviewees predicted, as the panels are filled with people who they said are variously "lazy" or a "complete waste of rations." Others celebrated inconsistency as a virtue, or at least something that can never be totally eliminated from any legal system (with some noting inconsistent rulings by US district courts as support for this perspective). Another questioned whether such negotiations could be successfully initiated:

> Do we want to get into this thing and waste five years of our time to end up with a solution that might be worse than what we have now? Because all kinds of people will have all kinds of wishes of provisions they might like to amend. So if you have a big international conference to amend the Washington Convention, watch out. You don't know what you're going to get.

Summing Up

This chapter used a combination of interviewee evidence and case data to determine what sustains investment law. It showed that arbitrators retain substantial autonomy from states, benefiting from imprecise treaties, multiple competing overseers, and a network of treaties.

There are relatively few instances of states attempting to challenge the system in a fundamental way, which makes rigorous tests of my claims difficult. Yet for present purposes, it is sufficient to show that any attempted reforms would be highly unlikely to be successful unless led by a coalition of powerful countries willing to question the system's fundamentals and make costly changes. Such structural barriers can help us account for non-contestation. This is akin to New York University sociologist Steven Lukes' account of the third face of power, where structural constraints foreclose resistance before it starts (Lukes 2004). This is contrasted with a first-face power: through observable coercion; second-face power: through agenda control; and fourth-face power: through discourse (Hafner-Burton et al. 2012).

Is there hope for change?

References

Abbott, Kenneth W., Robert O. Keohane, Andrew Moravcsik, Anne-Marie Slaughter and Duncan Snidal. 2000. "The Concept of Legalization." *International Organization* 54 (3): 401–19.

Alchian, Armen A., and Harold Demsetz. 1972. "Production, Information Costs, and Economic Organization." *American Economic Review* 62 (5): 777–95.

Alter, Karen J., and Sophie Meunier. 2009. "The Politics of International Regime Complexity." *Perspectives on Politics* 7 (1): 13–24.

Bello Janeiro, Domingo. 2012. Daimler Financial Services AG v. Argentine Republic (Bello Dissent). ICSID.

Breyer, Stephen. 2014. BG Group PLC v. Republic of Argentina. U.S. Supreme Court.

CAITISA. 2017. "Auditoría Integral Ciudadana de Los Tratados de Protección Recíproca de Inversiones y Del Sistema de Arbitraje En Materia de Inversiones En Ecuador." Quito: CAITISA.

Charlotin, Damien. 2017. "BIT Award against Kyrgyzstan Is Annulled in Paris, with Court Giving Weight to Money-Laundering Allegations That Had Earlier Failed to Persuade Arbitrators." *Investment Arbitration Reporter*, February 23.

Commission, Jeffrey P. 2007. "Precedent in Investment Treaty Arbitration—A Citation Analysis of a Developing Jurisprudence." *Journal of International Arbitration* 24 (2): 129–58.

Contreras, Rudolph. 2017. Crystallex International Corporation v. Bolivarian Republic of Venezuela (Memorandum Opinion). U.S. District Court for the District of Columbia.

Crawford, James R., Stanimir Alexandrov, and Pierre-Marie Dupuy. 2016. Blusun S.A. v. Italian Republic (Award). ICSID.

Daele, Karel. 2014. "Saint Gobain v Venezuela and Blue Bank v Venezuela—The Standard for Disqualifying Arbitrators Finally Settled and Lowered." *ICSID Review* 29 (2): 296–305.

Derains, Yves, Guido Santiago Tawil, and Claus von Wobeser. 2016. Isolux Infrastructure Netherlands, B.V. v. Kingdom of Spain (Award). SCC.

Dezalay, Yves, and Bryant G. Garth. 1996. *Dealing in Virtue: International Commercial Arbitration and the Construction of a Transnational Legal Order*. Chicago: University of Chicago Press.

Drezner, Daniel W. 2009. "The Power and Peril of International Regime Complexity." *Perspectives on Politics* 7 (1): 65–70.

Ecuavisa. 2017. "UE, 'Sorprendida' de Que Ecuador Haya Denunciado Tratados Bilaterales Con 7 Países Europeos." *Ecuavisa*, May 11.

Elsig, Manfred. 2011. "Principal–agent Theory and the World Trade Organization: Complex Agency and 'Missing Delegation.'" *European Journal of International Relations* 17 (3): 495–517.

Fazal, Tanisha M. 2013. "The Demise of Peace Treaties in Interstate War." *International Organization* 67 (4): 695–724.

Fortier, L. Yves, James Crawford and Jose Carlos Fernandez Rozas. 2002. Compania de Aguas del Aconquija S.A. and Vivendi Universal v. Argentine Republic (Vivendi I) (Decision on Annulment). ICSID.

Gaillard, Emmanuel, and Yas Banifatemi. 2003. "The Meaning of 'and' in Article 42(1), Second Sentence, of the Washington Convention: The Role of International Law in the ICSID Choice of Law Process." *ICSID Review* 18 (2): 375–411.

Galanter, Marc. 1974. "Why the 'Haves' Come Out Ahead: Speculations on the Limits of Legal Change." *Law & Society Review* 9 (1): 95–160.

Ginsburg, Tom, James Melton and Zachary Elkins. 2011. "On the Evasion of Executive Term Limits." *William and Mary Law Review* 52 (6).

Goldstein, Judith L., and Lisa L. Martin. 2000. "Legalization, Trade Liberalization, and Domestic Politics: A Cautionary Note." *International Organization* 54 (3): 603–32.

Graham, Erin R. 2015. "Money and Multilateralism: How Funding Rules Constitute IO Governance." *International Theory* 7 (01): 162–94.

Griffith, Gavan, Patrick L. Robinson and Per Tresselt. 2010. Enron Creditors Recovery Corp. Ponderosa Assets, L.P. v. Argentine Republic (Decision on Annulment). ICSID.

Guillaume, Gilbert, Nabil Elaraby and James Crawford. 2007. CMS Gas Transmission Company v. Argentine Republic (Decision on Annulment). ICSID.

Hafner-Burton, Emilie M. 2009. "The Power Politics of Regime Complexity: Human Rights Trade Conditionality in Europe." *Perspectives on Politics* 7 (1): 33–37.

Hafner-Burton, Emilie M., David G. Victor and Yonatan Lupu. 2012. "Political Science Research on International Law: The State of the Field." *American Journal of International Law* 106 (1): 47–97.

Haftel, Yoram Z., and Alexander Thompson. 2017. "When Do States Renegotiate International Agreements? The Impact of Arbitration." *Review of International Organizations*.

Hanotiau, Bernard, Tiunade Oyekunle and Klaus Sachs. 2016. TECO Guatemala Holdings, LLC v. Republic of Guatemala (Decision on Annulment). ICSID.

Hawkins, Darren G., and Wade Jacoby. 2006. "How Agents Matter." In *Delegation and Agency in International Organizations*, edited by Darren G. Hawkins, David A. Lake, Daniel L. Nielson and Michael J. Tierney, 199–228. Cambridge: Cambridge University Press.

Hawkins, Darren G., David A. Lake, Daniel L. Nielson and Michael J. Tierney. 2006. "Delegation under Anarchy: States, International Organizations, and Principal-Agent Theory." In *Delegation and Agency in International Organizations*, 3–38. Cambridge: Cambridge University Press.

Helfer, Laurence R., and Anne-Marie Slaughter. 2005. "Why States Create International Tribunals: A Response to Professors Posner and Yoo." *California Law Review* 93 (3): 899–956.

Hepburn, Jarrod. 2016. "In Mesa Award, Waste Management Reading of FET Is Embraced." *Investment Arbitration Reporter*, April 28.

———. 2017. "Indian BIT Negotiator Clarifies Country's Stance on Exhaustion of Remedies, and Offers Update on Status of Country's Revamp of Bilateral Investment Treaties." *Investment Arbitration Reporter*, March 31.

Hepburn, Jarrod, and Luke Eric Peterson. 2017. "Investigation: As New Cases Emerge under Islamic Investment Treaty, Initial Viability of Claims Seems to Hinge on Willingness of Respondents to Appoint Arbitrators." *Investment Arbitration Reporter*, March 2.

Hirschl, Ran. 2004. *Towards Juristocracy: The Origins and Consequences of the New Constitutionalism*. Cambridge, MA: Harvard University Press.

Horn, Norbert. 2008. "Current Use of the UNCITRAL Arbitration Rules in the Context of Investment Arbitration." *Arbitration International* 24 (4): 587–602.

Hwang, Michael. 2007. Malaysian Historical Salvors Sdn, Bhd v. Government of Malaysia (Award on Jurisdiction). ICSID.

ICSID. 2006. "ICSID Convention, Regulations and Rules." 15. Washington, DC: World Bank.

———. 2014. "ICSID 2014 Annual Report." Washington, DC: World Bank.

Johnson, Tana. 2014. *Organizational Progeny: Why Governments Are Losing Control over the Proliferating Structures of Global Governance*. Transformations in Governance. Oxford: Oxford University Press.

Kabra, Ridhi. 2017. "As Argentine Bond Case Comes to a Formal Close, Arbitrators Spar over Whether They Had Failed to Render a Merits Award in a Reasonable Time." *Investment Arbitration Reporter*, January 4.

Karton, Joshua D. H. 2013. *The Culture of International Arbitration and The Evolution of Contract Law*. Oxford: Oxford University Press.

Kim, Jim Yong. 2013a. Blue Bank International & Trust (Barbados) Ltd. v. Bolivarian Republic of Venezuela (Decision on the Parties' Proposals to Disqualify a Majority of The Tribunal). ICSID.

———. 2013b. Burlington Resources, Inc. v. Republic of Ecuador (Decision on the Disqualification of Professor Francisco Orrego Vicuna). ICSID.

———. 2013c. Repsol S.A. and Repsol Butano S.A. v. Republic of Argentina (Decision on the Proposal to Disqualify a Majority of the Tribunal). ICSID.

Langford, Malcolm, Daniel Behn and Runar Hilleren Lie. 2017. "The Revolving Door in International Investment Arbitration." *Journal of International Economic Law* 20 (2): 301–32.

Levesque, Celine. 2014. "'Correctness' as the Proper Standard of Review Applicable to 'True' Questions of Jurisdiction in the Set-Aside of Treaty-Based Investor–State Awards." *Journal of International Dispute Settlement* 5 (1): 69–103.

Levy, Laurent, and Laurent Aynes. 2014. Caratube International Oil Company LLP and Devincci Salah Hourani v. Republic of Kazakhstan (Decision on the Proposal for Disqualification of Bruno Boesch). ICSID.

Lukes, Steven. 2004. *Power: A Radical View*. Second edition. London: Palgrave Macmillan.

Lupu, Yonatan, and Erik Voeten. 2012. "Precedent in International Courts: A Network Analysis of Case Citations by the European Court of Human Rights." *British Journal of Political Science* 42 (2): 413–39.

Lyne, Mona A., Daniel L. Nielson and Michael J. Tierney. 2006. "Who Delegates? Alternative Models of Principals in Development Aid." In *Delegation and Agency in International Organizations*, edited by Darren G. Hawkins, David A. Lake, Daniel L. Nielson and Michael J. Tierney, 41–76. Cambridge: Cambridge University Press.

Mattli, Walter, and Thomas Dietz, eds. 2014. *International Arbitration and Global Governance: Contending Theories and Evidence*. Oxford: Oxford University Press.

McCubbins, Mathew D., Roger G. Noll and Barry R. Weingast. 1987. "Administrative Procedures as Instruments of Political Control." *Journal of Law, Economics, & Organization* 3 (2): 243–77.

Nolan, Beth, Gene Sperling, Bill Marshall, Peter Rundlet and John Duncan. 2000. "Memorandum for John D. Podesta: Urgent Need for Policy Guidance to Resolve Interagency Litigation Strategy Dispute in Loewen NAFTA Arbitration," February 10.

Orrego Vicuna, Francisco. 2010. "Softening Necessity." In *Looking to the Future*, edited by Mahnoush H. Arsanjani, Jacob Cogan, Robert Sloane, and Siegfried Wiessner, 741–52. Alphen aan den Rijn, the Netherlands: Brill.

Orrego Vicuna, Francisco, Kenneth W. Dam, and J. William Rowley. 2010. Merrill & Ring Forestry L. P. v. The Government of Canada (Award). UNCITRAL ad hoc.

Paparinskis, Martins. 2011. "MFN Clauses and International Dispute Settlement: Moving beyond Maffezini and Plama?" *ICSID Review* 26 (2): 14–58.

Parra, Antonio R. 2013. "Participation in the ICSID Convention." *ICSID Review* 28 (1): 169–78.

Pauwelyn, Joost, and Manfred Elsig. 2013. "The Politics of Treaty Interpretation: Variations and Explanations across International Tribunals." In *Interdisciplinary Perspectives on International Law and International Relations: The State of the Art*, edited by Jeffrey L. Dunoff and Mark A. Pollack. Cambridge: Cambridge University Press.

Pelc, Krzysztof J. 2014. "The Politics of Precedent in International Law: A Social Network Application." *American Political Science Review* 108 (3): 547–64.

Peterson, Luke Eric. 2009. "Divided ICSID Annulment Committee Annuls Malaysian Salvors Award; Controversial 2007 Award Had Declined Jurisdiction." *IA Reporter*, April 20.

———. 2013a. "Russia Secures Set-aside of Hedge Fund's Modest Yukos-Related Arbitral Award, as Investor Declines to Spend Funds to Defend Pyrrhic Arbitral Win." *IA Reporter*, September 10.

———. 2013b. "After Settling Some Awards, Argentina Takes More Fractious Path in Bond-Holders Case, with New Bid to Disqualify Arbitrators." *IA Reporter*, December 30.

———. 2016a. "Energy Charter Treaty Award Is Set aside in Seat of Arbitration." *Investment Arbitration Reporter*, April 13.

———. 2016b. "As Domestic Courts Second-Guess Arbitral Verdicts in Past Yukos Cases." *Investment Arbitration Reporter*, April 25.

———. 2016c. "India Liable for Expropriation and Unfair Treatment in Satellite Dispute, but Majority of Tribunal Says 'Essential Security' Defence Scales Back Liability." *Investment Arbitration Reporter*, July 26.

Pohl, Joachim. 2013. "Temporal Validity of International Investment Agreements." OECD Working Papers on International Investment 2013/04. Paris: Organisation for Economic Co-operation and Development.

Polanco, Rodrigo. 2014. "Is There a Life for Latin American Countries After Denouncing the ICSID Convention?" *Transnational Dispute Management (TDM)* 11 (1).

Port, Nicola Christine, David Fuhr and Jessica R. Simonoff. 2010. "Article XIII." In *Recognition and Enforcement of Foreign Arbitral Awards: A Global Commentary on the New York Convention*, edited by Herbert Kronke, 531–40. Alphen aan den Rijn, the Netherlands: Kluwer Law International.

Poulsen, Lauge N. Skovgaard. 2015. *Bounded Rationality and Economic Diplomacy: The Politics of Investment Treaties in Developing Countries*. Cambridge: Cambridge University Press.

Puig, Sergio. 2014. "Social Capital in the Arbitration Market." *European Journal of International Law* 25 (2): 387–424.

Raustiala, Kal, and David G. Victor. 2004. "The Regime Complex for Plant Genetic Resources." *International Organization* 58 (02): 277–309.

Rezek, Francisco, Thomas Buergenthal and Peter Trooboff. 2000. Compania de Aguas del Aconquija S.A. and Vivendi Universal S.A. v. Argentine Republic (Vivendi I) (Award). ICSID.

Rosenne, Shabtai. 1970. *The Law of Treaties: A Guide to the Legislative History of the Vienna Convention.* Alphen aan den Rijn, the Netherlands: Brill Archive.

Rowley, J. William, Gabrielle Kaufmann-Kohler and Carlos Bernal Verea. 2007. Compania de Aguas del Aconquija S.A. and Vivendi Universal S.A. v. Argentine Republic (Vivendi II) (Award). ICSID.

Saldarriaga, Andrea. 2013. "Investment Awards and the Rules of Interpretation of the Vienna Convention: Making Room for Improvement." *ICSID Review* 28 (1): 197–217.

Sattorova, Mavluda. 2012. "Defining Investment Under the ICSID Convention and BITs: Of Ordinary Meaning, Telos, and Beyond." *Asian Journal of International Law* 2 (02): 267–90.

Schreuer, Christoph H. 2011. "From ICSID Annulment to Appeal: Half Way Down the Slippery Slope." *The Law & Practice of International Courts and Tribunals* 10 (2): 211–25.

Schreuer, Christoph H., Loretta Malintoppi, August Reinisch, and Anthony Sinclair. 2009. "Proposal to Amend Convention." In *The ICSID Convention—A Commentary*, Second edition. Cambridge: Cambridge University Press.

Schwebel, Stephen M., and Peter Tomka. 2009. Malaysian Historical Salvors SDN BHD v. The Government of Malaysia (Decision on the Application for Annulment). ICSID.

Shahabuddeen, Mohamed. 2009. Malaysian Historical Salvors Sdn, Bhd v. Government of Malaysia (Dissenting Opinion). ICSID.

Sibelesz, Hugo Hans. 2014. Valeri Belokon v. The Kyrgyz Republic (Decision on Challenges to Arbitrators Professor Kaj Hober and Professor Jan Paulsson. PCA.

Simson, Caroline. 2017. "Arbitration Opt-In Could Let NAFTA States Skirt Hang-Ups—Law360." *Law360*, August 31.

Soderlund, Christer, David A. O. Edward, and Andreas J. Jacovides. 2010. Sempra Energy International v. Argentine Republic (Decision on Annulment). ICSID.

Speidel, Richard E. 2006. "International Commercial Arbitration Implementing the New York Convention." In *Arbitration Law in America: A Critical Assessment*, edited by Edward Brunet, Richard E. Speidel, Jean R. Sternlight, and Stephen J. Ware. Cambridge: Cambridge University Press.

Teles, Steven. 2010. *The Rise of the Conservative Legal Movement: The Battle for Control of the Law.* Princeton, NJ: Princeton University Press.

Tomka, Peter. 2013. CC/Devas (Mauritius) Ltd., Devas Employees Mauritius Private Limited, and Telecom Devas Mauritius Limited v. Republic of India (Decision on the Respondent's Challenge to the Hon. Marc Lalonde as Presiding Arbitrator and Prof. Francisco Orrego Vicuna as Co-Arbitrator). PCA.

Veeder, V. V. 2013. "The Historical Keystone to International Arbitration: The Party-Appointed Arbitrator—From Miami to Geneva." *Proceedings of the Annual Meeting (American Society of International Law)* 107: 387–405.

Waibel, Michael, and Yanhui Wu. 2017. "Are Arbitrators Political?" *Working Paper.*

Yusuf, Abdulqawi Ahmed, Cecil W.M. Abraham, and Rolf Knieper. 2016. Tidewater Investment SRL and Tidewater Caribe, C.A. v. Bolivarian Republic of Venezuela (Decision on Annulment). ICSID.

Chapter Six

TOWARD GLOBAL POPULAR CONSTITUTIONALISM

I hate when organizations say, "Investor–state dispute settlement restricts sovereignty, human rights, environment, and so forth." Bullshit! That is in a sense a criticism of the whole system of treaty or international law. You gave something to get something. You have voluntarily agreed to have what you do judged by certain standards. If you don't want that, then don't enter into the treaty. When you see how hard environmental organizations work to get treaties concluded? To ban various substances? They want states bound, okay? So it is a question of, what is your cause?

—Investment arbitrator interviewed for *Judge Knot*

Is another investment law possible? Up to this point, we have seen how investment arbitration builds on long-standing and increasingly conservative projects in Western liberal thought about the appropriate balance between state and market (chapters 2 and 3), represents an ingenious but asymmetric and complex substitute for missing governance institutions in the global economy (chapters 4 and 5) and tangles up domestic politics and law (chapter 1).

The downsides of this system are increasingly getting notice. Witness chapter 1's opening quote from comedian John Oliver, fuming over controversial tobacco arbitrations and raging that investors even have the option of second-guessing democratic decisions in international arbitrations. But this last chapter's leading quote reminds us that second-guessing states is precisely what the international law project is all about. Putting constraints on carbon emissions, war and child labor are just some of the achievements of a project that goes back centuries. Is our discomfort with investment arbitration about something specific and isolatable to it, or a vestigial Biblically inspired dislike of those that would dare to judge us (or our democratic choices)?

We can split the criticism of investment law into what I will call an abolitionist ("judge not") camp and an institutionalist ("judge knot") perspective. The first viewpoint is implicit in much contemporary criticism of investor–state dispute settlement (ISDS). It sees any international review of domestic regulations as illegitimate. It wonders why states ever allowed themselves to be internationally judged, let alone by clubby untenured arbitrators (partly) paid for and appointed by the corporations that bring the caseload. For the abolitionists, such a regime can only end in a chilling of government regulations, and the only solution is for countries to pull out of investment treaties posthaste.

The institutionalist critique views the problem somewhat differently. It looks at Ira Rennert suing the government of Peru in international arbitration to derail a suit by La Oroyan victims of his pollution in Missouri courts, and wonders how that became

a viable strategy for the world's richest people. It questions the democratic compatibility of strong forms of judicial review in the nations where domestic judges asserted
them, and why many of these same countries would agree to *not* judicially review the
work of arbitrators—effectively creating judicial supremacy domestically and arbitrator
supremacy internationally. The institutionalist critique suspects that many supposed
biases of arbitrators reflect those of the legal profession writ large who (along with
economists and pop editorialists) have rewritten history to view adjudicators of all varie-
ties as checks on the irredeemable belligerence and market-interventionism of pandering
politicians. Judge knotters do not worry about arbitrators solving difficult questions over
a bottle of wine, but fear that the asymmetries and complexities of investment law's
regime complex mute the feedback from the states that have to actually do politics and
development. Policy reforms would therefore target these problematic elements.

Historical institutionalism can help us assess which reform path is more viable—
blowing up investment law or untying the judge knot. If we were at a critical juncture—
think early days of European colonialism or the destruction of a world war—then
abolition of investment law might indeed be doable. Whatever institutions existed before
would have been swept away, opening up (in the jargon we learned in chapter 2) a permissive condition for a complete remaking of a social democratic international order.
But just because such an outcome is possible does not make it likely. Business owners
and the legal profession might still be able to draw on public support for neoliberalism—
the notion that government is incapable of delivering social democratic outcomes and
must instead prioritize the needs of market participants. In such a case, the productive
conditions for an egalitarian turn would not be present. Of course, countries can always
opt out of the system one-by-one. But as we saw in chapter 5, the costs are high to doing
so. And, as Brexit demonstrates, de-linking from transnational neoliberal projects creates
the possibility, but not necessity, of a progressive nationally focused order.

As this book went to press, newspaper reports indicated that the renegotiations of the
North American Free Trade Agreement (NAFTA) may include removing investor rights
from the deal. While this might appeal to some populists within the Trump administration (and the Democratic Party), it seems likely to infuriate the business interests whose
support would be needed to get a new deal through Congress. Why, these groups will
surely ask, would Americans give away rights for their businesses that their competitors in
Europe still get? Indeed, their talking points (there are thousands of treaties, the US has
never lost a case, etc.) have already been written, and refuting them is not easy.

So, is the status quo locked in? Is investment law like the QWERTY keyboard, so
widely in use it cannot be replaced (even though it is suboptimal)? I do not think so.
Ideas like the Investment Court System proposed by Canada and the European Union,
along with admirable reform ideas coming out of the Organization for Economic
Cooperation and Development and United Nations, show momentum for change. Yet
there also are risks to making the international investment regime look more like a
court, with an appellate structure and tenured judges. This would further separate the
judges from the public and risk the locking in of wrong or short-sighted decisions. In
short, it would make the regime more like the World Trade Organization, where complainant countries lose 90 percent of the time and governments' defenses are given little

meaningful weight. And, like the WTO, an investment court would neither be required (or well-suited) to be attentive to the popular legitimacy and scientific-regulatory merit of domestic policies.

A better path forward would leverage and adapt what works about investment arbitration, namely its relative informality and porousness. When states are ruled against by an investment tribunal, they do not have to change their laws. When an investment tribunal produces an extreme or untenable award, its reasoning is not locked in. Because investment standards are imprecise, they can be applied both to violations of the letter as well as the spirit of international rules. Arbitrators can document ways that governments fall short of best practices without having to necessarily rule against them and force the coughing up of taxpayer funds. And instead of being stuck with the same group of people, fresh blood and new talent can always be brought into the system. While 28 individuals have served on the WTO's Appellate Body, more than 340 have served on investment-treaty arbitrations. True, a smaller cohort of arbitrators does tend to be regularly reappointed. But there is nothing that requires this, and arbitrators who prove themselves weak or unskilled risk losing reappointments.

All these features could be adapted to serve more social democratic ends, while preserving sovereignty. Imagine an invigorated international labor, environmental and consumer protection that built on the investment arbitration template. Instead of states only being named and shamed when they interfered with property rights, they would get a spotlight put on them for failure to have a fulsome economic democracy. And rather than handing this mission to a narrow group of technocratic adjudicators who might get it wrong or burn out, states could open up the doors to hundreds or even thousands of labor lawyers, environmental protectors and consumer advocates tasked with incrementally sketching in new rules for the global economy. Thus, even if one cares not a whiff about investment law, one can look at its success as a model to emulate for other goals.

To be sure, some aspects of investment law have to be changed to address legitimate abolitionist-oriented criticism. The role of money, for one, has to be lessened to keep financial speculation at bay. And arbitrations (whether on investment, labor or any other matter) should not be the final word. Instead of careening towards difficult-to-reverse judicialization with neoliberal leanings, citizens need a more porous global public square. With a proliferation of competing ideas about how to "do development" and "do policy," there is lower risk that any one idea is wrong.

This chapter proceeds as follows. First, I contrast two visions of the role of law in democracy: popular constitutionalism versus judicial supremacy. I argue that the former is more desirable, especially for political systems still struggling to build their legitimacy, as the US federal government was in its early days (the focus of the section below) and as the global liberal economic order is today. Instead, what we have is a prematurely judicialized global governance system. Accordingly, the second section looks at lessons we can learn from the successes and failures of past attempts to curb or amplify judicialization from the labor, trade and tax spheres. I conclude by offering a global popular constitutionalism that would reorient international economic law away from excessive judicialization and toward citizens and the working class.

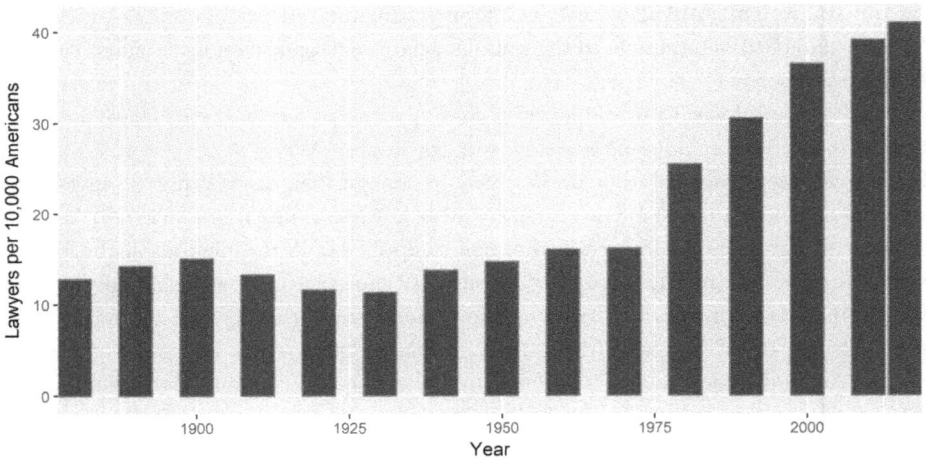

Figure 6.1 Rise of the American lawyers, 1880–2016
Source: Author's calculations using American Bar Association, Department of Commerce data.

Law in Democracy: From Popular Constitutionalism to Judicial Supremacy in the United States

Over the past five decades, the world has lawyered up—and nowhere more than in the United States. As the introduction noted, Americans have always been litigious, with the eighteenth-century observer Alexis de Tocqueville lamenting "there is almost no political question in the United States that is not resolved sooner or later into a judicial question." Yet there has been a quantitative shift over the past 50 years. In 1970, there were 16 lawyers for every 10,000 Americans, scarcely more than the 15 lawyers per comparable population numbers in 1900. By 2016, this figure had risen 250 percent to more than 40 per every American. (See Figure 6.1.)[1]

Before the explosion of lawyering, legal procedure and courts did not exert the dominance they do today. In colonial America in the 1700s, everyday citizens exercised control over their affairs and the affairs of business through juries that could pronounce not only on facts but also on the law. Far from rigidly applying rules, judges of the era revised the terms of contracts and debts to decide not only what was legal but also what was just (Horwitz 1979). This malleable approach to the law was reflected in how people thought about not only legal disputes but also about government itself. In the early 1800s, Thomas Jefferson advocated departmentalism, a theory that saw the three branches of government as co-equal representatives of the people, each permitted to have its own interpretations of what the law and constitution required (Engel 2011). In Jefferson's worldview, court rulings should not overturn democratically approved laws. Rather,

---

1. Other countries have also experienced growth in the influence of lawyers over the period (Ramseyer and Rasmusen 2010; Michelson 2013). But to bound the discussion in this chapter, I will focus on the US and international law settings.

judges should offer their judicial "take" on a law's constitutionality and invite the people themselves to hold legislators and presidents accountable through the electoral process.

But accountability through elections was not enough for early Americans. The eighteenth-century American revolutionaries were distrustful of concentrated power in a king or his judges. The Articles of Confederation thus had neither an executive nor a judicial branch. When this proved inadequate to advancing the national interest, the framers of the 1789 Constitution grudgingly accepted their creation. But the framers wanted more regular safeguards against abuse of power than elections every four years. Rather, the only way to get their majority support was to allow for impeachment of officers of both branches for treason, bribery and high crimes and misdemeanors. The Constitution does not define the latter terms, but legal scholar Cass Sunstein makes a convincing case that they do not relate only or even primarily to violations of the criminal code (Sunstein 2017). Rather, on the basis of the archival material, he concludes that the framers intended to capture both illegal and legal offenses against the public interest, including political abuses and maladministration. This could include recklessly firing cabinet officials, signing bad treaties and lying about foreign affairs. Over the course of US history, the US House of Representatives impeached 19 officers. Notably, judges represented the majority (13) of those impeached, and 100 percent (8) of those officers convicted by the Senate.

Legal scholar Larry Kramer calls these practices "popular constitutionalism," where ordinary citizens were given "a central and pivotal role in implementing the Constitution," as were their representatives, through safety valves like impeachment (Kramer 2005, 8). The rationale for this role at the time was not total egalitarianism, since blacks, women and the unpropertied did not enjoy the privilege. Rather, the involvement of the non-judicial population derived from the central role that common law accords to popular custom. In ascertaining the precise balance of power in law between governments and citizens, judges and other observers looked to the balance that citizens in practice permitted through jury verdicts, votes, social movements and petitioning. Custom evolved, and the way it evolved was through what the people (through their actions) allowed or blocked. Indeed, and as Kramer documents, the framers of the Constitution understood their undertaking was a novel one in world history—an experiment that would require ongoing revision if violent change were to be avoided. Thus, the document could be amended in "an easy, regular and Constitutional way" (in the words of George Mason, the author of the first 10 amendments, also known as the Bill of Rights). The methods: a two-thirds vote by the people's representatives (Congress) or by the people themselves (through constitutional conventions). Amendments could replace or add to what came before, thereby updating the old social compact to address new challenges (ibid. 53).[2]

---

2. Legal scholar Adrian Vermeule has called for more amendment activism for reasons motivated by contemporary social science scholarship: the bounded rationality and cognitive capacity that affects all humans. If only a relative handful of judges clarify what the Constitution means, then there is a high probability that individual idiosyncrasies will distort the development trajectory of the law. In contrast, by having 535 members of Congress and the public take on the task, individual failings matter less.

While popular constitutionalism was strongest in the early days of the American republic, glimmers of it could be found much later. In Abraham Lincoln's first inaugural address, in 1861, he sought to limit the implications of legal decisions primarily to the litigants directly involved rather than the country as a whole:

> The candid citizen must confess that if the policy of the Government upon vital questions affecting the whole people is to be irrevocably fixed by decisions of the Supreme Court, the instant they are made in ordinary litigation between parties in personal actions the people will have ceased to be their own rulers, having to that extent practically resigned their Government into the hands of that eminent tribunal.

That President Lincoln could state the point so baldly was indicative of a broader popular conception of the appropriate role of judges at the time. And the Supreme Court itself was responsive to the mood, scrutinizing (in Kramer's view) "laws that no longer had popular support" (Kramer 2005, 214), and striking down as unconstitutional only two laws between 1789 and 1860, four in the 1860s, seven in the 1870s, four in the 1880s, and five in the 1890s. This contrasts with 30 in the 1990s.[3]

Even today, presidents are occasionally willing to limit their deference to the court. As President Barack Obama stated in his 2010 State of the Union Address after the controversial *Citizens United* decision (which determined that the government could not constitutionally limit independent political expenditures):

> We face a deficit of trust—deep and corrosive doubts about how Washington works that have been growing for years. To close that credibility gap we must take action on both ends of Pennsylvania Avenue to end the outsized influence of lobbyists; to do our work openly; and to give our people the government they deserve [. . .] Last week, the Supreme Court reversed a century of law to open the floodgates for special interests—including foreign corporations— to spend without limit in our elections. Well I don't think American elections should be bankrolled by America's most powerful interests, or worse, by foreign entities. They should be decided by the American people, and that's why I'm urging Democrats and Republicans to pass a bill that helps to right this wrong.

Nonetheless, the default mode of US politics today is not popular constitutionalism, but rather judicial supremacy, which began to rear its head as early as Chief Justice John Marshall's assertion of the Supreme Court's authority over the US Constitution in the landmark 1803 case *Marbury v. Madison*. Kramer and other scholars identify various factors that encouraged this development. First (and as I explored in chapter 3), experts encouraged experts to view politics as a distasteful competition by interest groups and bureaucrats as self-seeking profit maximizers. In contrast to this unflattering portrayal, the men and women in robes seemed austere and disinterested. Popular and scholarly

---

3. As for international law, US politicians were scarcely more favorable towards adjudication-centrism, with progressives such as Woodrow Wilson and Franklin D. Roosevelt looking skeptically at lawyers having too much of a role in their designs for postwar orders (Mazower 2013; Marceau 2015).

conceptualizations of "democracy" drifted away from the dictionary definition of majority rule, and toward liberalism's concern with the protection of minorities' rights (including those of economic elites).

Second, while conservatives in the nineteenth and twentieth centuries had long relied on judges to restrain popular impulses, progressives found their own reasons to join the judicial admiration club. In the 1890s, labor lawyers and trust busters began to see courts as one venue for balancing against employers after decades when they had been seen as the home court for railroad companies and combinations. The amount of litigation finance available to progressive groups then expanded after the New Deal in the 1930s, driving up demand for legal services (Epps 1998). The New Deal and insurance markets had led to a reconceptualization of business liability. Instead of injured workers left fending for themselves, businesses could purchase insurance to cover their medical expenses—regardless of which party was proximately at fault (Friedman 1994). Similarly, progressives began to see delegation to courts as a way to lock in and carry over legislative victories won during favorable political years into years of electoral loss (McCubbins et al. 1987).

There are still other structural features that made the United States especially reliant on what political scientist Robert Kagan calls "adversarial legalism" (Kagan 2003). The separation of authority between federal and state governments means that "where the buck stops" on regulation is often unclear. So instead of relying on administration, mediation, markets or politics to resolve disputes and assign blame, Americans use courts to seek "total justice." The generally lax regulatory environment means that citizens are encouraged to seek post-facto resolution to problems through the courts instead of ex ante protection by regulatory bodies. The deregulation process itself can lead to more lawyering, as arms-length relationships between the state and the private sector lead to a proliferation of rules to govern that conduct (Vogel 1996).

The height of this ceding of power to judicial authority was the contested presidential election in *Bush v. Gore* in 2000. As Kramer notes, prior periods of history would have seen calls for impeachment, making the justices' lives more difficult through overwork, ignoring the ruling, cutting the court's budget, packing its bench or stripping its jurisdiction. Today, few contest the court's power, even if they dislike its policies.

Pervasive legalism was even on display in reaction to the #MeToo anti-sexual harassment movement. Senator Al Franken (D-Minnesota) was accused of harassing female colleagues and constituents just as his party was hoping to beat the alleged multiple child molester Roy Moore in the race for one of Alabama's long-red Senate seats. While Franken's infractions fell well short of rape or extreme abuse, fellow Democrats nonetheless called on the former comedian to step down. Their hope: to present a clear anti-sexist brand to voters in Alabama and beyond. This was an imminently political decision, but some commenters advocated for it be a more legal one. In their preference, Franken would have had a semi-property right to his seat, which he would get to keep unless a long-drawn-out legal hearing under due-process protections proved his culpability beyond a shadow of a doubt. But his "crime" was not a violation of a law, but of a rapidly evolving political norm. For countless generations, women had been made to feel that tolerating unwanted advances and touching (or worse) was the price of moving through the world. Men are not rightfully entitled to this advantage, any more than politicians are to their elected office. Thankfully, and without any change in law, this is starting to change. And, luckily for Democrats, the politicians bested the legalists in time for Moore's opponent to win the Alabama election.

Great moral reckonings happen when the old ways get swept away, and where being on the wrong side of history matters as much if not more as being on the wrong side of the law. Lincoln freed the slaves without compensating slaveholders, and Koreans (and others) solved land hoarding by elites by redistributing it to the people. Indeed, the history of economic development is full of examples where old rules are thrown out the door. As the planet confronts rampant inequality and climate catastrophe, expect many more reckonings to come.

Three Tales of Judicialization

When politics becomes overly judicialized, how to reverse course? In the sections below, I consider three instructive case studies: US labor law, international trade and international taxation. In each case, political actors increased, decreased or otherwise modified the degree of judicialization in the policy domain. Like investment arbitration, all three areas involve powerful business actors with entrenched interests in the pre- or post-reform outcomes. Each example provides useful road maps of how to think of moving to new social equilibriums.

Labor: From More Judicialization to Less, and Back Again

US labor law is a prime illustration of how to (and how not to) reduce the level of judicialization in a policy domain.[4] In early US history, businesses were able to get courts to issue injunctions to break up strikes. Such procedures were not based on any statute, but rather common-law tradition inherited from England (Naidu and Yuchtman 2016). As detailed below, courts were adept at blocking Congress from curtailing this judicial power over the early part of the twentieth century. By then, however, workers' organizations concluded that courts were not merely failing to solve a problem created by greedy industrialists, but themselves were the problem. With partners in Congress, they passed legislation that for a time loosened the judiciary's grip on labor policy, enabling a near quadrupling of the unionization rate[5] (see Figure 6.2).

---

4. This section draws on (Lovell 2003).
5. Alternative explanations for the increased focus on a business–union pact during the war, but this does not fit the temporal sequence. The percentage of workers belonging to a union went from 7.5 percent in 1930, to 9 percent in 1936, to 15.1 percent in 1937, to 19.2 percent in 1939—the eve of the 1940 Lend-Lease Act that facilitated foreign arms sales and the 1941 US entry into World War II. Thus, nearly three-quarters of the trough-to-peak percentage gains predated entry into the war. In contrast, by the end of World War II, the unionization rate edged up "only" 40 percentage points (to 27 percent of workers) and would not reach its peak of 28.3 percent until 1954, nearly a decade after the war. Thus, while the war may have

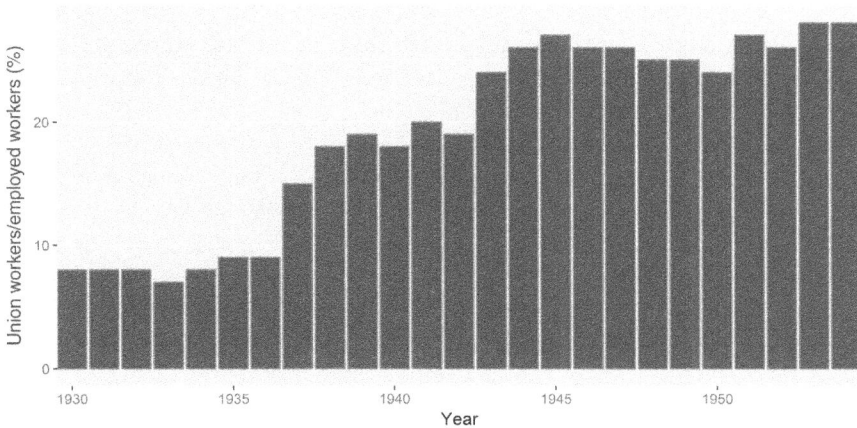

Figure 6.2 Unionization's jump after courts tamed, 1930–1954
Source: Author's calculations based on Congressional Research Service data.

It took a series of reactions and counter-reactions before policy makers got to the desired outcome of lessened judicialization. Before 1890, courts ruled on labor issues on the basis of common law and custom, but by 1890 they had a statutory basis for anti-labor injunctions: the Sherman Act. Under this act, judges blocked workers from combining together to sell their labor only at certain higher wage rates—just as they did businesses combining together to sell their goods at fixed prices (Cox 1955). Unions responded on multiple fronts. In 1894, they launched a strike on the railroads that paralyzed interstate commerce. The public sided with the unions, and Congress responded in 1898 by passing the Erdman Act, which criminalized the blacklisting of union members on the railroads. Yet the US Supreme Court rolled back the provision in *Adair v. the United States* (1908), arguing that it interfered with liberty of contract.

The 1914 Clayton Act seemed to make progress for labor. The law specified that "the labor of a human being is not a commodity or article of commerce. Nothing contained in the antitrust laws shall be construed to forbid the existence and operation of [unions] or to forbid or restrain individual members of such organizations from lawfully carrying out the legitimate objects thereof." But yet again, in 1921, the Supreme Court in *Duplex Printing v. Deering* gutted the law, finding that the Clayton Act exemption applied only to those few workers in disputes with their actual or prospective employer, not to the activities of unions (which typically involve union staff and other sympathetic unions). Moreover, in this decision, the court decided that the employer's property rights were not only in his factory but also in his business plan, which required "unrestrained access to the channels of interstate commerce"—access made more difficult when unions engage in secondary boycotts (Pitney 1921). Ironically, Congress had considered but ultimately

---

increased unionization, the lion's share of the percentage gains predated Pearl Harbor but followed Roosevelt's court-packing threats of February 1937.

rejected a clearer formulation that antitrust laws shall not "be construed to apply" to labor. Instead, a perfectly legitimate reading of the Clayton Act's language was that an injunction would do nothing to limit the "existence" of unions, even if it made organizing them through proven tactics more difficult.

In *Duplex*, there was a progressive path not taken—just as there had been in 1914. A dissent by Supreme Court Justice Louis Brandeis argued for judicial sensitivity and modesty when it came to social policy, noting that the Clayton Act "was the fruit of unceasing agitation, which extended over more than 20 years and was designed to equalize before the law the position of workingmen and employer as industrial combatants." Brandeis added that "the social and economic ideas of judges [. . .] were prejudicial to a position of equality between workingman and employer [. . .] and that, in any event, Congress, not the judges, was the body which should declare what public policy in regard to the industrial struggle demands." These echoed early Americans' skepticism of judges in the era of popular constitutionalism, now sidelined to a minority report.

After such limited success in forty years of campaigning, the labor movement and its allies began proffering still more radical solutions. In 1927, Senator Henrik Shipstead of Minnesota introduced legislation developed with Andrew Furuseth of the Seamen's Union. The legislation stated: "courts shall have jurisdiction to protect property when there is no remedy at law; [but] for the purpose of determining such jurisdiction, nothing shall be held to be property unless it is tangible and transferable, and all laws and parts of laws inconsistent herewith are hereby repealed." The connection to *Duplex* was clear—a business plan was not a tangible thing, thus the state could not protect ways that labor might have interfered with it.

Such a proposal might have changed the course of history, including in investment law. As we saw earlier in the book, an expansive interpretation of the already expansive US property rights (to include protections against even incidental interference with business plans) has gained currency in some investment tribunals. Had property been narrowly circumscribed to real estate and physical holdings, according to the Shipstead Act, then there would have been less of a precedent for expansive regulatory-takings jurisprudence to take root.

But it was not to be. In lieu of the Shipstead Act, Congress gave US workers a more mixed resolution to judicial interference in their affairs. First, in 1932, a coalition of progressive Republicans and Democrats passed the LaGuardia–Norris Act, which addressed the *Duplex* decision by stating that "No court of the United States shall have jurisdiction to issue a temporary or permanent injunction in any case involving or growing out of a labor dispute" unless five specific exceptions are met. This more blunt restriction on judicial power was effective. In University of Washington political scientist George Lovell's telling:

Even judges who appeared to be quite hostile to organized labor had a difficult time ruling that employers met the entire gauntlet of procedural and jurisdictional limitations specified in the statute [. . .] Even when confronted with provocative and violent behavior that judges would have routinely enjoined as "coercive" or "unlawful" a decade earlier, judges adhered to the statutory procedures and refused to issue injunctions when they could not make the required findings of fact. (Lovell 2003, 180–82)

Second, in 1935, Congress passed the Wagner Act, which established the National Labor Relations Board (NLRB). In lieu of the judiciary governing labor law, specialized NLRB adjudicators appointed by the executive and likely more favorable to unions would do so. Indeed, early decisions by the board were strongly pro-labor and useful for gathering evidence about harmful business practices. How would the court respond? While the conservative majority had ruled against various early New Deal policies, President Franklin D. Roosevelt threatened to pack the court with more favorable judges in February 1937. Two months later, the court responded by confirming the constitutionality of the Wagner Act, sparking the coining of the quip "a switch in time that saved nine" and upholding the constitutionality of the labor programs.

The decision was close. Four justices still held onto their anti-New Deal views (Hughes 1937). Moreover, the court managed to assert a power of review of NLRB decisions, which it began overturning within a year. Over time—and after Congress affirmed the legality of US states undercutting one another's labor standards in the Taft-Hartley Act in 1947—the unionization rate in the private sector dropped back to under 10 percent, its pre-New Deal levels, by the 1990s (Dubofsky 1994). As of early 2018, the Court is considering rolling back the last remaining protections for public sector workers, a move which could reduce unions to almost nothing.

In sum, de-judicialization of labor law was at its most effective when it set multiple clear obstacles to jurisdiction (as in the 1932 Norris–LaGuardia Act). Moreover, the aborted 1937 court-packing plan was a critical juncture that reinjected politics into court affairs and jolted the judiciary off its extreme anti-labor positions. But the norm, both before and after the 1930s, was a court that insinuated itself back into the class struggle on the side of economic elites.

Trade: From No to Lots of Judicialization

Trade is now arguably the most judicialized area of international law. Unlike other international courts that have a narrow regional focus, the World Trade Organization has nearly universal membership, is the only major international court that has ready jurisdiction over the United States, and issues rulings that impact a wide range of government activities.

It was not always so. At the 1944 Bretton Woods Conference, the Roosevelt administration's Harry Dexter White and the progressive British economist John Maynard Keynes proposed a new global order that would include the World Bank to fund economic development and reconstruction projects, the International Monetary Fund to deal with macroeconomic issues, and an International Trade Organization to govern trade. Their vision was more technocratic than legalistic, prioritizing agreement between diplomats and experts over legal dispute settlements. This reflected a concern that including lawyers would turn "problems of an economic character" into legal ones (Marceau 2015, 6). The Bretton Woods negotiators were mindful of the role in the national context that non-judges played in checking and balancing judges' remit (through legislative override and impeachment), and knew that the new international structure would not have anything as formal as a unified executive or legislative branch to perform that function.

Nevertheless, lawyers eventually made their presence felt. When Congress made clear it would reject the International Trade Organization in 1950, this left only the tariff-reductions framework of the 1948 General Agreement on Tariffs and Trade (GATT) in its place (Diebold 1952). In the early years, the absence of an institutional home and rules was not a problem, as most of the policy makers attending to the pact's affairs had drafted the rules, a process that built mutual trust. But shortly thereafter, staff at the GATT Secretariat argued that gaps in the law and the complexities of applying the law to factual disputes necessitated adjudication. In 1952, the first dispute panel was formed—a process that was adopted with modifications by member states in a 1955 meeting (Marceau 2015).

It was not long before policy makers began wondering if the trade regime could be expanded to include rules on more than just tariffs. Policies such as tax rebates on exports to promote trade surpluses were not duties, as such, but nonetheless affected trade. As the United States began running its first postwar trade deficits, the Richard Nixon administration in the late 1960s and early 1970s wondered whether these "non-tariff" rules could be behind it all. But how to get other countries to agree to expand the reach of the General Agreement on Tariffs and Trade? President Nixon created a sense of urgency by imposing an across-the-board import surcharge in 1971 and launching a series of GATT cases, including one that produced a favorable ruling for the United States against European countries' tax rebates. Europeans pleaded for mercy, and Congress sought to normalize the situation by authorizing Nixon to negotiate a formal expansion of GATT rules into nontariff areas such as subsidies, product standards and government procurement (Hudec 1980).

This institutional shift led to reactive sequences that furthered judicialization. When the Tokyo Round of the GATT concluded in 1979, countries had agreed to formalize dispute settlements in new policy areas beyond goods. But rather than a single court, separate mini-dispute-settlement bodies were established for goods disputes and the other areas covered by the Tokyo codes. These bodies, which consisted of panels of ad hoc adjudicators, were not required to come to agreement with one another, and their decisions were not always seen as well reasoned. This became a problem to be solved.

Negotiators in the subsequent Uruguay Round of trade negotiations, from 1986 to 1994, placed improved dispute-settlement mechanisms on the agenda, although on a separate track from the economic and trade issues that most interested national capitals. In 1989 Canada proposed the idea of an Appellate Body as a way of ensuring the high quality of legal decisions. As University of Bern political scientist Manfred Elsig recounts from interview research with negotiators, the United States was not a strong supporter of the idea, but reluctantly agreed to the appellate idea after predicting it would more likely be a complainant rather than a respondent. American negotiators thought appeals would be rare and believed that adjudicators would tend to confirm the lower panels' decisions (Elsig 2017). Europeans were scarcely more enthusiastic. But without compelling alternative proposals, the Appellate Body became a part of the final undertaking of the Uruguay Round.

One of its members has called the decision to create the seven-member Appellate Body "an inspired afterthought, rather than the reflection of a grand design to create a strong new international court" (Van den Bossche 2005, 65). But that is precisely what it became. Since then, more than 500 disputes have been launched, many against the United States and Europe. More than 90 percent of the challenges to defendant governments' policies have been successful. For some areas of policy, this reflects a selection effect of governments bringing only strong cases all the way to Geneva (Allee 2004). In others, however, there is genuine surprise at the doctrinal innovations that the Appellate Body has produced.

Some legal scholars argue that the existence of the Appellate Body may aggravate rather than lessen trade friction (Alter 2003), while evidence that on net it has helped increase trade is lacking (Anderson 2016, 57). The US Supreme Court issued scarcely any rulings against government in its first century, but the Appellate Body's very first ruling 16 months after its creation found against the US government's anti-pollution policy for gasoline (Wong et al. 1996). A few years later, it found against antitrust penalties that Congress had passed in 1916 but the executive branch had never even deployed. Because the Appellate Body found against the law itself (not the way it was applied), the only compliance option was full repeal, which the adjudicators determined must be completed in months even as the United States reeled from the contested *Bush v. Gore* decision (Lacarte-Muro et al. 2000; Ganesan 2001).

A recent suite of decisions has expanded the remit of World Trade Organization rules particularly far into the domestic policies of national governments. India's renewable-energy policies got a scolding, as did Europe's anti-seal cruelty laws (Graham et al. 2014; Van den Bossche et al. 2016). But the United States has come in for a particular stinging. Its regulations to protect dolphins, label meats, ban Internet gambling and regulate flavored tobacco have all been labeled trade barriers, in startling demonstrations of adjudicator independence from its most powerful member (Tucker 2014).

Because working procedures and WTO law are sticky (costly to renegotiate), the United States has resorted to expressing its displeasure through blocking the reappointment of Appellate Body members. The practice originated under the Obama administration and has been embraced by the Trump administration. On the one hand, blocking reappointments comes across as a bullying move, but on the other it appears to have worked. In 2017, the United States reversed its losing streak on defense when the Appellate Body sided with the country on airplane subsidies. Much like President Franklin D. Roosevelt's "switch in time that saved nine," the Appellate Body's response to President Obama and President Trump could be called a "switch in heaven that saved seven," the "heavens" in reference to the aircraft case, the "seven" for the members of the Appellate Body.

Only time will tell if the US pressure campaign will continue to work. And even then, what the United States gains in deference as a defendant it may lose as a complainant. After all, the Trump administration has a number of claims against China's industrial policy where the Appellate Body's newfound deference to states may not come in so handy (Tucker 2017a).

In short, from an original design of the General Agreements on Tariffs and Trade, which explicitly foreclosed judicialization, the World Trade Organization ended up becoming among the most judicialized of international courts. Lawyers began framing trade frictions in legal terms even before the Tokyo Round, a state of affairs that governments blessed after the fact. To make sure it worked well, states reluctantly agreed to stronger rules. Once the delegation to adjudicators happened, it was difficult to reverse—even in the face of unanticipated results. To some, this very binding to adjudication has made forward momentum on liberalization virtually impossible (Goldstein and Steinberg 2008). In any case, it has given states few ideal solutions for dealing with excessive adjudicator independence.

Tax: Selective Judicialization

A final comparison—this time from the tax realm—shows a more moderate type of judicialization. International tax treaties were introduced shortly after major economies' introduction of the corporate income tax nearly a hundred years ago. Many taxpaying entities operate in multiple jurisdictions, which creates substantial downside risks from a tax perspective. In the 1920s, the International Chambers of Commerce began to raise concerns about the costs that multinational corporations faced when two or more governments attempted to tax the same income, obviously leading to double taxation. As multinational firms became more complex, and as they entered into an arms race with governments by deploying increasingly sophisticated tax-planning structures and other measures to counter the corporate income tax, the potential for double taxation grew.

One key area of dispute occurs when the two government taxing authorities on either end of a corporate transaction assess its value differently, based on the various rationales for determining the so-called "transfer price" contained in domestic laws and in transnational guidance from the Organisation for Economic Cooperation and Development, comprised of developed and advanced developing nations. Tax treaties help address these issues by creating a common set of definitions and rules, but doing so necessitates a political settlement between the signatories over which tax authority should sacrifice tax revenue when both have a competing claim (Picciotto 1992).

In principle, the enforcement of tax treaties is resolved in domestic courts, since these treaties become a part of the domestic tax code once in force. Every year there are hundreds of court cases around the world in which taxpayers successfully invoke tax treaties to challenge a revenue authority's assessment of their tax liabilities. But these treaties also include an administrative procedure through which taxpayers can request that tax diplomats from the two countries attempt to negotiate an agreement to resolve an instance of double taxation. For taxpayers, this "mutual agreement procedure" (MAP) has several advantages over taking a case to court: it is less costly, the taxpayer retains anonymity, and it focuses on relieving double taxation, which even a successful court challenge may not fully resolve because it only takes place in one of the two jurisdictions concerned. Because it is an administrative decision, not a legal one, taking the MAP route does not generally preclude subsequent recourse to the courts, and in some countries the two can take place in parallel.

It has recently become apparent that the institutional design of the mutual agreement procedure is problematic. Because the administrative authorities are not obliged to reach an agreement, they have little incentive to both devote sufficient resources to these negotiations and to be flexible in those negotiations. And if the negotiations fail to resolve the policy differences, then the burdened taxpayer has no recourse other than the domestic court systems of the two countries concerned. A growing backlog of unresolved cases involving mutual agreement procedures among OECD countries reached five thousand in 2014, the last year for which complete data are available (OECD 2016).

This is why binding third-party arbitration began to be seriously discussed by tax authorities in recent decades (Park 2001). The European Union introduced arbitration for intra-EU disputes in 1990, and then individual EU countries incorporated the same procedure into their treaties with non-European countries thereafter. In the late 2000s, the United States amended its tax treaties with four European countries to include arbitration (Mulvihill and Wrappe 2011). By one count, only 158 tax treaties out of thousands include arbitration provisions (Pit 2014, 448), but this is set to increase dramatically following a pledge by OECD member states in 2017 to introduce arbitration into their tax treaties over the next few years.

Tax arbitration has some superficial similarities with investment arbitration, but many important differences. The appointment mechanism is similar, with each disputant picking an arbitrator who together appoint a chairman. Yet the non-state entity plays a more passive role in tax arbitration relative to investor–state arbitration. While some treaties allow multinational taxpayers to ask for international arbitration to be initiated, the two governments are ultimately the disputants.[6]

But perhaps the biggest difference is the reduced scope of tax arbitration's decision making compared to investment rulings. Arbitrations in US tax treaties do not produce written awards or provide legal reasoning. Their role is reduced to picking which state's tax law interpretation is correct. This system is called "baseball arbitration rules," which derives from US baseball teams' practice of negotiating salary increases for ball players. Rather than producing a detailed legal argument, tax arbitration amounts to picking a number (Ault and Majdanska 2015).

There are pros and cons to tax arbitration's relatively narrow scope. By not producing written rulings, states retain more control over interpretations. But it does not fulfil the traditional legal system role of clarifying obligations in a public manner, making economic life more predictable. This reduced scope may help explain why investment law has produced hundreds of cases, while international tax law mere dozens. In the absence of stronger dispute settlement, states have incentives to advance tax-rule interpretations that are most favorable to them. For instance, in 2016 Europe became fed up with lax taxation of US multinational corporations and unilaterally hiked the tax bill of companies such as Apple. In response, the United States claimed this higher taxation came

---

6. This contrasts also with domestic legal procedures, which allow private taxpayers to challenge tax assessments of a single state or (more controversially) double taxation between US states. See Howard (2005) and Alito (2015).

at the expense of taxes that the US government itself might claim. The dispute led the Obama administration to scuttle its cooperation in OECD efforts to combat tax avoidance (Cobham 2016).

Reforming Investment Law: Can Knotty Be Nice?

Can investment law be de-judicialized? Is some global version of popular constitutionalism possible? Everything in this book thus far suggests the barriers are high. We have learned how thousands of treaties are on the books, hundreds of arbitral tribunals have been convened, and various national laws permit and, indeed, demand deference. Third-party funders bankroll investor–state dispute-settlement cases and can triple their investments by doing so. Claimants can get around states' reform efforts by treaty shopping and nationality planning. States that threaten cancellation of their treaties risk capital flight. Proposals to further judicialize the system through an investment court system have historically found scant support in the United States, where policy makers are warier of international law than trading partners across the Atlantic.[7] And the business and legal communities effectively mobilize to defend their advantages under the current system, as shown by the virulent corporate opposition to Trump's NAFTA renegotiation proposals.

Indeed, systems that provide concentrated benefits and dispersed costs are notoriously difficult to reform. The move toward a lower tariff environment for the US economy required decades of institutional innovation to take care of displaced workers—with decidedly poor results—and mobilize support from export industries. Similarly, the investor–state dispute-settlement system provides a concentrated benefit to the narrow band of firms with substantial overseas presence and available finance for litigation. This is consistent with recent research showing outsize elite influence on policy (Gilens and Page 2014). No one should be surprised to see interest groups successfully mobilize to defend their investment law benefits.

Nonetheless, I propose there is a way to design a mostly win–win solution. My strategy could be described by the improv comedy concept of "yes, and." This captures the notion that the negation of a starting proposition stops a conversation, while affirming the proposition and adding to it moves things forward. Thus, instead of countering the argument that "ISDS supports the rule of law" with "no it does not," one could instead say "yes, and it illuminates how the 'rule of law' sometimes produces funny results, such as treating pollution as a legal entitlement."

Indeed, there is more banality than evil in investor–state arbitration. Many of the decisions are predictable when lawyers with little knowledge of a country are forced to come

---

7. Moreover, to the extent that the substantive standards direct adjudicators' inquiry in certain pro-investor ways, it is unclear that an international bureaucracy would be more legitimate than arbitrators. Indeed, constant reappointment pressures are one of the few tools respondent states currently have at their disposal to partially check arbitrator behavior. If this is removed, adjudicators will be more insulated from affected countries and groups on the ground, likely weakening rather than increasing their legitimacy. (See Lupu 2013 for an examination of the insulation dynamic more generally.)

to a legal conclusion about its domestic policies. (As we learned in chapter 5, investment law rules typically forbid arbitrators from finding no legal conclusion is possible.)

Here are three "yes, and" proposals, which I develop below and which can help evaluate reform proposals. The first is "yes investment law has benefits, and it can do more to boost efficiency." Adapting political scientist Dan Drezner's formulation, efficiency means getting to better policy outputs (through arbitration decisions) and better policy outcomes (through capital investments allocated according to economic fundamentals not legal rents) via low-cost policy processes, such as ensuring that the reform itself is efficiently enacted by satisficing incumbent interests while mobilizing new ones—all at minimal costs to policy makers with scarce time and resources (Drezner 2014).

The second is "yes, investment law can produce useful remedies, and more people should be involved and benefit from them." Fairness means that the policy outputs and outcomes should help not only the interests of foreign investors but also a broader cross-section of politically and normatively important actors. These results are more likely if the policy process (via access to arbitration) is expanded to include additional actors, such as labor and environmental experts.

The third is "yes, investment arbitration has benefited from self-reinforcing tendencies, and so should any reforms." Chapter 2's discussion of historical institutionalism illustrated three ways change does happen or does not. Critical junctures are one path, where the past is imploded, and the future is up for grabs. Incrementalism is a second, where new directions are possible but more strongly bound by decisions that came before. Path dependence is a final possibility, where lock-in of prior decisions is a real risk. As detailed in the previous section, judicialization is not impossible to reverse, but it is sticky. Once judicial review was in place in US courts, Congress had to be very explicit about not wanting it applied in the labor context. Where the legislature left any ambiguity, the jurisdiction-stripping decision itself was subject to review.

Similarly, once judicial review was in place at the World Trade Organization, it was difficult to curtail without scoring an "own goal": the flip-side of winning policy space as a state defendant (or coercing it out of the WTO's Appellate Body) is extending that benefit to others, which can cost states as complainants. But the other extreme—no international rule development at all, as in the international tax arena—hurts cooperation efforts. Accordingly, policy reform's rollout needs to be systematic (not treaty-by-treaty), needs to anticipate and channel likely objections and needs to make the right order of incremental changes, which create their own beneficial feedback loops and path dependencies.

Global Popular Constitutionalism: A Roadmap

If global governance is going to be both legitimate and effective, but without creating a utopian global federalism,[8] it needs a design that uses what works about the current system and discards what does not. My recommendation: a fluid and permeable system

---

8. This is unlikely to materialize, as it requires political leaders from diverse countries to agree upon collective constitutional strictures. But, if seriously attempted, it should include a tenured global court and global constitutional document to ensure stability. But it should also

built on arbitration, where lots of ideas and personalities cross-pollinate, but where the risk of lock-in of any one idea or set of personalities is minimal. I believe such an option is workable, and meets the three "yes, and" criteria I identified above. It would promote efficient policy outcomes by encouraging prompt compensation where economically merited and leveraging the knowledge of investment lawyers even where not. It would lead to better policy outputs by involving a more diverse set of actors than just foreign investors and investment arbitrators. Finally, it would involve an efficient process, rolling out reforms in a useful reactive sequence that ultimately leads to its own lock-in (see Figure 6.3).[9]

I contend such a proposal would rein in the worst abuses of the system while upholding a right-sized amount of investor rights. This is a piece of what I call global popular constitutionalism, which refers not to a single global constitutional text but rather a structure and practice that allow everyday people (and representatives of their interests) to demand accountability from powerholders in the global economy. And, to be sure, all three elements (rightsized damages, more equal access and multilateralization) must go together. Picking any one of them (without the others) would make for a poor use of scarce policy maker time and could make current flaws with the system worse.

The first component of my proposal builds on provisions of US administrative law (Bruff 1988). I propose the enactment of an *equitable investment act*, which would give third parties a new right to petition US courts to vacate arbitration awards that affect broader public interests. This would be a big move, shaking up the system and simulating a critical juncture. Nonetheless, this would require just a few sentences of legislation. Here is how it would work. Say a French bank sues Argentina under a Franco–Argentine bilateral investment treaty, alleging that a new Argentine administration's signature financial-regulation plan cuts into profits more than under a previous lighter-touch regime. Under the current system, the bank could sue Argentina and benefit from the possibility (however remote) that arbitrators would side with it and order cash payment. And under current federal arbitration laws, the bank would enjoy the near certainty that national courts would help enforce the award— with no review of the policy merits of the underlying claim.

Under an equitable investment act, in contrast, a US court would be empowered to set aside the arbitrators' award if Argentine consumer groups showed it would harm their interests in a stable financial system back home. The legislation would presume that the United States has jurisdiction to take such an action, which would render the award unenforceable anywhere in the world.[10] Congress could order courts to allow standing

---

feature all the safeguards that America's founding fathers put in place to ensure accountability: impeachment, amendments to the constitution, and leaders ready and able to use both on a regular basis.

9. For the legal language for each of these proposals, see Tucker 2016. I use the US as an example, but complementary efforts could be made in any country.

10. In contrast, under the New York convention, the US would have to be specified in the award as the "seat of arbitration" for a US court to be so empowered. And under the Washington Convention, as we saw in chapter 5, only the International Centre for the Settlement of Investment Disputes procedures allow for annulment of awards.

Initial condition:
Investor-state dispute settlement, with cash remedies, unequal access, national court deference

The US passes the Equitable Investment Act allowing award set-aside, building off of US administrative law and arbitration enforcement rules

Critical Juncture

US simultaneously proposes Equitable Investment Convention, which any country can join without costly treaty-by-treaty renegotiations

REACTIVE SEQUENCE OF STICKS AND CARROTS

CONVERSION OF EXISTING INSTITUTIONS

So if... French bank beats Argentina in ISDS; may move towards US court enforcement

Then... Argentine consumers ask for set-aside

Deters cases that undermine the public interest from being brought

If... court sides with them, award not enforceable

States whose investors are often on winning end eventually join to get around Act

States often on losing end will voluntarily sign to avoid paying damages

And French banks demand France sign Equitable Investment Convention

More efficient expropriation case management

Case law and custom continue developing, but with more diverse users and defenders than present system

Path Dependence of Equitable Investment

Investors retain ability to embarrass states over non-expropriation claims

Arbitrators, states, investors, and others pushed into multi-direction dialogue (unlike judicial supremacy) and collective reasoning can sort out which treaty or domestic obligations to prioritize (unlike regime complex)

Labor and environmentalists get same naming-and-shaming rights

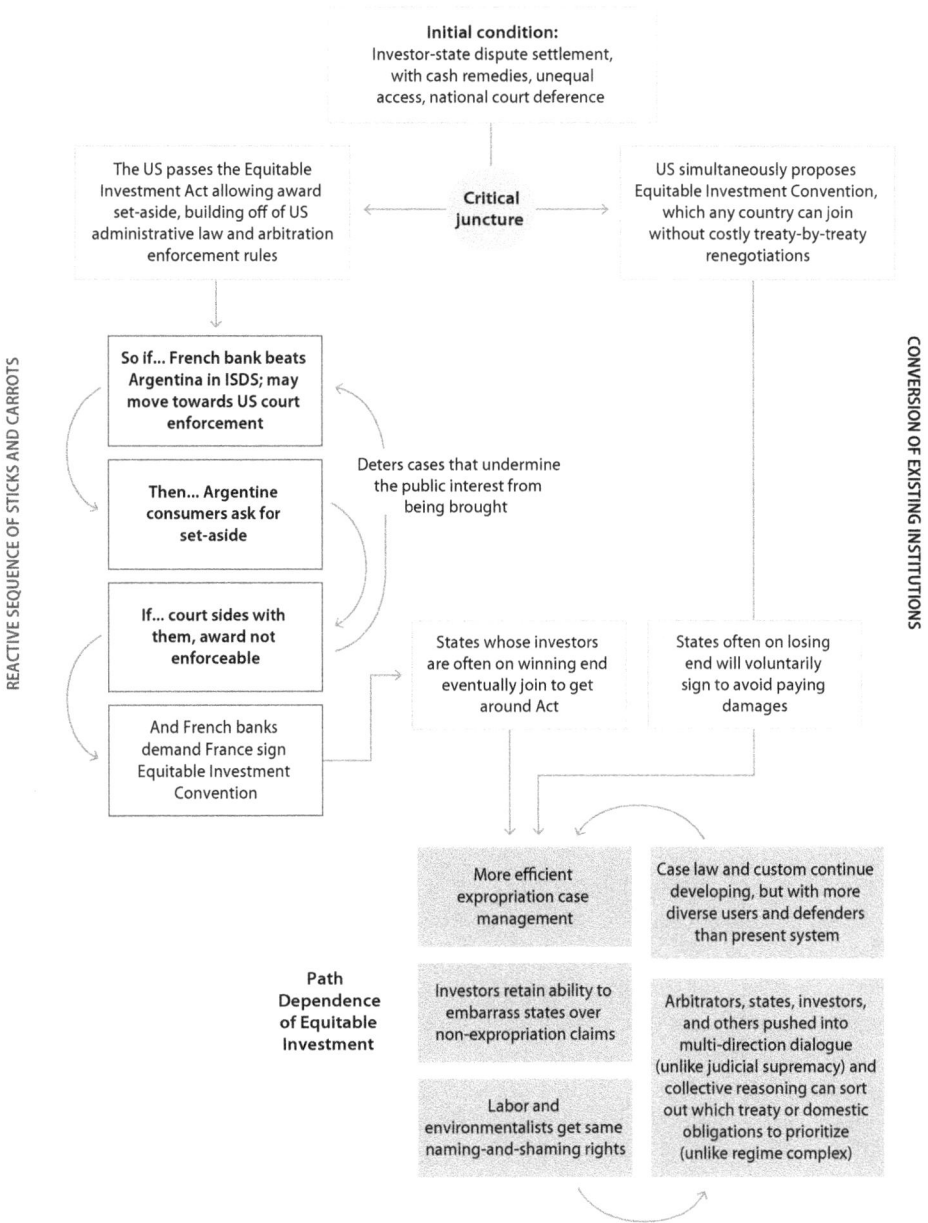

Figure 6.3 Roadmap toward a better investment law: An institutionalist proposal
Source: Author's analysis.

in such cases. If the Argentine consumer groups prevail, then the French bank would be ordered to pay the legal fees of the consumer group.

While innovative, the proposal builds on existing practice. Already, US courts are involved in investment arbitration, because French (and other) investors can ask them to enforce awards. The reform would simply expand their oversight role to take into account a broader set of interests. And the matter of standing and legal fees reflects what US law provides for in lawsuits by US citizens under, for example, the Clean Water Act—providing a model to emulate (Greenfest 2013). Even if Argentine activists never used these rights, the possibility (and uncertainty of the outcome) would deter foreign investors from launching arbitration claims against popular public-interest policies in the first place.

It is possible that an equitable investment act would put the United States in violation of its international obligations. Under domestic law, there should be no problem, as courts have interpreted later statutes as trumping earlier inconsistent treaties (Kesavan 2006). But the Washington and New York conventions require judicial deference to arbitration. If US judges suddenly applied stricter review, French and other foreign investors might challenge this practice with further ISDS claims (Park 2007). But these challenges would take years to play out, giving the United States breathing room to pursue and further develop the strategy. Moreover, the very act of enacting such legislation would send a signal to foreign investors that the US would resist paying claims under an old system deemed illegitimate, thereby deterring claims in the first place.

In the long term, though, an equitable investment act would not be enough. New treaty rules also would be needed to put investment governance on a more sustainable footing and avoid the risk of long-term US non-compliance with international obligations. Among other things, foreign investors would be eager to move toward a system in which treaty outcomes are more certain. As part of a one-two punch with the changes to domestic arbitration law, the United States also should propose a global *equitable investment convention* and call on other countries to sign up.

This new proposed convention would separate investor gripes into two tracks, both of which would better mirror our national laws' balance of property rights and democratic decision making. On one track, states that expropriate property would have to compensate investors promptly and fairly, just as the Fifth Amendment to the US Constitution requires. Instead of investment law proceedings that take years to resolve and often deliver only a fraction of investors' claimed damages, teams of accountants would work to precisely tally the value of what investors sank into their projects. If there is some value left in the investment, then an expropriation would be deemed to not occur, and the investor would be responsible for the accountants' expenses. But if there is no value left (the definition of expropriation under the new rules), then the state would get a bill and be responsible for the expenses of the accountants and for appropriate compensation ordered by them at the end of a six-month study period. If the state balked at paying, the investor would be able to seek enforcement and attachment in US courts or elsewhere, as under the current system.

If a respondent state wishes to dispute that an expropriation took place, then the new convention would allow it to request an arbitration to defend itself. If a tribunal found that no expropriation took place, then the investor would be responsible for the tribunal's costs, and no damages would be awarded. But if the tribunal finds against the state, then the state pays the tribunal's costs, and the damages assessment would be doubled. What is the logic here? It boosts the legitimacy of arbitration by forcing the state to be the one that requests it. This is in contrast to the current system, which allows a host state government to be sued for treaties negotiated by administrations decades (or centuries!) before. Making states' consent more proximate in time will increase the confidence of all parties. In any case, retaining the residual possibility of arbitration allows tribunals to continue to clarify the contours of what constitutes an expropriation under international law, thereby enhancing predictability. Of course, the state could also just roll the dice with the accountants instead of going through litigation, which would speed up justice for the investor. And if states drag cases out when the facts are not on their side (which they would be in a good position to know), they would face steep penalties.

On a second track, if a state harmed an investor in less-severe ways, then arbitrators could still rule on whether and how the government fell short of its obligations, just as they do now. But unlike the current system, arbitrators would not award damages and would produce an advisory decision in six months. This finding would not only establish any international law problem posed by the government action, but also recommend specific reforms governments could make to come into compliance. This targets a central weakness of the current system, where tribunals fault states for falling short of international law standards but without identifying a reasonable and democratically feasible alternative available to domestic decision makers. If arbitrators were forced to systematically put themselves in the state's shoes, rulings would likely become more modest.

States could accept or reject the advice, but they would be required to explain their choice. Arbitrators would then respond in kind, either affirming the state's compliance or addressing its excuses. All correspondence would be made public. If the state chooses to exercise its sovereign right to not comply, then it would be responsible for the tribunal's expenses. If the state does comply by changing its policies, the tribunal tab is on the investor.

As with the expropriation track, this alternative track would encourage efficient decision making. Corporations would not over-invest in lawyering for the sake of large damages claims, because these would no longer be allowed to be made in the first place. But in cases where tribunal review actually leads to finding a policy at fault and a willing state's policy change, the investor would benefit and thus be responsible for the tribunals' costs. Unlike my proposed standards for the reimbursement of expropriation costs, which are designed to help companies that were truly forced out of an investment, my recommendations for non-expropriation costs would require companies that benefitted from a change to the policy environment to pay for a fair share of a legal system that brought this about. States' financing of tribunal expenses when they do not change policies is akin to membership fees in an international legal body, subsidizing the global public good of better and more defined international law. Removing the high-stake remedies from the system would lessen third-party speculation on litigation and allow lawyers to develop norms that could inform, but not paralyze, government operations.

This bifurcated procedure would have subtler benefits as well. Proponents of current investment law often claim that their awards are as much about improving domestic institutions as it is netting investors' and lawyers' money. Or as I quoted one earlier in the book: "This is a good government operation. Fucking little countries should be grateful! We are to teach them how to govern themselves." Whether or not this has been the case is debatable. Nonetheless, critics of the current system are left in a difficult spot if they are seen as defending states' rights to be predatory and govern poorly—an argument with limited constituencies anywhere, but especially among these legal elites. Retaining investors' right to have a tribunal rule on fair and equitable treatment, for example, would allow the good government operations to go on. At the same time, the public and iterative nature of arbitrators' recommendations and states' responses would discourage arbitrators from making wild anti-state and anti-development arguments.[11]

Most importantly, a global equitable investment convention would fix the current double standard vis-à-vis labor and environmental interests. Labor standards in trade deals, for example, are rarely enforceable, and when they are, the rights of workers are sidelined in favor of highly judicialized proceedings that favor foreign investors (Vogt 2015). Instead of foreign investors enjoying rights that domestic investors, unions and environmental groups do not, the proposed new convention would level the playing field. Just as a foreign investor can now ask a tribunal to determine whether capital controls violate a state's obligations, a union would be able to request a second opinion on collective bargaining rights. Similarly, an environmental group could shine a spotlight on weak carbon-emissions plans. And domestic investors could complain about preferential treatment received by wealthy foreign companies.

Like foreign investors currently enjoy, labor and environmental interests as well as domestic investors should benefit from both precise rules (to target known bright lines) and imprecise rules (to make sure the intent of those bright lines is also captured). For labor interests, a precise rule could be "no banning of unions," and an imprecise rule could be "no actions that make unions less likely." This change reorients the debate away from bashing imprecise norms such as fair and equitable treatment, and towards leveraging imprecision in the service of more diverse interests. These more inclusive proceedings would allow citizens to name and shame bad governments. Arbitrators would help them, by building a paper trail of states' deeds and misdeeds (just as foreign investors would retain the right to do) without compromising sovereignty.

A global equitable investment convention would make for better and more inclusive legal decisions. As we learned earlier in this chapter, juries in early US history helped

---

11. Finally, the nature of the horse-trading we learned about in chapter 4 would also be altered. Currently, state-appointed arbitrators can trade their vote for a finding against the state on the merits for a reduced damage award. Under the new system, damages would not be allowed for non-expropriation claims. As such, the horse-trading and bargaining between arbitrators would take place at the merits stage itself, producing more balanced interpretation of the rules for good behavior.

establish the parameters of law and custom. Different branches of government were assumed to be not only able but also obligated to come to their own determinations on constitutional questions. Rather than expecting judges to right every wrong, courts provided judgments to inform the public debate, with any political consequences of their decisions flowing from voters. Likewise, in an investor-plus-others system of arbitral-advice-and-state-response, the public would have a tool to push for institutional reform at home (rather than states getting off the hook for "bad" policies by paying an investor off), and foreign investors would know which countries to be wary of. Throughout all of these tracks, the norm laboratory of international law would go on—just in the service of a broader constituency than multinational investors.[12]

The proposed new convention also would create openings for new blood to be brought into the arbitral pool and acquire experience that would build their reputations. Say progressive non-governmental organization advocates have expertise in labor law. In the current institutional setup, there is no formal role for them to play. If, however, labor disputes were arbitrated, then there would be a new demand for their skills. Over time, as the pool of international adjudicators became more diverse, this would bubble up into national and international public service. After all, adjudication experience looks good on the CV. This also is why a more open and porous system (including one open to non-investment specialists and non-attorneys, as in my proposal) is preferred to an institutional investment court of five or nine judges, as in Europe and Canada's current reform proposals. Instead of the blinkered development ideologies we learned about in chapter 3, we could have actual development and politics experts. Instead of the 120 tribunal types we learned of in chapter 4, we would have virtually unlimited combinations. Partisan labor wingman with neutral investment wingwoman with a managerial chair. Socialite chair with turncoat investment wingman and neutral environmental wingwoman. The possibilities abound.

Finally, an equitable investment convention would offer a path toward systemic reform of the more than three thousand investment treaties that already exist, with all the treaty shopping possibilities this network allows. Countries that joined the proposed convention would spare their investors from being dragged into US courts under an equitable investment act. For any two countries that joined the convention, their past deals would be automatically superseded without time-consuming country-by-country negotiations. There is a precedent for such a docking mechanism within investment law. In the early 2010s, UN negotiators developed the Mauritius Convention, which updates the transparency provisions of all past investment treaties for any two countries that join (Kaufmann-Kohler and Potesta 2016). Nonetheless, this structure suffers from a fatal flaw: a lack of attention to political incentives. Years later, only a handful of countries have ratified the pact. In my proposal, the introduction of an equitable investment act is what herds countries into a global equitable investment convention.

---

12. Additionally, progressive national judges looking for international precedents would have much more material to scour.

Complementary Policies

Global popular constitutionalism is not only about reformed investment rules. It is also about a broader agenda that contributes to de-rigging the liberal international order in perception and reality by bringing the people themselves into it. A range of complementary policies would help reduce the bias in favor of foreign investors, a bias that sits at the heart of the current liberal order.

The first set of policies would target corporations. An equitable investment convention might help highlight wrongdoing by governments while an *equitable recognition act* would do the same (and go further) for corporate wrongdoing. Today, multinational investors can pollute a local environment or abuse workers and then strategically declare bankruptcy in a given jurisdiction in order to avoid paying out tort claims there (Stiglitz 2008). This is one reason why the *Renco* case discussed in chapter 1 ended up in US courts. But a better development policy would use and strengthen local courts. Peruvian courts should determine whether Renco broke local law, and US courts should help in the collection of damages. The main barrier to enforcement at present is that the recognition standards vary by US states (Moghaddam 1987). The United States and other countries with large financial hubs should federalize and streamline this system through making it easier to recognize judgments across jurisdictions.

The second set of policies would target taxes. Illicit tax flows are estimated to cost hundreds of billions of dollars a year (Spanjers and Kar 2015). As a condition for joining new trade agreements, countries would have to agree to divide up taxing rights on the basis of where goods are sold, automatically share tax information and maintain a wealth registry of the global assets of their corporations and citizens. If tax havens from outside the trading bloc chafe at these rules or attempt to game the system, then their financial institutions should be blocked from conducting business in the trading bloc. This carrot-and-stick approach would maximize the chances of best practices spreading globally. That is the static change negotiators can control. But as this book makes clear, subsequent post-negotiation matters are less under state control. In adjudication over these terms, tax arbitrators should be empowered to utilize imprecise rules, such as ensuring multinationals pay their fair share of tax in countries where they operate, and not act to frustrate the goals of tax justice.

Third, there needs to be a set of policies governing monopolies. Economic and political theory has long recognized the threat of market power to individual and societal wellbeing. This is largely an issue of domestic rules and enforcement, but there are international dimensions as well. For instance, in 2014, US plaintiffs brought an antitrust case against two Chinese vitamin manufacturers. A US lower court found the two firms guilty of cornering the global market and price-fixing. On appeal, the US Court of Appeals for the Second District noted such behavior would have been an open-and-shut case under US antitrust law, where price fixing is illegal. Nonetheless, the court found that because the Chinese government had ordered the price-fixing the Chinese plaintiffs would not be able to comply with both US and Chinese law simultaneously. On grounds of inter-judicial comity—respect for one another's legal systems—the court denied remedy to the US plaintiffs (Hall 2016).

Under a new set of international monopoly guidelines, the United States should insist on strong and enforceable rules on the degree of allowable industry concentration. Rather than relying on government lawyers and diplomats to bring the case, US plaintiffs could automatically trigger international consultations. If those consultations did not yield satisfactory outcomes, then the cases could go to US courts, where judges would be instructed not to apply comity principles. Here, as with the taxation recommendations, precise rules on industry concentration would be supplemented with imprecise rules such as "separate companies shall not by actions other than per se combination act to limit competition."

Finally, there would need to be a new set of financial policies. In 2008, Wall Street speculation brought the US economy to its knees and reverberated around the globe. The Dodd-Frank Act addressed some of the root causes, but not all of them—and even those rules are now being rolled back by Republicans in Congress. Legal scholar K. Sabeel Rahman has called for a third way between technocratic elitism and deregulation. His vision would involve clearer rules and greater direct participation by financial institutions and regulators with communities across the country. Hard caps on bank size, for example, would be more comprehensible to everyday citizens than complicated tests of systemic risk. With a clearer threshold that even journalists and citizens could easily see, civic organizing and accountability is easier (Rahman 2016).

Unfortunately, current trade rules could be used to label size limitations as impermissible market access akin to "quotas of zero" (Tucker 2011). While trade and investment pacts have some defenses that countries can use if their prudential regulations are challenged, there is substantial ambiguity about how protective these defense clauses are—especially when countries are regulating in novel ways. Indeed, in a recent trade case by Panama against Argentina's anti-tax haven rules, the Obama administration sought to keep adjudicators from clarifying what policies are and what are not prudential (Tucker 2015). This could be smart for plausible deniability: sometimes it is better to not know when you are breaking the rules. But clarifying what the rules of the global economy are and are not can boost its legitimacy with the public. In any case, the United States instead should formally commit to not enforcing these rules, and ask other countries to do the same, until bank regulators can agree on appropriate and enforceable new international norms.

Finally, getting the US financial regulatory house in order is great foreign policy. The 2008 financial crisis cost other countries more than $8 trillion (Luttrell et al. 2013)—an amount that dwarfs foreign aid flows and even the most optimistic projections from trade agreements such as the Trans-Pacific Partnership.

Addressing Objections

There are numerous possible objections to the proposals I have made in this chapter. First, investors' advocates could argue that foreclosing damages payments for states' violations of standards like fair and equitable treatment could lessen predictability and stop capital from flowing to emerging markets that need it. But the system at present is already unpredictable, with arbitrators telling me that whether investors get favorable rulings or not depends entirely on which arbitrators hear their case. As shown in their answers in chapter 3, no one was able to provide a clear template for how states should regulate that would avoid arbitration claims. Moreover, investors lose more cases than they win and (even when they win) recover mere pennies on the dollar As insurance, this is not great. So while investment-treaty rules have raised sovereignty concerns for governments, they have not been a great gift to investors either.

A second related objection is that the proposal, by softening the enforceability of investment rules, would weaken the rule of law. As already noted, ISDS can force governments to pay, but only after the breach has happened. Offending governments are not forced to change policy. So the ability of investment law to incentivize correct behavior seems limited, at least outside of the payment of compensation for expropriation.

But this second objection also reflects an infatuation with legalism whose day has passed. Leaders in the West have long had excessive faith in the ability of rules to trump interests. Faced with a rising China, Bill Clinton held out hope that the WTO would force the market interventionist country to have its actions "subject to rules" (Clinton 2000). Barack Obama called the Trans-Pacific Partnership a way to get China to "play by the rules that America and our partners set, and not the other way around" (Obama 2016). Yet as former State Department officials Robert Blackwill and Jennifer Harris have documented, countries like China and other rising powers put following of national interests above the niceties of globalization's supposed rules. The result: growing economies and expanded geopolitical influence. Their prescription: the United States should stop pretending that it will sacrifice its economic and geopolitical standing in the name of rule following (Blackwill and Harris 2016). To be clear, neither the authors nor I advocate for willy nilly disregard for rules and norms. But, as political scientist Ian Hurd has documented in the national security space, gradual contestation and reshaping of the rules in the name of national interests is the normal state of affairs. The same should be true of economic affairs in the face of competitors that look very different than those faced by the US in the past.

In some ways, such a policy shift would be just a concession to reality. As we saw in chapters 1 through 3, the twentieth-century economic idea that economic development was all about getting the prices, institutions or other golden straitjackets right is belied by the history of today's rich states, wherein highly consequential interruptions to markets and the rule of law were the norm. Far from checking power, domestic courts shielded political branches from legal liability until relatively late in the development process. And the nineteenth-century idea that law can somehow substitute for politics is contradicted by the fact that both operate in tandem. From the World Trade Organization to the World Bank, litigation operates in the shadow of power, and diplomats use law as but one tool among others (Jandhyala et al. 2015). As the planet's major powers wrestle with which, if any, economic model will become hegemonic, my equitable investment convention could help. Rather than stale debates about whether China or the United States are following rules made decades ago for different economies, we would have thousands of citizen arbitrators helping to contest and define what the new rules should be, without risking their irreversible lock-in.

A third objection is the argument that loading up the trade and investment regime with responsibilities beyond trade and investment makes for a poor fit. In this view, each issue area should get its own institutional home. I have a number of responses to this line of argument. For one thing, trade and investment deals already reach far beyond trade and investment. Indeed, virtually any public policy on any matter can come under the scrutiny of these pacts' rules. We are already part of the way toward a global governance system, but it just represents one set of interests. Moreover, the traditional international bodies that tackle labor and other social issues tend to be weak relative to their trade and investment counterparts. Better integrating the different pockets of global governance (while adding safeguards for democracy and sovereignty) can lessen fragmentation and boost cross-issue expertise.

Fourth, investment law abolitionists could point out problems my proposal does not solve and wonder how precisely the problems in chapter 5 would not be replicated here. For instance, investors could still use contracts of the threat of a treaty proceeding to bully governments. This is true, but keeping monetary damages mostly out of the picture will reduce the incentives for investors to do so. And venal investors will tend to bully no matter what; government officials have to be capable of standing up to them when it makes policy sense. The transparency revolution of the equitable investment convention will bring that bullying into clear public view. As for whether my proposal is adequate to the problems I have identified, I would say yes. We get around the principal complex and regime complex hurdles to change by asserting a fix on a global scale, such that arbitrations would not simply be rerouted to the most deferential countries. We enhance the public's ability to screen, monitor and sanction arbitrators through boosting review powers of domestic courts (under the act) and greater transparency and arbitrator diversity (in the convention).

Ultimately, abolitionists are unlikely to be satisfied with any policy reform that leaves ISDS intact. This is understandable. Indeed, the system's standards on sensitive matters like regulatory takings seem almost designed to trigger rejection from social democrats. Still, as US Treasury Secretary Timothy Geithner once said, "plan beats no plan." What he meant was that criticisms alone (in his time of the Wall Street bailouts) are unlikely to gain as much intellectual traction with policy makers than proactive solutions (even imperfect ones). At its core, the abolitionist case counsels doing away with investors' rights at the international level, leaving them to plead their cases in domestic courts. At the same time, progressive abolitionists want to boost the enforceability of labor and environmental rights, although by relying mostly on setting conditions on other countries' market access to developed country markets. This is like replacing something with nothing. It is unlikely to go over well with investors, especially with legitimate concerns about the expense and time of pursuing domestic litigation. And it is unlikely to go over well with developing countries, many of whom have built their economies around a symbiotic relationship with US companies. In contrast, global popular constitutionalism offers lots of alternatives that could conceivably replace the functions that ISDS' advocates think it is fulfilling, while avoiding angering allies with trade-restricting threats future administrations are unlikely to follow through on. And as historical institutionalism teaches us, structures already in place that have constituencies defending them are hard to fully erase. Layering on top of what works and converting what does not are generally more promising strategies that praying for a critical juncture that may not come.

Fifth and finally, observers on both sides of the debate might question whether a reform that begins with a unilateralist move like the equitable investment act and ends with a social democratic globalization is politically plausible or legally desirable. If the charge is audacity, I plead guilty. As a growing body of research demonstrates, rising economic inequality is hollowing out democracy, as elites capture governing institutions for their own benefit. Hoping for this captured system to do progressives' work for them is unrealistic, so the alternative vision and program must be big and at scale. Neoliberalism is a system of policies, values and means of favoring constituencies to support its program. Progressives must offer alternatives on each of those levels, not simply produce a laundry list of policies or hope that the clock can be rewound to an earlier era. Global popular constitutionalism is an effort to go further. As for the international legality of the equitable investment act, this is a valid concern. Nonetheless, the historical experience of Roosevelt and Nixon explored earlier in this chapter suggests critical junctures often need to be engineered in order to get change moving. A controlled disruption to create negotiating leverage in a discrete area of policy is far preferable to risking a more chaotic and systemic disintegration of the liberal global order if persistent legitimacy deficits are left unaddressed.

Nonetheless, more research is certainly needed. *Judge Knot* sheds new light on investment arbitration, but we need to know more. How do businesses and private law firms think about the remedies the system offers and about possible alternatives? What are the obstacles and solutions to easier international recognition of judgments against companies? How precisely might standing rules be clarified to allow civil society groups to push for set-aside of objectionable ISDS awards? While scholars have worried that the availability of these remedies might chill public interest regulation, systematic evidence for this is lacking. Indeed, the evidence we do have tends to come from countries like Canada, where the government is relatively transparent and where officials openly speak to researchers. In such settings, democratic governments that admit to experiencing regulatory chill can also be pushed in the opposite direction. It is really the less transparent and democratic countries where regulatory chill would be most concerning, but these countries are also where researchers would be less likely to know about it happening. In short, much more research is needed.

Signing Off

I started this book project with concerns about international investment law and the ways it might interfere with democratic decision making. By the time I sent the manuscript to the publisher, I became increasingly convinced that this was a more generalized problem of valuing legal resolution and certainty over the messiness of democracy. The United States resolved its top election of 2000 in the courts, as did Ukraine in 2005, Austria in 2016 and Kenya in 2017. When the Trump administration proposed modest changes to NAFTA, economists and lawyers panicked at anything that would remove an unyielding certainty from business planning (Tucker 2017b). I believe it is possible to reinvigorate our democracies, but it will require comfort with more pluralism and contestation and less legal finality and one-size-fits all solutions.

In my nearly twenty years at the forefront of policy and academic debates around globalization, I have regularly noted how uncivil the conversation can be. Proponents of trade and investment pacts deem themselves the defenders of job creation and the rule of law and tar opponents as luddite protectionists. Critics of these same pacts see themselves as the guardians of the disenfranchised and smear proponents as shills for corporate offshoring. Both sides accuse the other of idiocy and bad faith. To be sure, the economics profession bears its share of blame. Economists are often distrustful of government. They elevate individual utility over institutional and political sustainability. And a macho culture dominates. But an overly legalized system of global governance may also contribute to the problem. It could make these conflicts worse, since any policy or even rhetorical concession made by one side is seen as a benefit accruing to the other.

Conflict is not necessarily bad. Indeed, it is the lifeblood of the political process. But recall the different modes of governance and dispute settlement: politics, law, mediation, markets and administration. Before and after the political process figures out the balance of power in society, politicians and policy makers need to flip the switch to administration to get the design features right. This is the kind of expert guidance that helped countries such as South Korea and Taiwan along their development paths (discussed in chapter 3). It is hard to make progress in issue areas where polarization is the norm, and where groups attribute bad motives, unreasonableness and more influence to their opponents than is rational—a phenomenon policy scholars call the devil shift (Sabatier et al. 1987). To bring more legitimacy to global cooperation, all the players need to be capable of casting the devil out.

The weaknesses of the international economic law system are real. Business voices are louder on the international stage than are voices with stakes in democratic economic policy making, such as labor unions and environmental groups. Business-friendly rulings—if not accompanied by a steady stream of labor-friendly rulings, peasant-friendly rulings, and more—risk tarnishing the international law project more broadly, and confusing the through-line of our public diplomacy. Even if no one in the US State Department signs off on rulings like *Metalclad* or *Bilcon*, there is a risk that the newspaper-reading public in Mexico and Canada will see such rulings as a projection of US power, since they happened under a treaty with the United States. Finally, even businesses may not be getting much out of the system. They spend lots of money, lose lots of cases and, even when they win, do not get policy change.

So who benefits, if not people, companies or our diplomacy? Lawyers, those trained skeptics of politics and change. If arbitrators' decisions are too legalist and constraining of states' room for maneuver, then policy makers and the public more generally should have ways of offering alternative perspectives informed by the history of economic development and democratic practice. By subjecting both perspectives to public scrutiny, we can get better and more reasoned results. Just as markets have not been the most important institution in triggering socioeconomic change, the law is also a lagging indicator. In the most consequential decisions, politics and administration matter as much if not more.

To paraphrase De Tocqueville, not all political matters (or indeed many at all) need to be turned into judicial questions. Democracy is messier than litigation, but it also delivers a legitimacy that the courts cannot.

Let us end the last chapter by returning to the story that started the first. Imagine if the global popular constitutionalist policies had been in place when the Renco Group sued Peru. Under the equitable recognition act, the citizens of La Oroya could have brought their claim in Peruvian courts, knowing that US courts would not flinch at enforcing them. Under the equitable investment act, the lawyers representing the people of La Oroya could be standing by at a US courthouse with a set-aside motion for any award an arbitral panel produced in Renco's favor. Under the equitable investment convention, the company could not plausibly claim damages from Peru unless there had been an expropriation, so would not be wasting the time of so many. Moreover, Judge Catherine Perry or her Missouri judicial colleagues could hear the La Oroyan kids' case even as the treaty arbitration proceeded, with each level secure in the knowledge that neither venue's conclusions would trump the other. Investor rights would not disappear, but they would coexist alongside the rights of others in society, and not receive greater weight. Indeed, the content of the rights themselves would be debated democratically, both in and out of these courtrooms. La Oroya's citizens would be getting their health care paid for today, instead of waiting for a day in court that never comes.

References

Alito, Samuel. 2015. Comptroller of Treasury of Maryland. v. Brian Wynne et ux. U.S. Supreme Court.

Allee, Todd. 2004. "Legal Incentives and Domestic Rewards: The Selection of Trade Disputes for GATT/WTO Dispute Resolution." Manuscript. University of Illinois.

Alter, Karen J. 2003. "Resolving or Exacerbating Disputes? The WTO's New Dispute Resolution System." *International Affairs* 79 (4): 783–800.

Anderson, Kym. 2016. "Contributions of the GATT/WTO to Global Economic Welfare: Empirical Evidence." *Journal of Economic Surveys* 30 (1): 56–92.

Ault, Hugh J., and Alicja Majdanska. 2015. "Arbitration and International Institutions." Working Paper.

Blackwill, Robert D., and Jennifer M. Harris. 2016. *War by Other Means: Geoeconomics and Statecraft.* Cambridge, MA: Belknap Press.

Bruff, Harold H. 1988. "Public Programs, Private Deciders: The Constitutionality of Arbitration in Federal Programs." *Texas Law Review* 67: 441–98.

Clinton, Bill. 2000. "China Speech." Johns Hopkins University, March 8.

Cobham, Alex. 2016. "The US Treasury Just Declared Tax War on Europe." *Tax Justice Network* (blog). August 24.

Cox, Archibald. 1955. "Labor and the Antitrust Laws. A Preliminary Analysis." *University of Pennsylvania Law Review* 104 (2): 252–84.

Diebold, William. 1952. *The End of the ITO.* Vol. 16. Essays in International Finance. Princeton, NJ: International Finance Section, Department of Economics and Social Institutions, Princeton University.

Drezner, Daniel W. 2014. "The System Worked: Global Economic Governance during the Great Recession." *World Politics* 66 (1): 123–64.

Dubofsky, Melvyn. 1994. *The State & Labor in Modern America*. Chapel Hill: University of North Carolina Press.

Elsig, Manfred. 2017. "Legalization in Context: The Design of the WTO's Dispute Settlement System." *The British Journal of Politics and International Relations* 19 (2): 304–19.

Engel, Stephen M. 2011. *American Politicians Confront the Court: Opposition Politics and Changing Responses to Judicial Power*. Cambridge: Cambridge University Press.

Epps, Charles. 1998. *The Rights Revolution*. Chicago: University of Chicago Press.

Friedman, Lawrence M. 1994. *Total Justice*. New York: Russell Sage Foundation.

Ganesan, A. V. 2001. United States—Anti-Dumping Act of 1916 (Award of the Arbitrator under Arbitration under Article 21.3(c) of the Understanding on Rules and Procedures Governing the Settlement of Disputes). WTO.

Gilens, Martin, and Benjamin I. Page. 2014. "Testing Theories of American Politics: Elites, Interest Groups, and Average Citizens." *Perspectives on Politics* 12 (03): 564–81.

Goldstein, Judith L., and Richard H. Steinberg. 2008. "Negotiate or Litigate? Effects of WTO Judicial Delegation on US Trade Politics." *Law and Contemporary Problems* 71 (1): 257–82.

Graham, Thomas R., Seung Wha Chang,and Yuejiao Zhang. 2014. European Communities— Measures Prohibiting the Importation and Marketing of Seal Products (Appellate Body Report). WTO.

Greenfest, Seth W. 2013. "The Politics of Judicial Supremacy: Congress, the Supreme Court, and Standing to Sue." Working Paper.

Hall, Peter M. 2016. In Re Vitamin C Antitrust Litigation. U.S. Court of Appeals for the Second Circuit.

Horwitz, Morton J. 1979. *The Transformation of American Law, 1780–1860*. Cambridge, MA: Harvard University Press.

Howard, Robert M. 2005. "Comparing the Decision Making of Specialized Courts and General Courts: An Exploration of Tax Decisions." *Justice System Journal* 26 (2): 135–48.

Hudec, Robert E. 1980. "GATT Dispute Settlement after the Tokyo Round: An Unfinished Business." *Cornell International Law Journal* 13: 145–204.

Hughes, Charles Evans. 1937. NLRB v. Jones & Laughlin Steel Corp. U.S. Supreme Court.

Jandhyala, Srividya, Geoffrey Gertz and Lauge N. Skovgaard Poulsen. 2015. "Does Arbitration Reduce Diplomatic Pressure in Investment Disputes?" In *Annual Meetings of the International Studies Association*. New Orleans.

Kagan, Robert A. 2003. *Adversarial Legalism: The American Way of Law*. Cambridge, MA: Harvard University Press.

Kaufmann-Kohler, Gabrielle, and Michele Potesta. 2016. "Can the Mauritius Convention Serve as a Model for the Reform of Investor–State Arbitration in Connection with the Introduction of a Permanent Investment Tribunal or an Appeal Mechanism?" Geneva: Center for International Dispute Settlement.

Kesavan, Vasan. 2006. "The Three Tiers of Federal Law." *Northwestern University Law Review* 100: 1479–1636.

Kramer, Larry D. 2005. *The People Themselves: Popular Constitutionalism and Judicial Review*. Oxford: Oxford University Press.

Lacarte-Muro, Julio, Claus-Dieter Ehlermann and Florentino P. Feliciano. 2000. United States— Anti-Dumping Act of 1916 (Report of the Appellate Body). WTO.

Lovell, George I. 2003. *Legislative Deferrals: Statutory Ambiguity, Judicial Power, and American Democracy*. Cambridge: Cambridge University Press.

Lupu, Yonatan. 2013. "International Judicial Legitimacy: Lessons from National Courts." *Theoretical Inquiries in Law* 14 (2): 437–54.

Luttrell, David, Tyler Atkinson, and Harvey Rosenblum. 2013. "Assessing the Costs and Consequences of the 2007–09 Financial Crisis and Its Aftermath." *Economic Letter* 8 (7).

Marceau, Gabrielle, ed. 2015. *A History of Law and Lawyers in the GATT/WTO: The Development of the Rule of Law in the Multilateral Trading System.* Cambridge: Cambridge University Press.

Mazower, Mark. 2013. *Governing the World: The History of an Idea, 1815 to the Present.* New York: Penguin Books.

McCubbins, Mathew D., Roger G. Noll, and Barry R. Weingast. 1987. "Administrative Procedures as Instruments of Political Control." *Journal of Law, Economics, & Organization* 3 (2): 243–77.

Michelson, Ethan. 2013. "Women in the Legal Profession, 1970–2010: A Study of the Global Supply of Lawyers Symposium: Women in Legal Practice: Global and Local Perspectives: Part II: Global Perspectives." *Indiana Journal of Global Legal Studies* 20: 1071–1138.

Moghaddam, Behrooz. 1987. "Recognition of Foreign Country Judgments—A Case for Federalization Note." *Texas International Law Journal* 22: 331–50.

Mulvihill, Paul, and Steven Wrappe. 2011. "Arbitration in Tax Treaties: The Canada–United States Income Tax Convention." *Corporate Business Taxation Monthly* 13: 25–32.

Naidu, Suresh, and Noam Yuchtman. 2016. "Labor Market Institutions in the Gilded Age of American Economic History." Working Paper 22117. National Bureau of Economic Research.

Obama, Barack. 2016. "President Obama: The TPP Would Let America, Not China, Lead the Way on Global Trade." *The Washington Post*, May 2.

OECD. 2016. "Mutual Agreement Procedure Statistics 2006–2014."

Park, William W. 2001. "Income Tax Treaty Arbitration." *George Mason Law Review* 10 (4): 803–74.

———. 2007. "Respecting the New York Convention." *ICC International Court of Arbitration Bulletin* 18 (2).

Peterson, Luke Eric, and Vladislav Djanic. 2017. "In an Innovative Award, Arbitrators Pressure Uzbekistan." *Investment Arbitration Reporter*, June 22.

Picciotto, Sol. 1992. "International Taxation and Intrafirm Pricing in Transnational Corporate Groups." *Accounting, Organizations and Society* 17 (8): 759–92.

Pit, Harm Mark. 2014. "Arbitration under the OECD Model Convention: Follow-up under Double Tax Conventions: An Evaluation." *Intertax* 42 (6): 445–69.

Pitney, Mahlon. 1921. Duplex Printing Press Co. v. Deering. U.S. Supreme Court.

Rahman, K. Sabeel. 2016. *Democracy against Domination.* Oxford: Oxford University Press.

Ramseyer, J. Mark, and Eric B. Rasmusen. 2010. "Comparative Litigation Rates." Discussion Paper 681. Cambridge, MA: John M. Olin Center for Law, Economics, and Business at Harvard Law School.

Sabatier, Paul A., Susan Hunter and Susan McLaughlin. 1987. "The Devil Shift: Perceptions and Misperceptions of Opponents." *The Western Political Quarterly* 40 (3): 449–76.

Spanjers, Joseph, and Dev Kar. 2015. "Illicit Financial Flows from Developing Countries: 2004–2013." Washington, DC: Global Financial Integrity Project.

Stiglitz, Joseph E. 2008. "Regulating Multinational Corporations: Towards Principles of Cross-Border Legal Framework in a Globalized World Balancing Rights with Responsibilities." *American University International Law Review* 23: 451.

Tucker, Todd. 2011. "How to Reform WTO and FTA Rules to Confront Too-Big-To-Fail Banks." Washington, DC: Public Citizen.

———. 2014. "The WTO Ruling on the United States' Flavoured Cigarettes Ban." In *The Global Tobacco Epidemic and the Law*, edited by Tania S. Voon and Andrew D. Mitchell, 87–104. London: Edward Elgar Publishing.

———. 2015. "WTaxO Lesson #4: Use Your Defenses." *Under Two Ceilings* (blog). October 7.

———. 2016. "Accountability in a Regime Complex: Charting Policy Reforms for Investor-State Dispute Settlement." In *APSA Annual Conference*. Pittsburgh.

———. 2017a. "On Labor Day, Switch in Heaven That Saved Seven at the WTO?" *Medium* (blog). September 4.

————. 2017b. "Why NAFTA Needs an Expiration Date." *Politico*, October 26.

Van den Bossche, Peter. 2005. "The Making of the 'World Trade Court.'" In *Key Issues in WTO Dispute Settlement: The First Ten Years*, edited by Rufus Yerxa and Bruce Wilson. Cambridge: Cambridge University Press.

Van den Bossche, Peter, Seung Wha Chang, and Thomas R. Graham. 2016. India—Certain Measures Relating to Solar Cells and Solar Modules (Report of the Appellate Body). WTO.

Vogel, Steven Kent. 1996. *Freer Markets, More Rules: Regulatory Reform in Advanced Industrial Countries*. Syracuse: Cornell University Press.

Vogt, Jeffrey S. 2015. "The Evolution of Labor Rights and Trade—A Transatlantic Comparison and Lessons for the Transatlantic Trade and Investment Partnership." *Journal of International Economic Law* 18 (4): 827–60.

Wong, Joseph, Crawford Falconer, and Kim Luotonen. 1996. U.S.—Standards for Reformulated and Conventional Gasoline (Panel Report). WTO.

Appendix

METHODOLOGY

When I began this project in 2012, I was interested in the link between investment treaties and economic development. Namely, did these pacts make it more or less likely that countries would move up the income ladder? As I dug in, it became rapidly apparent that there were two ways of approaching this question. First, one could look at whether the act of signing or ratifying investment treaties actually succeeded in bringing in investment. This research area was already well trod by political scientists and economists, who tended to black-box what investment law was really about. A second approach (the one I took) looked instead at how much discretion do investment-treaty arbitrators have, and what are the potential implications of this discretion for development?

This question required that I speak to the individuals who are in the room—the arbitrators themselves. This Appendix reviews how social scientists have historically studied adjudicators and how I extended and modified their approach in my primary research, including through assembling original datasets of investment arbitrator interviews and case outcomes.

How Do Social Scientists Study Adjudicators?

The dominant myth of the legal profession is that judges just apply the law. This legalist ideology assumes the law is a coherent and integrated set of rules, as if it had been drawn up by a single author. Each legal problem will have a correct answer, which is simply found by judges who reason by analogy to other cases. In this view, judges also strive for stability, predictability and finality in the law, and ensure that like cases are decided in like ways. They will assume a disinterested posture, and even rule against powerful interests in order to maintain their own legitimacy. They are socialized through educational and professional institutions to decide cases in accordance with legal doctrine, and to defer as much as possible to officials from elected branches of government.

Many social scientists see this legalist account as untenable. Judges decide similar cases differently from one another, issue decisions even when the law is not clear, and involve themselves in political matters. This was clearly demonstrated by the US Supreme Court decision in *Bush v. Gore*, where a conservative majority of justices made the legally questionable decision to hand the US presidential election to the Republican candidate.

Interviews with adjudicators can generate valuable data, but their legalism can cloud the full truth. Within-interview validity checks can help. The distinguished legal researcher Lee Epstein recommends avoiding verbal and nonverbal cues that could reveal the interviewer's personal views, and to ask open-ended questions that allow multiple interpretations and help to reveal underlying attitudes (Epstein 1990, 198). Rutgers University political scientist Milton Heumann recommends asking questions that invite reminiscing and "war stories"—an interview tactic that has been found to help overcome judges' professionally inculcated aversion to speaking about their work (Heumann 1990). And political scientists Donald Songer and his colleagues recommend not-for-attribution interviews, as being on the record can encourage strategic rather than honest answering (Songer et al. 2012, 61).

University of Dayton political scientist Jason Pierce offers the most detailed guidance. He states that, in setting up interviews, interview requests needed to be written and succinct, as judges are busy (so do not want to be forced to guess what you are asking for). Because judges are rarely interviewed, he recommends avoiding using or minimizing use of the word "interview" in the letter. He found he had to promise anonymity in order to secure 70 percent of his interviews. The letter should also be ambiguous as to ultimate goals of the research. This avoids getting biased answers or outright rejections (Pierce 2002).

Likewise, unless specifically demanded, Pierce did not send interview questions ahead of time. He also offers other guidance for conducting interviews. He used open-ended questions with more loquacious interview subjects, and more pointed ones with more reserved judges—all the while following from a basic set of core questions. Social-science words such as "agenda," or questions about specific colleagues would tend to cause the judges to button up. The same was true for predictably controversial questions, which Pierce delayed until the end. Despite requiring anonymity, most of his interview subjects were willing to be recorded. Pierce states that recording was essential, as judges speak in a "complex and lengthy" manner "often laced with caveats and qualifications" (ibid. 137).

Because the interviews Pierce conducted were relatively long, averaging an hour, he could test for internal validity and consistency. The longer an interviewee talks, the more likely they will say something that contradicts an earlier statement. Such later statements can be seen as especially reliable if they go against the speaker's own interests. This also is the case when the interviewee would be fired or experience hardship if the statement became public (Bleich and Pekkanen 2013, 98).

My Method

In conducting the interviews and analysis, I used grounded theory methods. Although rarely discussed in political science,[1] this approach is an invaluable set of qualitative procedures for the collection and coding of observational data. While originally used in medical sociology, it has also been applied to studies of legal phenomena (Ewick and Silbey 1998; Popescu 2012). Glaser and Strauss (1967) crafted the grounded theory method in response to a concern that, instead of coming up with useful new theories, scholars were

---

1. Eckstein (2009 [1975]: 140) notes in passing that the method stimulates the theoretical imagi-
   nation by utilizing comparisons across a large volume of data, which gets around some of the
   bias concerns in case study selection.

merely quantitatively testing deductive theories based on shaky empirical premises (like rational choice). However, scholars tackling new areas could be accused of making unsystematic and impressionistic readings of phenomena of interest. Glaser and Strauss' solution was to create a new toolbox for innovative and pragmatic research capable of new theories. The core of their technique is structured comparison of fragments of interview and other textual data to build a theory from the ground up, where abstract analytical concepts are always linked back to variance in primary sources. Grounded theory traces its intellectual roots to pragmatism (that the value of an analytical framework depends on it being useful for understanding dynamic social processes) and symbolic interactionism (that individuals have some agency within their perception of their opportunities and constraints in the world around them, which is in turn constituted by the interactions of the individuals) (Corbin and Strauss 1990).

Grounded theory employs a purposive (rather than random) sampling strategy, in order to keep the analysis open to theoretically interesting distinctions that emerge over the course of the research. Prior scholarship on investment arbitration, for example, emphasized the importance of arbitrators' nationality and place in the tribunal—party appointed or chairman (Franck 2009; Waibel and Wu 2017). Accordingly, my initial sampling strategy sought to maximize variance on those dimensions. After completing interviews with 20 of the most frequent arbitrators, my subjects told me repeatedly that every tribunal had its own unique culture, so it was impossible for them to generalize in response to my questions about how they conducted their work. Accordingly, I shifted my sampling strategy to include a person from nearly every one of the finalized arbitrations. This broad sampling helped me produce the diversity of arbitrator ideologies and types described in chapters 3 through 5.

All told, I requested interviews of 95 arbitrators, received 68 acceptances and three rejections and conducted 44 interviews. These individuals served in 261 cases, or roughly 80 percent of the 347 cases finalized at the time this book was going to press. Well before the 44th interview, arbitrators were repeating each other enough that I believed I had reached the point that grounded theorists call theoretical saturation, where the marginal additional interview time fails to produce new conceptual information. In each case, I promised not-for-attribution interviews and to keep my notes confidential, as it seemed unlikely the arbitrators would speak openly otherwise. Moreover, because several interviewees argued that the numbering or dating of interviews would make it possible for their peers to identify them, I exclude such citations. According to my interviewees, arbitrators used forensic methods (taking advantage of dates and numbering) to determine the identities of the interviewees in an early examination by legal scholars Yves Dezalay and Bryant Garth of international commercial arbitration (Dezalay and Garth 1996).

In order to maximize reliability and comparability of my results, I asked a core set of eight questions in my interviews (varying only slightly if absolutely necessary to maintain a conversational flow). These are discussed in the next section. This allows the study to be (in principle) replicated, a possibility that will help validate, nuance or correct my account in *Judge Knot*. My hope is that that goes at least part of the way towards reducing the transparency concerns that are a necessary hazard of close qualitative research on elites (Moravcsik 2014).

In order to create a warm, conversational tone, I began each interview with an open-ended biographical question about the arbitrator's background:

1.   "To get started, I was hoping you could tell me how you first became interested in investment-treaty arbitration?"

I followed this with open-ended questions about inter-collegial norms within arbitration:

2.   "What are some of the different ways arbitrators divide labor, and is one more common than another?"
3.   "What are some of the differences between a good and a bad chair, and what about for a party-appointed arbitrator?"

Question 2 frames the topic of interest, while question 3 helps to avoid uninformative answers (such as, "We just apply the law") by imploring arbitrators to acknowledge and discuss the variance within the arbitral profession. Together, these questions yielded many of the findings in chapter 4.

I then moved to progressively more-pointed questions:

4.   "When you are looking at an imprecise provision such as 'fair and equitable treatment,' what are some of the techniques you use to put meat on the bones of what it means?"
5.   "If a developing country came to you outside of your arbitral capacity, and asked for some tips or rules of thumb for avoiding arbitration when they are formulating and rolling out a new policy, what are some of the things you would say?"

These questions helped differentiate views on interpretive flexibility within tribunals and then subtly introduced the politics and economy questions that informed the analysis in chapters 3, 4 and 5.

The next questions looked at arbitrators' discretion in the broader institutional frame-work in which they operate:

6.   "Some have advocated the creation of an appellate system to review arbitral awards. Is that something you are in favor of? Why or why not?"
7.   "When I talk to political science colleagues about investment arbitration, and I note that investors are the only ones that bring the cases, and that they have a hand in picking the arbitrators, they predict that investors must win all the time. But I have to point out the statistics that say that states win more than they lose. Does that outcome surprise you? Why?"

These questions helped shed light on arbitrators' perceptions of the utility of attempting to rein them in, and whether they even needed to be reined in at all. These questions help shape the work in chapter 5, as well as the recommendations in chapter 6.

I then moved to the final questions:

8. "The historic rationale for investment treaties was because developing countries had weak institutions, and the treaties would compensate for that and bring in more investment. But increasingly, you see investment treaties being contemplated between pairs of rich countries. Do you think this is useful or necessary?"

Number 8 called back to number 5: What, if any, ideology do arbitrators have about the state and development? Because several questions were inserted in between the two, this served as an internal validity test. After all, if the whole point of investment treaties is to help development, treaties would not be necessary between already-developed countries. The combination helped to reveal convergences and divergences between arbitrators on the ultimate purpose of their work.

I used grounded theory techniques to qualitatively code the interview transcripts in the nVivo software package. In this method, conceptual labels are imposed on every word, sentence or paragraph within a document(s), and are allowed to overlap. In a first phase, inductive "open coding" produces "en vivo" concepts (which closely match the words used by the subjects). As the researcher develops what is typically a large number of concepts over an initial sample of texts, she constantly compares each to the others to look for similarities, differences and negative cases. This invites recoding, collapsing, merging and renaming of the concepts. The coding fractures the original transcripts so that units of text (words, sentences) can be read in isolation from their original interview or another context. (This process is evident in this book, where splices of different interviews are counterpoised with one another.)

While open coding is inductive, the next two phases (axial and selective coding) are deductive. These stages require the researcher to put all the inductively derived concepts back into a recognizable social-science shape. Concepts that seemed anomalous are probed for what they say about a subjects' ability to use agency or be constrained by structures, to cause some consequence to happen, or to create social meaning. If open coding produces a detailed inventory of social facts, axial coding begins to link up these facts to one another and selective coding turns these linkages into a theoretical story. At these stages, preexisting theories (such as amount of wealth leading to more social power) are not brought in, as they may not be operative in the phenomenon under investigation. All tentative conclusions must be based on the data, and all data must be used or accounted for in the story.

Finally, there is "theoretical coding," whereby the researcher compares their story to preexisting scholarly work and can borrow concepts if they earn their way into the grounded theory. Some grounded theorists even postpone their literature review until this stage. Of course, this is an idealization of the research process, as even committed grounded theory practitioners do not go into a field completely ignorant of existing scholarly work. But these tools indicate an attempt to not let existing scholarship dictate the contours of new research (Strauss and Corbin 1998; Charmaz 2006). The interplay between the creative generation of open coding and the disciplining of axial, selective and theoretical coding, is what makes grounded theory a uniquely potent qualitative tool.

Here is one example of how I implemented this method from the bottom up. One arbitrator told me, "some of the times, the party appointed arbitrator feels he is the watchdog [...] That I think is a big mistake. Because in the end, they provoke the reaction of the chair, who may tilt the other way." My initial label for this text in open-coding was "watchdog." That exact word did not come up in later interviews, but other interviewees described situations where partisan wingmen were more or less successful in their attempts to influence their tribunals. In axial coding, I compared these responses to the original "watchdog" comment, in order to ascertain what types of strategies were available to arbitrators. In selective coding, I attempted to draw consequences from the strategies. How would these strategies affect case outcomes? Was the residue of these interactions evident in the final awards themselves? Finally, in theoretical coding, I compared these dynamics with the work of other scholars in the judicial politics field. (This literature became quite literally part of my data, the analysis of which is evident in the exposition style of chapter 2.) Each stage pushed me closer to the core concept of the judge knot, the notion that what sets investment arbitration apart from other forms of judging was its curious combination of finality and knotty anarchy.

Below I provide descriptive statistics about my interview subjects, including their nationalities and how often they served in cases that produced final awards. Thirty-one were conducted in person in Washington, DC, Geneva, Boston, Miami, Toronto, Seattle, and Montreal, and the remainder by telephone. (See Table A.1.)

Finally, in order to externally validate these conclusions drawn from the internal world of arbitration, I assembled a dataset of all finalized investment treaty cases (defined as an award dismissing a case on jurisdiction or making a determination as to the merits). When I began this project, there was not yet a usable and public repository of case-outcome data. Accordingly, I set to constructing one myself. This required reading and coding nearly 200 outcome variables and case characteristics of nearly 350 awards, a process that took years of work and involved triangulating between archives of publicly available awards and industry reporting of nonpublic awards (for which some case data was nonetheless available) at sites like IA Reporter, ITALaw, UNCTAD and others. Gus Van Harten and Susan Franck were also generous in sharing data for me to get a sense of different coding possibilities. In the meantime, a number of other scholars and agencies have made more data available and in more usable formats. UNCTAD, for instance, now has much more accessible and usable data than when I started this project. Please visit www.toddntucker.com for a repository of the data and replication files I am able to make available.

A hazard of all of our work is an unquantifiable risk of selection bias. To paraphrase former US Defense Secretary Donald Rumsfeld, do the public awards (the known knowns), nonpublic awards we know about (known unknowns), and the totally secret awards (unknown unknowns) vary in a systematic or random way? If the variation is random, then our conclusions should be largely unaffected by the revelation or not of additional awards. But if the nonpublic awards vary in some systematic way from the others, new revelations could force us to change our conclusions. This might be the case if, for instance, governments are more likely to keep awards secret when they involve embarrassingly large damage payments to investors.

When I began this project, my interviewees and other experts were of the opinion that most awards eventually find their way into the public domain. With many hands and

Table A.1 Interviewees, by country and appointments

Chair Appointments	Investor Appointees	State Appointees	Total Appointments
162	123	89	374

By Country (various appointment arrangements)

Australia	1
Austria	1
Bangladesh	1
Belgium	1
Canada	5
Chile	1
Costa Rica	1
Egypt	1
France	2
Germany	1
Mexico	2
Netherlands	1
Spain	3
Sweden	4
Switzerland	4
Thailand	1
UK	3
USA	11
Grand Total	44

Source: Author's analysis; appointments refers to my original dataset of finalized investment treaty cases.

eyes on the documents (at arbitration centers, in governments, in companies), it seemed likely that someone somewhere in the chain would leak. Arbitrators themselves use the awards as calling cards with law firms, so they themselves have an interest in seeing their work go public. By the time *Judge Knot* went to publication, however, the consensus seems to have frayed a bit. Today, scholars are employing a suite of empirical techniques to improve our understanding about potential impacts of secrecy on our conclusions (Hafner-Burton and Victor 2016). In the meantime, the best remedy for this methodological problem may ultimately be political. Indeed, one distinct advantage of my proposed Equitable Investment Convention is bringing an end to secret payments of taxpayers' money to foreign corporations.

References

Bleich, Erik, and Robert Pekkanen. 2013. "How to Report Interview Data." In *Interview Research in Political Science*, edited by Layna Mosley, 95–116. Ithaca, NY: Cornell University Press.
Charmaz, Kathy. 2006. *Constructing Grounded Theory: A Practical Guide through Qualitative Analysis (Introducing Qualitative Methods Series)*. London: SAGE Publications.
Corbin, Juliet M., and Anselm L. Strauss. 1990. "Grounded Theory Research: Procedures, Canons and Evaluative Criteria." *Qualitative Sociology* 13 (1): 3–21.
Eckstein, Harry. 2009. "Case Study and Theory in Political Science." In *Case Study Method*, edited by Roger Gomm, Martyn Hammersley and Peter Foster, 118–64. London: SAGE Publications.

Epstein, Lee. 1990. "Interviewing U.S. Supreme Court Justices and Interest Group Attorneys."
    Judicature 73 (4): 196–98.

Ewick, Patricia, and Susan S. Silbey. 1998. *The Common Place of Law: Stories from Everyday Life.*
    Chicago: University of Chicago Press.

Franck, Susan D. 2009. "Development and Outcomes of Investment Treaty Arbitration." *Harvard
    International Law Journal* 50 (2): 435–89.

Glaser, Barney G., and Anselm L. Strauss. 1967. *The Discovery of Grounded Theory: Strategies for
    Qualitative Research.* Chicago: Aldine Transaction.

Hafner-Burton, Emilie M., and David G. Victor. 2016. "Secrecy in International Investment
    Arbitration: An Empirical Analysis." *Journal of International Dispute Settlement* 7 (1): 161–82.

Heumann, Milton. 1990. "Interviewing Trial Judges." *Judicature* 73 (4): 200–202.

Moravcsik, Andrew. 2014. "Transparency: The Revolution in Qualitative Research." *PS: Political
    Science & Politics* 47 (01): 48–53.

Pierce, Jason L. 2002. "Interviewing Australia's Senior Judiciary." *Australian Journal of Political Science*
    37 (1): 131–42.

Popescu, Mihaela. 2012. "Judicial Discourse as Feeling Rules: Obscenity Regulation and Inner Life
    Control, 1873–1956." *Law, Culture and the Humanities.*

Songer, Donald R., Susan J. Johnson, C. L. Ostberg and Matthew E. Wetstein. 2012. *Law, Ideology,
    and Collegiality: Judicial Behaviour in the Supreme Court of Canada.* Montreal and Ithaca, NY: McGill
    Queens University Press.

Strauss, Anselm L., and Juliet M. Corbin. 1998. *Basics of Qualitative Research: Techniques and Procedures
    for Developing Grounded Theory.* Second Edition. London: SAGE Publications.

Waibel, Michael, and Yanhui Wu. 2017. "Are Arbitrators Political?" Working Paper.

INDEX